D0561243

"Wellington Webb, the first African American mayor in Denver's history, worked tirelessly to reduce crime in his city and across the country, and I was proud to appoint him to chair the U.S. Conference of Mayors' Task Force on Violent Crime. His autobiography is a candid and compelling account of the remarkable life of a good man, an energetic, intelligent leader who served his beloved city and our nation well."

—President William J. Clinton

"Wellington Webb has written a memoir that is both inspiring and instructive. He reminds us that passion and purpose are paramount."

—Tavis Smiley, author, television and radio host

"This is a unique story of American politics and the life of a boy who … became mayor of Denver, the president of the United States Conference of Mayors, the National Conference of Black Mayors, and the National Conference of Democratic Mayors, a first in American politics, which makes him a 'triple-crown mayor.'

"This is a moving, human, and, at times, funny story. Webb is blessed with a most strategic mind and God-given leadership talents, which make him, in my opinion, a political giant of mayors across our nation and on our globe."

—Tom Cochran, executive director of the
U.S. Conference of Mayors

"Wellington Webb came from obscurity to fame without ever forgetting his roots. He grew from a black activist to a well-known and well-respected mayor who left an indelible stamp on Denver. His story is inspirational, educational, and well told."

—Richard D. Lamm, former governor of Colorado

"I was very proud to serve with Wellington Webb as he both led Denver and served as an important voice for all of America's cities in the 1990s, a time of renaissance for Denver. Everywhere Wellington served, he was the leader, offering sage counsel and a principled, progressive, and pragmatic approach to solving the difficult problems that cities faced as the twentieth century came to a close. Aspiring politicians everywhere should study his mastery of multiracial coalition politics, [a] key to Wellington's electoral and governing successes."

—Marc Morial, mayor of New Orleans, 1994–2002, and president of the National Urban League

"During a twelve-year span as Denver mayor, Wellington Webb faced a period of historic challenges to American cities and created a legacy of achievement that still shapes the lives of Denver citizens. As the city's first black mayor, he embraced diversity and promoted social awareness. His commitment to the city's children was unmatched as he advocated for early-childhood education to maximize every child's full potential. Wellington Webb exemplifies the impact of a dynamic leader on an urban city."

—Reg Weaver, president, National Education Association, Washington, D.C.

Wellington Webb

The Man, the Mayor, and the Making of Modern Denver

An Autobiography with Cindy Brovsky

Fulcrum Publishing
Golden, Colorado

Text © 2007 Wellington Webb
Photographs © 2007 Wellington Webb, unless otherwise noted

All rights reserved. No part of this book may be reproduced, stored in a retrieval system, or transmitted in any form or by any means, electronic, mechanical, photocopying, recording, or otherwise, without written permission from the publisher.

Library of Congress Cataloging-in-Publication Data

Webb, Wellington E.
  Wellington Webb : the man, the mayor, and the making of modern Denver
/ by Wellington E. Webb with Cindy Brovsky.
      p. cm.
  Includes index.
  ISBN-13: 978-1-55591-634-3 (alk. paper)
  ISBN-10: 1-55591-634-1 (alk. paper) 1. Webb, Wellington E. 2.
Mayors--Colorado--Denver--Biography. 3. Denver (Colo.)--Politics and
government--20th century. 4. Denver (Colo.)--Biography. I. Brovsky,
Cindy. II. Title.
  F784.D453W43 2007
  978.8'033092--dc22
  [B]
                              2006033717

Printed in the United States of America by Malloy Incorporated
0 9 8 7 6 5 4 3 2 1

Editorial: Sam Scinta, Katie Raymond
Cover image and interior design: Jack Lenzo

Fulcrum Publishing
4690 Table Mountain Drive, Suite 100
Golden, Colorado 80403
800-992-2908 • 303-277-1623
www.fulcrumbooks.com

To my wife, Wilma, and our children,
Keith, Anthony, Allen, and Stephanie.

To my grandchildren, my brothers,
and all of our family members and friends
who have been an important part of my life's journey.

To the Mile High City, where I arrived as a sickly child
from Chicago and whose voters later gave me the opportunity
to be the city's leader for twelve years.

To the people who supported my efforts
and to those who worked for me and with me—
as well as those who opposed me and fueled my desire to succeed—
in opening city government to all people.

To my employees, cabinet members, and friends
whose names do not appear in these pages:
be assured that your important work and continued
support is invaluable and appreciated.

To the trailblazers who came before me
and to those who will come after me
to help America fulfill its promise
to embrace opportunity for all of her people.

Contents

Foreword

In *The Man, the Mayor, and the Making of Modern Denver*, Wellington E. Webb provides a scintillating review of the last quarter of twentieth-century Denver and the dawn of twenty-first-century Denver. In that time, Wellington played a herculean role in the creation of the world-class modern-day twenty-first-century Denver. Most important, Wellington taught those of us who knew and worked with him the importance of being a public servant, championing civil rights, and never accepting defeat. These life lessons for me and so many others are the true legacy of Wellington Webb.

As a state representative, governor's cabinet officer, presidential appointee, and mayor, Wellington led as a true servant of the people. He knew his mission was to enable other people to develop their full human potential. While the great monuments of modern Denver—Denver International Airport, the renaissance in the Central Platte Valley, the restoration of the South Platte River, the revitalization of downtown Denver, and many others—were all important to his legacy, he was most proud of his legacy in helping the people of Denver and the United States recognize that they had the power within themselves to achieve their God-given potential.

That mission of an "enabler" came from his most basic values, including the love he constantly displayed for his family and his community. The people closest to Wellington played an inspirational role in helping him reach for the stars as he confronted his own personal and political challenges. They also taught him, as he taught us, never to accept defeat. For many of us, the 1991 campaign for mayor is forever etched in our minds. In that campaign, most political leaders looking at a 7 percent standing in the polls would have given up. Yet Wellington's determination and his famous sneaker walk through the city proved all of his doubters wrong. He went on to victory and to lead the city and county of Denver in its march through history that concluded the twentieth century and began the twenty-first century.

For me, I will always cherish Wellington as a champion of civil rights. He held the baton in the march for civil rights with people like Martin Luther King Jr., Nelson Mandela, César Chávez, and Rosa Parks. He fought to make sure that diversity enriched our society, and he worked tirelessly against the agents of hate and division who would have turned the clock backward on the progress of American civil rights.

While Wellington knew and worked with famous people such as presidents of the United States and other world leaders, he never forgot the common person. Throughout his book, we find the common person whom he celebrated in every neighborhood of Denver. For him, these common persons were the true heroes he served.

As we are taught in the Book of Proverbs, "Wisdom resides in the heart of the discerning and truly wise gentleman." Wellington Webb became that wise gentleman through his life experiences. From the 100-pound sickly twelve-year-old who arrived in Denver to the halls of national power, Wellington gained tremendous wisdom, and we are blessed that he shared that wisdom with all of his community.

—United States Senator Ken Salazar

Introduction

At six-foot-four and as Denver's first African American mayor, mayor for twelve years, I never blended into a crowd. I never traveled without police security, because I'd received death threats. I never dropped my strong facade, because of my fear of failure, my desire to succeed, and the impact my success or failure would have on future minority leaders.

My wife, Wilma, and I were accompanied by police detectives Ken Chavez and Bobby Bogans on July 21, 2003, to Denver International Airport (DIA). It was fitting that the $5 billion airport that consumed my first term would be the setting where one chapter in my life ended and a new journey began. The city's new leader, John Hickenlooper, kindly allowed the officers to drive us to the airport following his inauguration earlier that day.

That morning, the detectives picked up Wilma and me at our home, which is not far from where my grandmother Helen Williams Gamble raised me. Many thoughts were running through my head as we drove past the modest homes in northeast Denver, a primarily black and immigrant working-class neighborhood during my youth that had changed over the years and become more gentrified with middle-class Anglos and Latinos.

These detectives had seen me at my highest points, from ribbon cuttings for new parks and professional sports facilities to Super Bowl and Stanley Cup victory parades. They walked with me in a thriving downtown anchored by new lofts and businesses and accompanied me to visit doctors at the city's public hospital, which I helped to keep open.

I always take pride when I see the tented roof at Denver International Airport (DIA). At the tenth anniversary of the opening in 2005, I reflected on all the hurdles we jumped to get the airport opened and what a great facility it is today. Photograph courtesy of Chris Carter, DIA

They also saw me at my most vulnerable, following funerals for children killed in gang shootings and feeling exhausted from twenty-hour workdays at city hall. The officers had watched me unwind with a stiff drink late at night at Pierre's Supper Club following political battles.

These detectives were like family, sharing home-cooked meals with me, Wilma and our children, Keith, Anthony, Allen, and Stephanie, and other relatives.

When we got to the passenger escalator at DIA, their important role in my life was over. I glanced back at the stoic men who had guarded me for twelve years, and the emotion in their faces brought a tear to my eye. Their presence was my last link to city hall, and as they walked away, they knew that my life, as well as their own lives, had changed forever.

I arrived in the Mile High City in 1953 as a sickly 100-pound twelve-year-old with asthma. Denver had a small, tight-knit black community that comprised 11 percent of the population by 1991. So not only were the odds against me in terms of growing from a skinny kid into a healthy adult, but also in terms of being one of two African American men in a mayoral runoff. I was proud that race never became an issue in this predominantly white city.

I was the underdog in the campaign, despite my election to the Colorado state legislature and my election as Denver's auditor. I ignored the advice of longtime friends to quit the mayor's race. Instead, I took my campaign to Denver's streets and walked more than 300 miles citywide. I slept in the homes of more than forty city residents. A Hispanic family served me tortillas and green chile for breakfast. A middle-class Anglo family gave me their only bedroom while they slept on a sofa bed in the family room. A wealthy couple allowed me to sleep in their luxury guest bedroom. And I brought my own army cot to a homeless shelter when I stopped there one night.

During my dozen years as mayor, Denver went from being

perceived as a cow town to being in the worldwide spotlight by hosting Pope John Paul II for World Youth Day in 1993, President William Clinton and world leaders for the Summit of the Eight in 1997, the Oklahoma City bombing trial in 1997, and massive parades for the Denver Broncos' two Super Bowl victories (1998 and 1999) and Colorado Avalanche's two Stanley Cup championships (1996 and 2001).

We also painfully and successfully addressed the ugly social issues of the Ku Klux Klan rally on Dr. Martin Luther King Jr.'s birthday, the gang warfare that claimed innocent lives, and the nearby tragedy of the Columbine High School shootings.

I was sued for asking for a day of prayer to end gang violence. I was sued for seeking more minority contracts for city projects. I surprised many when I proposed ending court-mandated busing for the public schools.

My first act as mayor in 1991 was to convene a Downtown Summit to map out a plan to revitalize the core of our city. Representatives from cities nationwide now visit Denver to see how we preserved our historic buildings and created a vital downtown, whereas their downtowns are turning into ghost towns.

"If elected mayor, what do you want Denver to be like?" I was asked during the 1991 mayoral campaign. "Do you want Denver to be like San Francisco or New York or Chicago or Santa Fe?"

I didn't hesitate with my response.

"I don't want Denver to be like any of those cities," I said. "I want Denver to be proud simply of being Denver. I want to create a city that other cities will want to emulate."

My goal was to make Denver residents feel so confident that any criticism of the city would seem trivial. At the end of my twelve years in office, I felt successful because Denverites had a little extra swagger in their walks that reflected their pride in their city.

The redevelopments of Stapleton International Airport and the former Lowry Air Force Base into residential and commercial communities with ample park space have received national and international awards.

"Some people never thought Wellington Webb would be a good manager," said Bill Hornby, former *Denver Post* newspaper editor and longtime Denver Planning Board chairman. "Maybe some of it was racism and Denver's conservative business community. He sure proved them wrong."

But on that hot July morning of Hickenlooper's inauguration, I was damned tired after three terms as the city's mayor. I was exhausted from the expectations, the demands, and staff changes.

We built just about everything we had wanted to, from DIA to nearly 2,500 acres of new parks; the addition to the Central Denver Branch Library; the Blair-Caldwell African American Research Library; a twenty-six-foot-tall Dr. Martin Luther King Jr. sculpture; the 1,100-bed Hyatt convention center hotel; and expansions to the Denver Art Museum, Colorado Convention Center, and the Denver Zoo. The Cherry Creek Shopping Center opened on my watch, along with new police district stations and recreation centers. Instead of people flocking to the suburbs, more than 100,000 people moved to Denver during my three terms.

We didn't leave much to be done. We pushed the envelope and always had multiple projects under way to stimulate the economy and create thousands of new jobs so no'one could question our work ethic and our vision.

Despite these accomplishments, I couldn't help but wonder what most politicians will never say: "What will be my legacy?"

In some cases, I felt I was lucky in my political career, which began with my election to the Colorado state legislature in 1972. Some people thought I was crazy to support a peanut farmer from Georgia for president. I was the first person in Colorado to make a donation to Jimmy Carter's campaign, and later served as his regional director for the U.S. Department of Health and Human Services (previously Health, Education and Welfare) under U.S. Secretaries

Joseph Califano and Patricia Roberts Harris.

Even though I walked out on Colorado governor Richard Lamm's first inauguration because he had not appointed any African Americans to his cabinet, he later asked me to join his cabinet as state director of regulatory agencies. Lamm also defended me in the face of negative campaigning during the 1991 mayoral race.

But luck only goes so far. I always tried to work harder than everyone else because I thought someone would say that I didn't belong. Again and again, I would think, "We will not lose; we will not fail." Not only would I have felt bad about failing, but as an African American, if I didn't do well, it would have made it even more difficult for those of color who sought leadership roles.

Polls showed I had only 7 percent in voter support seven months before the 1991 mayoral race, and I still trailed popular Denver district attorney Norm Early a month before the election. I knew it was sink-or-swim time. I laced up my tennis shoes and pledged to walk the city and not sleep in my own bed until after the election. The walk wasn't any brilliant strategy by my young campaign staff—we did it because we were broke. Every blister on my feet and my aching knee reminded me that this was my last shot at becoming mayor.

In 1983, I had mounted a late, unsuccessful campaign against Mayor Bill McNichols. Neither McNichols nor I could garner enough votes to make a runoff. Federico Peña, a former legislator, beat District Attorney Dale Tooley in the runoff, and as the city's first Latino mayor, Peña opened the door for other minorities. If I succeeded as the city's next leader, that door would not slam shut but would open wider for more people of color.

"Peña said, 'Imagine a great city,' and Wellington built it," said former Denver city councilwoman Joyce Foster. "And he built it in spite of all the negative press, the mean-spirited constituency, and people who were racist."

My work ethic came from my Grandmother Helen, who was a proud southern woman and whose pillars were dignity, pride, and good character. Whether you had a dime or more than $100 in your pocket, she believed that if you were of good character, you should walk the same and look the same, with dignity and pride. In doing so, others would look beyond economic status and see what really matters.

Except for my wife, Wilma, members of my family, and a few close friends, no one knows the difference between Wellington Webb the mayor and Wellington Webb the man.

The man started out as a shy kid from Chicago who relocated to Denver because of his asthma and parents' divorce. Few people thought I would grow into a political activist and fight for a number of social issues.

I learned as a child to conceal any weaknesses in my life. My childhood friends in Chicago and Gary, Indiana, didn't know I stayed indoors in the summer because the humidity triggered my asthma, even when I just walked around the block. I read a lot about the Roman heroes and the governing techniques of the Greek and Roman cultures, but I didn't tell anyone. They'd think a black kid from Chicago talking about Greek and Roman history was a square.

As a teenager, when my mother, Mardina, relocated to Denver with my four brothers, I didn't talk about the open bottles of liquor in our home or when her glass of "ice water" smelled like gin. She suffered a stroke in 1987 shortly after I was elected Denver's auditor.

Some of my Manual High School classmates recall me as a leader among the student body and a basketball star. Political success has a way of clouding people's memories. ... I was the introverted kid who sat in the back of the classroom—when I showed up. I nearly flunked out of high school, and I quit the basketball team as a senior because I didn't like the coach. During the graduation ceremony, only my grandmother knew that the neat leather folder designed to contain my diploma held a meaningless certificate.

My summer-school quest to get my diploma was nearly derailed when my grandmother let me sit in the city jail for a few days. My girlfriend had crashed my grandfather's car through a building while I was giving her a driving lesson. I unwisely lied to police about who was behind the wheel.

I became a father in my early twenties to twin sons, Anthony and Allen, with my first wife, Lyee. I seldom talk about the loss of our daughter, Felicia, who died from a sudden illness when she was two and a half. We married too young and divorced shortly after Felicia's death.

My grandmother introduced me to politics through her work as a Democratic district committeewoman, but, candidly, I initially got involved with political programs to help feed my family. The public schools didn't hire many African American male teachers in the mid-1960s. I had a college degree and was working in a potato chip factory. I supplemented my income by working with programs that addressed social issues and pushed for more job opportunities for minorities.

Wilma has been my partner in life and politics. Blending two families was not easy, and politics sometimes caused conflicts. Wilma's own successful political career was unfairly minimized after my election as mayor. Our young adult children also faced the burdens of their father being mayor, such as having to turn down jobs because of perceived conflicts of interest and our son Allen's public battle with substance abuse.

Perhaps the greatest misconception is that politicians are immune to criticism. Occasionally, I would get into moods where I was trying to figure out nine or ten issues and I wouldn't respond when someone said hello. Those are the days I probably shouldn't have been in public, because that's when I was seen as aloof.

There were times when I hurt and my family cried. It made me develop a thick skin; without it, I would have allowed the criticism to crush me. Politics is not for the weak.

Along with a thick skin came a mask. I didn't think it was appropriate for the public to see my tears when a child was shot by gang members, or my anger at receiving death threats against my family. The public needed to see the mayor as calm and in charge.

When Wilma and I arrived at the Denver Center for the Performing Arts for the 2003 inauguration, I heard someone call, "Mayor!"— and both Hickenlooper and I turned to respond. Denver was ending one chapter in its history and starting a new one.

My question of whether our work was valued was answered when Wilma and I were met by heartfelt applause from the crowd. I felt the appreciation was for all those hours of working seven days a week. When I was in office, some people applauded me. Others sucked up just because I had the title and the power. After I was no longer mayor was when I could really tell whether people appreciated what we did, because then there was nothing for them to gain.

As I approached the end of my tenure, I knew I wanted to temporarily get out of Denver after the inauguration of the new mayor. I didn't want to be around for anyone to ask me questions about how Mayor Hickenlooper, a successful businessman, was making the transition to city hall. This was Mayor Hickenlooper's time, not mine. Most people don't want the former coach making subjective statements about what the new coach is doing.

Fortunately for me, I was being given the highest recognition from my fraternity, Kappa Alpha Psi, at our annual meeting in Charlotte, North Carolina, the next day. So the timing was right. Wilma and I planned to leave Denver after the ceremony, and I would receive the Laurel Wreath Award, which had previously been given to other notable African Americans, including former congressman Louis Stokes of Ohio and the late, great attorney Johnnie Cochran.

I thought my life in politics was probably over on that day, and I was anxious to dive into the new challenge of starting a consulting business. Little did I know that nearly sixteen months later, I would take a shot at becoming chairman of the Democratic National Committee (DNC).

I saw this race as a once-in-a-lifetime opportunity for me to help shape the Democratic Party's message as a westerner who had led a major metropolitan city. I wanted to remind voters that Democrats are the party of the people. Democrats fight for such important issues as protecting Social Security and tackling the health care crisis. We are not antireligion but believe in civil rights for all Americans—whether Christian, Jewish, Muslim, Buddhist, or atheist.

Although party leaders encouraged me to enter the race, party members chose former Vermont governor Howard Dean. Dean already had his political machine in place from his failed presidential bid. Even so, I can still serve my party and the people in meaningful and useful ways.

When many people get to a certain age, they ponder, "Is my life story worth my writing a book? Do I have anything to say, and if I do, is anyone going to read it? Who am I writing for?"

With my life in transition after leaving the mayor's office, I began to reflect on my story.

I do believe that everyone's life is its own book. Each stage—whether high school, college, professions, marriage, or family—is a chapter.

Each person is different, as defined by his or her personal experiences, education, and environment. In some cases, it helps to explain why some people are in a room with a thousand people and feel lonely and others can be in a room by themselves and feel truly blessed.

My chapters are about the roots that helped a skinny asthmatic kid move to Denver to new friends, a new home, and how I often felt somewhat unsettled. I was always looking for something new, trying to stretch to see what's on the other side of the hill. At the top of one hill was my becoming leader of the Mile High City.

I was elected as the forty-second mayor of Denver against all odds and reelected in 1995 without the support of Denver's two major daily newspapers. In that reelection race, I faced the most vile, vicious, unprecedented attack on me and my family, not only by

Republicans, but by so-called liberal Democrats.

This story should come from me because the reality is that black politicians are judged by a different set of standards. I made some missteps with the media in my first term, but there's no denying that Mayor Peña and I were dissected and put under a microscope with critical and suspicious eyes.

Some would say that being scrutinized comes with the job of being mayor. But there are some glaring contrasts to how the media viewed my administration and the one that immediately followed.

After living in Denver for my entire adult life, I hired competent people whom I trusted and admired; the media called that cronyism. When Mayor Hickenlooper appointed some longtime friends to cabinet positions, they were referred to as his "brain trust." This is no judgment against Mayor Hickenlooper, because he had every right to pick bright people he trusts. He appointed my daughter Stephanie O'Malley as the director of excise and licenses, whereas she practically had to move out of state to get a job to avoid any appearance of conflict of interest during my twelve years in office. Other people tagged as cronies in my administration were asked by Mayor Hickenlooper to be part of his "brain trust." This is just one example of what minority politicians face.

Even two years after I left office, a newspaper reporter asked if I was related to a black developer who defaulted on a city loan. Unnamed sources started the gossip that the woman was my niece and that is why she got the contract when I was in office. I told the reporter our only common thread is that we are both black, and I did not do a "favor" for her or anyone—period. But I will fight to provide opportunities for those who are qualified and previously have been denied access. I will fight to guarantee access, but I won't guarantee outcome. My belief as a capitalist is to give all people the opportunity to succeed or fail based on their work ethic and intellect.

The reporter's question about the defaulted loan is no different from an insensitive police officer seeing a black man driving a Mercedes and jumping to the conclusion that the car is stolen. The question is akin to someone assuming a Latino man who has tattoos must be a gang member.

It may sting to hear that those stereotypes and racial attitudes still exist in Denver and cities nationwide. But ignoring these realities or shrugging them off as an old politician's sour grapes won't make things better for future generations.

To Denver voters' credit, they choose leaders who show they are willing to work hard and smart for the city. They don't base their choices on the color of the candidates' skin. But once a person of color gets into office, the double standards begin—and don't end once we become private citizens again.

The public got a glimpse of Wellington Webb the DNC chairman candidate, the mayor, the city auditor, a state department director, a federal regional department director, and a state legislator.

Here's my story about Wellington Webb the man.

My grandmother Helen Williams Gamble was a great influence on my life. She would have been proud her oldest grandson became Denver's forty-second mayor, and blown away that the city named a public office building in my honor.

Chapter One

Roots: From Alabama, Mississippi,
and Louisiana to Denver

When I was in my early twenties—long before Alex Haley's book *Roots* was made into a television series—I asked my grandmother to tell me about her family. This was a conversation I suspect most African American families have had with their parents or grandparents.

The dignified woman who raised me from the time I was twelve suddenly became upset and then defiant.

"I'm not going to discuss that with you," Grandmother Helen said. "Why do you want to know that anyway? What do you want me to tell you that you haven't already read in books?"

I ignored her reluctance and pushed her to tell me about her parents and grandparents.

"What do you want me to tell you about?" she said with anger and hurt in her voice. "How our mothers and grandmothers were raped? How we had no authority to define who we were? How our dads and grandfathers could not stand up for themselves as men? Why do you want to dredge all of that up?"

I later realized I was being insensitive because I really didn't prepare her for what I was trying to find out. I did not want to bring up the pain and misery of what she obviously experienced as a child. I was trying to get a sense of where she developed her strength, what she had experienced in her lifetime, and what drove her independence after her Chicago home burned down to move to Denver, where she didn't know a soul.

14

For anyone tracing a family tree, it can be difficult to find out information about your great-grandparents. My cousins, who were researching the Brazley family, became my library to my roots.

Isaac and Judith Brazley had five children in the small town of Little River, Alabama. Their names were Moses, Isaac, Ann, Edward, and Pleasant. Isaac married Rose Madison, and their youngest of ten children, Helen Mae Brazley, my grandmother, was born on October 2, 1894. Her siblings were Willie, Isaac, Peter, Carrie, Annie, James, Eugene, Clarine, and Rosa.

According to the 1900 census of Jackson County, Mississippi, my great-grandmother had her first child when she was seventeen, and the rest followed every two to four years. The children's ages ranged from five to twenty-eight in 1900.

As with most African Americans, I had no clue where in Africa my ancestors originated. It wasn't until I was older that technology helped give me a larger picture of my roots. By 2006, some blacks were having their DNA tested to trace their ancestry. My test showed that I inherited through my mother a segment of DNA that is found in the Bamileke people of Cameroon. The Bamileke people in coastal West Africa historically raised maize and peanuts and also were accomplished carvers of wood and ivory. They used elaborate masks in public ceremonies and funerals.

More surprising were the results of the DNA test on my father's side. My father's ancestry is traced back to England, Holland, Spain, and Portugal—some of the primary countries that traded slaves.

It was much less sophisticated and more difficult to find out information about my Grandmother Helen's youth. I was able to cobble together some of her family history during our short and infrequent conversations on the topic and from responses to my inquiries to my Brazley cousins.

Grandmother Helen was born in Selma, Alabama. Her parents both died when she was young, although I'm not sure of the circumstances. She was raised by her older brother, Peter, in a town called Carrolton, Louisiana. As an adult, I tried to find Carrolton and discovered that the once separate community incorporated in 1833 had became a neighborhood of New Orleans.

When she did talk about her childhood, my grandmother always gave credit to her brother for raising her with his own children, Florice and Jimmye. I was encouraged as a child to learn to play piano by Florice, who studied at Julliard and was a great opera singer. I always wanted to use my hands to bounce a basketball as opposed to playing piano keys. I went to only two piano lessons and played hooky from the rest.

I wasn't lucky enough to get the musical genes, but two cousins, who have never met each other, both studied classical music. Florice's son, Edward, "Big Ed," is an accomplished violinist, and my cousin Stanley Jordan is a well-known jazz guitarist. Jordan also earned a degree in classical music from Princeton.

I did inherit my grandmother's steady commitment to the Baptist church. Grandmother Helen was raised in the Baptist church; from there she derived her inner faith. She had faith in God, faith in the future, and faith that she could withstand the pressures of a racist society. I found a speech she wrote titled "Subject: Benefactors for Good." In careful cursive words written with a pencil, my grandmother outlined how Christians and the "Negro man" could succeed with faith.

> As benefactors for good, with a courage as great and a heart as fearless, you today can point the eyes of your people to unlimited opportunities and say to them as you go to and fro, beyond you lies success, take it! Success is not within the power of another man or race to give, it is within yourselves.
>
> As benefactors for good, do something! Hope for something! Achieve something and admonish our people against the habit of begging so much, which is a reflection upon individuals as well as the race. The paths of ages are littered with the memories of nations that achieved with less.

She graduated from Dillard University with a teaching degree, and she also took dressmaking and design classes. She worked as a modiste, a dressmaker and dress designer, in the Shoppe of Madam Loef'fell.

My grandmother was like many African Americans of her generation. She had a college degree but became a professional dressmaker because she could earn a higher income. Other blacks took jobs at the post office because, as part of the federal government, they were guaranteed a regular paycheck. Government was seen as somewhat of a protector for African Americans and minorities in general.

My grandmother preached the importance of education throughout her life. Yet it wasn't until my brother, Joseph, and I dallied with the Black Panther movement that she revealed her schooling wasn't always pleasant.

Joe, who is ten years younger, and I started leaning to the far left in the 1960s. We came to my grandmother's home in Denver with our black pants, black shirts, black leather jackets, and medallions around our necks.

"Did you join the Black Panthers?" she asked. "I don't know why you like that black stuff."

We started telling her about Black Power and how our race had been repressed. She shot back that in the South, not only was there prejudice against African Americans, but there was interracial prejudice among the blacks, especially in Louisiana, where she grew up. If you had light skin, you didn't associate with people of darker complexions. If you had dark skin, you didn't associate with light-skinned African Americans.

We just looked at her, confused, and then she told us that because she has light skin, she sometimes had to run home from high school. She said the students with dark skin would tell her she had no nation—she was a mongrel and half-breed, and she must have white blood in her.

"I go through all of that, and now I look at you two standing here with black leather jackets on," she said in disgust.

We were both stunned.

As an adult, I came across "The Speech" by Willie Lynch from 1712. Lynch, a British slave owner in the West Indies, was invited to the colony of Virginia to teach his methods to slave owners. His chilling speech talks about how the Ancient Romans used cords of wood as crosses for "standing humans along its highways in large numbers."

"You are here using the tree and the rope on occasion. I caught a whiff of a dead slave hanging from a tree a couple of miles back," Lynch said in his speech.

Lynch told the slave owners that killing their slaves was "losing valuable stock." He urged them instead to turn the slaves on themselves by making them question their differences, not only in age and sex, but in their skin color.

"Distrust is stronger than trust and envy is stronger than adulation, respect, or admiration," Lynch said. "The Black slave after receiving this indoctrination shall carry on and will become self re-fueling and self generating for hundreds of years, maybe thousands."

Grandmother Helen's traumatic experiences in her youth as an African American girl with light skin likely had roots in Lynch's speech.

Grandmother Helen grew into a serious young woman, but she found fun in her future husband, "Sweet Papa George" Williams. His father, Henry Williams, was a minister in Moss Point, Mississippi, which is basically separated by a railroad track from Pascagoula, Mississippi. Pascagoula is home port for many ships; Engles shipyard, located there, still produces many U.S. military vessels.

In my cousins' research, Brazley family members discovered that many of the relatives who grew up in Alabama were originally craftsmen. They eventually migrated to Mobile and Pascagoula to work in the shipyards as pipe fitters, plumbers, electricians, and carpenters.

Henry Williams's original last name was Hubbard, but that was the name of a plantation owner and he changed it, as did so many other black families during that time period.

George Williams's mother, Frances, my great-grandmother, was half white, including Irish.

George was about six-foot-two and was referred to as a lady's man, a dapper dresser, and in the early days, he had his hair processed, which was referred to as a konk. He was like a character in Spike Lee's movie *Malcolm X*. The movie gives you a sense of what the 1920s were like for many African American men. That was my grandfather—in a zoot suit with konked hair. He put too much of that processing stuff on his hair, burned it, and ended up bald before it was fashionable.

I never knew my grandparents when they were married, as they were divorced by the time I came along, but they always remained friends.

Out of their union, they had three daughters: Vernadette, Frances, and Mardina. Vernadette was the oldest. She was a sickly child and had a heart condition. As an adult, she died of lung cancer in Denver after years of smoking cigarettes. The middle child was Frances, who was independent throughout her life and protected both of her sisters. Vernadette and Frances were born in Pascagoula.

I only recently discovered that my grandparents separated in Pacagoula before my mother, Mardina, was born.

Grandmother Helen took her two daughters, Vernadette and Frances, and moved back to New Orleans to be near her family. She lived there until her older sister, Carrie, asked them to come live with her in Chicago.

My grandfather left Mississippi and reunited with his wife and two daughters in Chicago. My mother, Mardina, was born in Chicago on January 9, 1921. My grandfather worked for the R. R. Donnelley printing plant in Chicago before a final split with Grandmother led him back to Mississippi.

My grandmother made sure all of her girls were the most fashionable ones in school, and she made all of their clothes. She would comb through women's magazines such as *Harper's Bazaar* and *Vogue* and copy patterns for her daughters' clothes. They were not the most economically affluent, but they sure were the best-dressed girls in school.

19

Aunt Frances had one admirer she liked to tell us about. He played the piano, but she didn't particularly care for him because of his dark skin. His name was Nat King Cole. I can imagine how often she wondered why she let him get away. But then Frances was, as we say, "color struck"—she only was attracted to black men with light skin.

My mother had an interesting admirer too. John Johnson started a little magazine called *Negro Digest* that didn't do well. Then he started an offshoot magazine called *Ebony*, which became the most important publication in black America. In later years, Johnson followed my political career in Denver and ran stories about my tenure. He sent my grandmother 100 'American Beauty' red roses when she died.

Aunt Frances looked out for her two sisters, and she wouldn't hesitate to chase away any male she thought was unsuitable. She also wasn't afraid to fight any girls who gossiped about her sisters.

That was Frances, independent to the core. Her independence—and some would say her stubbornness—never let up, even when she faced terminal cancer. Frances knew she was dying, and in her eighties, she made a trip to visit family members, including her nephews and their families in Denver. She had had previous surgeries to treat her cancer and needed to use a walker because she was weak. But nothing was going to keep her from watching my grandson, Allen Jr., play quarterback for South High School.

"It's freezing outside," I warned her on a typical November day in Denver. "There's no way you can get up those bleachers with that walker."

She gave me that Aunt Frances look of determination. "You are either going to take me or I am going to throw my walker down your front steps, crawl to a taxicab, and get to the football stadium on my own," Aunt Frances warned me.

Well, the difference between Aunt Frances and most people is that what she said, she meant. We got her to the stadium and she sat on those cold bleachers, still covered with frost and snow, with the rest of us.

Aunt Frances epitomized the spirit of our family. Despite any obstacles, she would not be denied. Grandmother Helen could never control her. Come to think of it, she couldn't control any of her daughters. She wanted them to go to college, but they had their own plans.

Vernadette came to Denver and became a nurse's aide at Rose Memorial Hospital. Frances got married, didn't like her husband, fired him, joined the Women's Army Corps, and was stationed in Walla Walla, Washington. Her main job was folding parachutes for soldiers during World War II. She later married Eddie DeVille from Lake Charles, Louisiana, whom she met in the service.

My mother didn't want to go to college either, so Grandmother sent her to stay with her Aunt Rosie in Pasadena, California. Aunt Rosie got her ready to go to Pasadena Junior College, but a young man named Wellington Marion Webb changed that plan.

My parents met on a blind date in Chicago.

"My future husband, Henry Flowers, knew Wellington, and Dina was my childhood friend," recalled my parents' longtime friend Almeda "Boots" Flowers of Michigan. "I was the only one who called her Dina. I didn't want to deal with the whole Mardina name. We wanted to hook up Wellington with one of our friends and invited Dina to join us. It was Wellington and Dina who hooked up and was a twosome from then on."

My father, Wellington Marion Webb, was born on February 2, 1914, in Brighton, Alabama. His father, William Martin Webb, was born in Marion, Alabama, and was a graduate of the Tuskegee Institute in 1900. He actually named my dad Marion Wellington Webb.

"Why did you change your name?" I asked my father when I was older.

"Because Marion was a girl's name and I got tired of fighting other boys because I didn't like them calling me Marion," he said.

In the South, after the Civil War, many African American families named their kids after important people instead of with their slave master's name: George Washington Jones or Abraham Lincoln Smith, for example. In some cases, they would pick a Jewish name, such as Cohen, or an Irish name, such as O'Malley.

I didn't like my name when I was young. When I started playing sports, friends always referred to me by my last name because it was easier to remember.

"Shoot the damn ball, Webb," "Block the shot, Webb," "Get the rebound, Webb!" You can always tell my longtime friends because they still call me Webb.

But as I got older, I appreciated the name Wellington. It also made sense that my Grandfather Webb—whom I only met once—chose a unique name. He had a gift for words, and he was an advocate of education. He graduated as a tailor because Tuskegee at that time emphasized liberal arts and learning a craft. He also was an extemporaneous speaker, and people loved to hear him speak.

As I got older and researched the history of African Americans, I saw how both sides of my family identified with "The Great Debate of 1895" between black leaders W. E. B. DuBois and Booker T. Washington. DuBois said that getting an education and having the smartest 10 percent of African Americans leading the race would improve the black community. He was Harvard educated and went on to be one of the founders of the National Association for the Advancement of Colored People. Washington, unlike DuBois, was born a slave, claimed his freedom, and lived in the South. He was the founder of the Tuskegee Institute, one of the premier historically black colleges, which emphasized trades such as carpentry, brick masonry, and tailoring. In his response to DuBois's remarks about education, Washington urged blacks to plant their buckets down where they were and improve themselves through a trade.

Grandfather Webb saw both sides of the debate, having attended Tuskegee and having become a tailor. He was also an intellectual, like DuBois. He read about the Duke of Wellington defeating Napoleon in the Battle of Waterloo. That's why he named my father Wellington.

Grandmother Helen also related to DuBois and Washington. She graduated from Dillard University with a teaching degree, yet survived on her skills as a dressmaker. She believed, more like

DuBois, that her passion was education for her children and grand-children. She wanted them not only to be intellectually bright, but also gifted in leadership.

I also later learned that Grandfather Webb was a romantic. He married Gertrude Evans, and when my grandmother died, my father found some love letters my grandfather had sent her while he was at Tuskegee. He always started the letters with "My dear Gertrude" or "My darling Gertrude."

On February 6, 1897, my grandfather wrote:

> Your kind missive was received, contents noted and care-fully read. I need not say I was glad to hear from you, for indeed it always gives me consolation to hear from you or even think of you in any respect. Since your departure I have been thinking of you and consulted my self, how long will it be before we can be with each other not to be from one another so often.
>
> Gertrude I was glad to know you arrived home safely, finding Mamma better than she had been and hope she will continue. Although you hated to leave one, but, at the moment when I looked down up on my dear and said goodby there was never such an emotion before and since. Really when I was in Birmingham and was going to leave you I thought it was hard, but this was beyond all. How pleasant it would have been had I been along to accompany you, and then when you lay your head against a devoted breast which would have over looked you and protect you from harm.
>
> Gertrude you thanked one for my hospitality towards you, yes your thanks I appreciated, but my dear there is noth-ing under the sun I would not do for you if it was reasonable. Only one thing I regretted, was that I could not make your trip [any] more pleasant for you then it was. I shall not add any excuses for you know the condition of things or affairs with a person in school. You have returned home, I suppose

you are feeling much better and work is not so laborious, anyway I hope you will keep in good health and ever remember to always find yourself reading something and finally you will have formed one of the best habits in the world.

I saw Mrs. Young yesterday just after I received your letter, she was very polite just as always but it came to me what you said so kind, but know how to keep a person busy. Our communication was very short as the school bell rang, which you know everybody must turn. Ever since you left it has been raining and some what cold, and at present it is raining, although we must go. On the night you left my night's rest was not a good one, although with standing that you were present with me all of that night. Actually when I got to my room I thought of my books, but could not concentrate my thoughts on nothing but you.

Frank ask me to day when I had heard from you I replied and told him, now let him hear from you soon. Remember me to you Mamma, Miss Reid and their friends of mine. When you invite again let me know how Bessie enjoyed reading my letter. I will try to see you all in August. Good by my darling as I am going to Chapel and must close.

—Yours darling, W. M. Webb

After reading the letters, I told my brother Joe: "Hell, we didn't even really know our grandfather, but as well as he wrote, we would have married him too."

My grandfather died on January 22, 1955, in Brighton, Alabama. My mother was the first to sign the condolence booklet at the funeral. She also signed, "Masters Wellington and Joseph Webb," even though my brother and I didn't attend the service at Bradford's Funeral Chapel in Birmingham, Alabama. I wondered why the service wasn't at the Sixteenth Street Baptist Church. As I read the program, I noticed that Elder C. Sampson Myles, a Baptist minister who left the church to become a leading minister and scholar in the

Seventh Day Adventist Church, presided over the service.

My Grandmother Gertrude was from Alabama and was part Cherokee. My father's Indian heritage was evident in his red complexion.

During the 1940s and 1950s, many black people claimed they had Indian blood because at the time, being part Native American was considered better than being black. Some blacks went so far as to name their children after Native Americans. I can always tell how old someone is if they have a child named Cochise. Once I was at an airport in Chicago and saw that an airline reservation attendant's name tag said Sonseeahray.

"Your dad is about sixty-three years old and loves Western movies," I told the woman. "You may wonder where your name came from. It means "morning star," and he got the name from a movie with James Stewart and Jeff Chandler called *Broken Arrow*."

I loved that movie as a kid. It was one of the first films that showed Native Americans were intelligent and had principles they were fighting for. It wasn't the typical John Wayne movie where he killed 432 Indians with one six-shooter. Chandler had to play Cochise, because they didn't try to find a Native American actor. But the movie also featured Jay Silverheels, who went on to play Tonto in *The Lone Ranger*.

Yes, I am a Western movie buff, and I later learned that interest in the West extended to my father's family. My Grandmother Gertrude's brother, Frank, went to Arizona in 1919, became a cowboy, and lost touch with his family.

My father was very close to his mother because he was an only child and unexpected. I didn't know much about his side of the family until I tape-recorded a conversation with him in 1985. At the time, he was ill with prostate cancer but held on to see my daughter Stephanie graduate from Howard University in Washington, D.C.

We met in a terrace restaurant at the Washington Hilton Hotel, where he somewhat reluctantly agreed to talk about his past. It struck me how little I knew of my parents and ancestors. My father was hesitant to let me tape the conversation. He may have felt that his son was not proud of him working for the Chicago and North Western

Railway (C&NW) for forty-two years, considering I was a college graduate and his granddaughter now had a degree from Howard.

"I don't know much about my dad because he wasn't around," my father told me. "The only person around me when I got to the age of knowing was my mother and my grandmother, Blaney Kirk."

I learned that my father had a sister.

"She was older," he told me. "And I was born nine years after my sister passed. So Mother had her two kids fourteen years apart. She went to one doctor and the doctor told her she had a tumor and they were going to operate. So before having the operation, my mother went to another doctor and he told her she was pregnant."

My father went on to explain that Grandmother Gertrude worked for an undertaker in Birmingham, Alabama, and his grandmother was a nanny for Birmingham's wealthy families. They attended the Sixteenth Street Baptist Church, where in the 1960s four little girls were killed when the church was hit with a racial bombing.

The threesome moved to Chicago when my father was nine. He began attending Englewood High School in 1928 outside of Chicago and told me there were very few "colored students" there. That is what they called African Americans at that time—a reference later changed to "Negro," then "black," and ultimately "African American."

My father had to drop out of high school to help support the family. He was always disappointed he never got his high-school diploma, but was proud he found work to help feed his family.

He joined two Depression-area programs created by the federal government, the Works Progress Administration program and Civilian Conservation Corps at army bases in Illinois and St. Louis.

On May 29, 1937, he was hired by the C&NW to work in the club car and serve drinks. He was twenty-three years old, and his first trip was to Oakland, California, then Minneapolis, Minnesota.

I asked him what he remembered about the railroad, but before he could answer, I told him I didn't like the fact that most of the porters, a lower paying job, were black, whereas the better jobs, the conductors and stewards, were usually held by white people.

"Well, there wasn't any jobs for us black folks other than the post office or the railroad, and I went on the railroad," my father said. "I was making $72 a month, but the tips were good. And there wasn't any jobs open for us far as chefs, stewards, or in-charge men. But after being on the road for twenty-some years, the unions came in and broke that down. When I used to go back and forth to Birmingham, we couldn't go in the dining car. When we went in the dining car, they would put us behind a curtain, and that's where you would eat, separated from the white people. You'd be in the same dining car, but there would be a curtain between the tables where us blacks ate."

My father became noticeably uncomfortable talking about his past, and he suddenly stopped. It was just too painful.

For a young black man in the late 1930s and early 1940s, the railroad job was too stable for him to ever consider leaving, especially when he decided to get married.

"Dina's mother planned for sixteen bridesmaids," Boots Flowers recalled. "She had the material picked out to make the dresses and we were all measured."

In the meantime, my mother had different plans.

"She said she didn't want that, so she had a small wedding," Flowers said. "Her mother just about had a fit."

Flowers and her future husband attended my parents' wedding in the summer of 1940 in Chicago. I was born at 11:06 A.M. on February 17, 1941, in Cook County Hospital in Chicago.

Chapter Two

Childhood, Grandmother Helen, Divorce

I've been told I was nine pounds at birth, and as the first grandchild for both my mother and father's families, of course I was spoiled.

The year of my birth, Franklin Delano Roosevelt was inaugurated to a third term and M&M plain chocolate candies were introduced to the public. The Ford Motor Company signed its first contract with a labor union, and religious training in public schools was declared unconstitutional. When I was ten months old, the Japanese bombed Pearl Harbor and killed more than 2,000 U.S. seamen.

My father was working on the railroad when I was born. Aunt Frances picked up my mother and me from the hospital and started giving my mother instructions. She took us home to my Aunt Vernadette's house, where my mother and father were living. They later moved in with Grandmother Helen, who was still living in her sister Carrie's home, which was large enough for the whole family.

Grandmother Gertrude lived in a much smaller place that was called a kitchenette. A kitchenette is basically one room that serves as a living room and a bedroom. Off to one side is a little kitchen area with a small stove and a compact refrigerator. There were five or six apartments on one floor, and the renters shared one bathroom. You always had to remember to bring your own toilet tissue, and if you left the roll, it disappeared quickly. There was also only one bathtub for each floor, so Grandmother Gertrude had a bowl in her kitchen area to wash up in.

When Grandmother Helen bought her home in Denver, my

My mother and father wanted the popular photograph of the times. I was a
few months old when they had this shot taken for history.

mother rented an upstairs room that was larger than Grandmother Gertrude's entire kitchenette in Chicago.

My early years were spent in Chicago, going back and forth to the South on family vacations to the home of my mother's father in Moss Point, Mississippi, and to my grandmother's family in Pascagoula.

Like most people who relocated to Chicago, Grandfather Williams kept his property in Mississippi, to which he returned following his divorce. I remember the trips to see him in my youth. We would gas up in Chicago and plot our route so that we wouldn't have to stop for gas in segregated, unfriendly places. There was always fear until we got to our destination because of how many black people would disappear on trips between Chicago and Mississippi.

The night before the trip, my mother would make a meal of fried chicken and put it in a shoebox because we couldn't stop anywhere along the route to eat. We also never knew if we could use the restrooms at the gas stations or if we'd be greeted with "No Colored" signs.

After I moved to Denver to live with Grandmother Helen, I often returned to Chicago to visit my father and Grandmother Gertrude. During one of my summer visits, I remember seeing the newspaper headlines about a missing Chicago boy named Emmett Till. He lived right on Sixty-Third and Lawrence, which was a block from Grandmother Gertrude.

Till disappeared while visiting relatives in Mississippi. When he was reported missing, everyone in the neighborhood—many who had relocated to Chicago from Mississippi because it was the last train stop—feared the worst. They later found Till's unmercifully tortured and mutilated body. He was killed for allegedly whistling at a white woman. I thought that just as easily could have been me.

As I grew older and looked back on Till's death, I think that tragedy really raised the consciousness of America to the injustices experienced by blacks, especially those in the South. Till's mother was very brave to allow her son's beaten, bloated, unrecognizable face and body to be displayed in an open casket. Every black family I knew sat down their children and grandchildren and warned them of the dangers of traveling to other parts of the country, especially the South.

But as a child growing up in Chicago, I was sheltered from most of the racial problems of the 1940s and early 1950s.

My mother loved being the center of attention, and that also meant that I had the best birthday parties of anyone in my neighborhood. She always had an abundance of cake, ice cream, and a pile of presents to spoil her only child.

I remained the only child on both sides of the family for about ten years, so I got just about every toy the minute it hit the stores, whether it was a sled or a bike. I also had a set of thirty-six little toy soldiers from World War II, but my elementary school buddy had ninety-six. I was about six or seven years old and determined to go see his collection. After school, we crossed a busy street called South Park Way and went to see the troops. Of course, my parents had no clue where I was.

There was a circus in town at the time and there were rumors that the circus workers, commonly called gypsies, would steal your kids. My parents called the police, and neighbors were frantically looking for me. I came waltzing home, proud of myself for having borrowed some of my buddy's soldiers. The look of relief on my parents' faces faded quickly, and I got a good spanking that night.

Time with my father was scheduled around his trips running the railroad. Some of those trips teamed up with Union Pacific, which would require overnight stays in Denver. The black railroad workers stayed in the area of Denver that now houses the $16 million Blair-Caldwell African American Research Library. The neighborhood, near downtown Denver, is known as Five Points because of the intersection of major and neighborhood streets that form five points.

The Points neighborhood was made up primarily of black residents and had a national reputation for having some of the best jazz clubs in the country. The only time most white people would come to the area was to hear jazz greats such as Sarah Vaughn, Billie Holiday, Duke Ellington, Ella Fitzgerald, and nearly all of the other jazz stars

My father worked as a porter with the Chicago and North Western Railway for forty-two years. As a young boy, I cherished the time we had together when he wasn't out of town for his job.

In Chicago, my parents, Wellington
Marion Webb and Mardina Williams
Webb, lived with my Grandmother
Helen in a small apartment when I was a
child. We later moved to Gary, Indiana,
where my brother Joe was born.

of the 1930s to the 1960s.

When I was a young child in Chicago with my parents, Grandmother Helen was about fifty-one and basically living alone there because her daughters were grown. Her sister, Carrie, had died, and my grandmother inherited Carrie's home, but the house burned down and my grandmother lost everything. She thought this was a good time to start over outside of Chicago.

Before my dad told Grandmother Helen about Denver, Colorado, she had never heard of it. He explained to her that it was a really clean city and seemed like a nice place to live. If she wanted a fresh start in a new place, he told her Denver would be a good choice.

"Well, I think I'm going to try that," she said. "I'm going to start a new life."

Denver had its own version of segregation when my grandmother arrived. An invisible line kept blacks from owning homes in primarily white neighborhoods. At one point, the line was drawn at Downing Street; then it moved to Race Street. The line would later move to York Street. The other side of York to Colorado Boulevard was known as Sugar Hill. Sugar Hill is an area that whites decided to move out of and blacks would move in, but the owners doubled the prices. Blacks bought the houses anyway because they wanted to move out of the poor neighborhoods, even though they paid twice as much as the homes were worth.

Denver also had one of the most integrated neighborhoods in the country. To the credit of the Park Hill neighborhood, which runs from Colorado Boulevard to the old Stapleton International Airport area, whites decided to stay and let the diversity happen naturally and fairly.

Grandmother Helen bought a home in northeast Denver at 3220 Williams Street, and later another home at 3224 Williams Street. She was proud to be the second black resident in a neighborhood comprising primarily Italian and Irish immigrants and some Hispanic families. Grandmother was well known in the area because she served as a Democratic district committeewoman. She did the job Chicago-style, which meant that she knew everyone personally in the precinct.

"Wellington's grandmother was like the matriarch of the whole area," recalled my childhood friend Sam Batey, whose mother, Thelma, was a block captain for the Democrats. "Mrs. Gamble was the lady that everyone would go to for advice. She had the wisdom for all of the young families in the area."

Grandmother also continued her work as a dressmaker in Denver.

"Helen was a tall, gracious, beautiful, dignified, and very strong woman," recalled her longtime friend Ruby Kirk Gray. "She was the finest seamstress. Not only did she sew for the leading black women in town, but also for the rich, rich white women."

Grandmother was a member of New Hope Baptist Church, and she designed and created an elegant evening gown for Reverend M. C. Williams's wife, Anna Lee Williams. Anna Lee was an operatic singer whose desire to perform at Carnegie Hall was realized.

"She sewed little pearls all over that dress," Gray said. "Whatever Helen did, she did it with her whole heart. She pushed through the hard times with high character and principles."

My brother Joe recalled that a wealthy family offered to buy grandmother some stock in a start-up hamburger restaurant in gratitude for her sewing their daughter's wedding dress.

"My grandmother told them to just keep their money because it didn't sound like something to spend good money on," Joe said. "She felt that good money should be spent on shelter and food and not to take a risk. Cash was king and accepting that gift seemed foolish to her. The stock turned out to be in McDonald's."

She never dreamed that one by one, her family from Chicago would follow her to Denver, but that's exactly how it happened. She was the matriarch who relocated to a place where she didn't know anybody, and that took a lot of courage.

I was the first of my family to join my grandmother in the Mile High City. I spent one semester at Mitchell Elementary School. As I look back, it's clear my father and mother were having difficulties in

their marriage, and I was sheltered from that and sent to my grandmother, who provided stability.

"I thought he was a fine boy," recalled neighbor Ira Slack. "Even
back then, I thought, *Someday, this boy is going to be great.* He had
a look in his eyes that he was just one of those boys that you could
always depend on."

I later found out that my parents divorced while I was in Denver, but they would soon remarry.

My parents followed Aunt Frances and her husband, Eddie
DeVille, to Gary. They were both GIs, and after World War II, they
qualified to get homes on the GI Bill. My dad wasn't able to save a lot
of money from his railroad job, but Aunt Frances helped him get the
home. Frances and Eddie also opened a gas station, where I would
later arrive as a directionless teenager.

They had three children: David, Sheila, and Sharon, who were
closer to my four brothers' ages; I was their older cousin.

"The apartments in Chicago were small, and the children had
no yards to play in," recalled Evelyn Taylor, a Gary neighbor. "When
we got to Gary, the yards were so big. We were happy."

I left Denver and joined my parents in Gary. Then, after ten
years of being an only child, my brother Joe came along, and we
settled in as a family.

I was a good student at East Pulaski Elementary School. My
fourth-grade report card says I got As in arithmetic, spelling, reading, writing, and social studies and Bs in music and physical education. I got check marks that I was doing well in following directions,
doing neat work, and getting along with others. The only place I
needed to improve was in punctuality. (That issue dogged me as an
adult. When I was mayor, the media used to joke that all press conferences were on "Webb Time"—that usually meant I was running
behind fifteen to twenty minutes.)

My father was still working for the railroad, and my mother did
what many women did in those days: she was a homemaker. We had
a routine: church on Sunday at the Virginia Street Baptist Church

and Cub Scout meetings during the week.

Across the street lived the Thornton family, which included seventeen children. Dudley Thornton was my age, and we went to school together. I also hung out with his brother Gene. I always felt protected from bullies when I was with Dudley because if anyone messed with him or me, there were sixteen brothers and sisters to deal with.

A large part of Gary's population worked in Chicago and would take the train or drive into the city during the week. The main jobs in Gary were at the steel mills. Gary's population always increased after a strike—the steel mill would close down, and the men would get reacquainted with their wives.

I was about ten years old when something happened that would change my life forever. I remember this night like it was yesterday. I was asleep and suddenly woke up gasping for air. My mother grabbed me and propped me up between her legs so I could sit up and try to breathe before she called the hospital.

"It sounds like he's having an asthma attack," a nurse told her. "You can bring him into the hospital tomorrow. If it gets real bad, you can bring him in tonight."

All that night, I sat in my mother's lap, struggling to breathe. When future asthma attacks got worse, I had to go to the hospital to get shots that were given to me ten minutes apart. Sometimes I had to be placed in a hospital bed draped with plastic with oxygen pumped in to help me breathe. They didn't have small oxygen masks in those days.

The asthma affected my whole life. I couldn't run very far or do much activity in the summer because the humidity was so high in Gary. In those days, the newspapers and television news would post a daily pollen count, a ragweed count, and report on the number of new polio cases. My asthma was always worse when the pollen and ragweed counts were high.

We had one of the first televisions, and our friends would come by and watch. They used to broadcast a sign-off signal of a Native

American. We'd stare at that Indian for a long time. Maybe we thought he would say something, and if he did it would have probably scared us to death.

I would try to play games such as dodgeball, stickball, basketball, and baseball, but the wheezing would kick in and I'd have to sit down. Today, I am six-foot-four and 275 pounds. In those days, I was 100 pounds. I can thank Grandmother Helen, who was five-foot-eight, and both of my grandfathers, who were six-foot-two, for my physical stature. But as a child struggling with asthma, I was a skinny, sickly kid.

I never told any of my friends why I often didn't come out to play for three or four days and spent my time reading indoors.

"I didn't know he was sickly as a child," said Gwendolyn McCain, a Gary childhood friend. "Come to think of it, maybe that's why he was quiet. He was studious and I didn't see him play football with the guys. I thought he was shy."

McCain's parents, Evelyn and Manual Taylor, were active in politics and socialized with my parents. Fifty years later, McCain admitted that she had had a crush on me, which I never knew.

As my asthma got worse, my father sought a solution.

"I sent you and your mother to Tucson, Arizona, to see if that would help your condition," my father told me during a conversation in 1985. "You stayed there for a while, and when you came back, I thought it had changed somewhat."

My mother and I also traveled to the Mayo Clinic in Rochester, Minnesota, and to Nevada and Mexico to find out what climate would work best for me. Those were fun times with my mother. She bought me an Indian headdress in Arizona and then got me a sombrero in Nogales, Mexico. That trip was one of the best times my mother and I shared.

Back in Chicago, Grandmother Gertrude had hoped a preacher could heal my asthma, and he nearly scared me to death. She took me to an Evangelical tent set up near Lake Michigan and put me in a line of people going up to see the preacher. I kept letting people cut in front of me in line to delay meeting him. But Grandmother Gertrude walked beside me and kept nudging me toward the man.

"He has asthma," she told him. "Cure it!"

Then this man put his hand on my head and yelled, "Heal!"

It scared the hell out of me, and I started having trouble breathing because he was squeezing my head so hard. I thought lightning was going to come out of the tent ceiling. She also brought prayer cloths with us. In her own way, she was doing the best she could to help me.

When the asthma got worse, my parents talked about the family moving or sending me back to Denver to live with Grandmother Helen for a while. What I didn't know was that my parents were splitting up again—and this time for good.

"They married twice, and I thought they might try again," recalled my parents' friend Boots Flowers. "They were a couple who didn't get along, but they couldn't stand to be away from each other. It was kind of sad to see."

I don't remember putting up a fuss about leaving my parents, and that's probably because I had lived with my grandmother before. My father would remarry twice, and my brother Joe and I saw him on regular vacations to Chicago. My father adopted a boy, Frankie.

My mother also remarried twice. First to Samuel Crowell, and they had my brother Ron. After they divorced, she moved Joe and Ron to Denver to reunite with my grandmother and me. In Denver, she married Charles Frank Devereaux, and they had my two youngest brothers, Charles and Michael.

I sometimes wonder what would have happened if my grandmother had decided to stay in Chicago or move to New Orleans, where some of her family still lived, instead of coming west to Denver. Older family members change the course of life for the next generation, and we often never think about what might have been. ...

Chapter Three

Growing Up in Denver

Denver's climate gave me back my childhood. Instead of being cooped up in the house, reading, to avoid the humidity of Chicago and Gary, Indiana, I was playing basketball and baseball in the streets with my new friends. My childhood friends Sam and Charles Batey used to meet me in an alley or at a nearby Catholic school playground for pickup games.

"Webb wanted to be a basketball star, just like everybody in the neighborhood," recalled classmate Jim McNally.

I attended Cole Junior High School, which was a big change from the school in Gary. All of my classmates in Gary were black. Cole was a mixture of cultures: black students, Hispanic students, Japanese students, and white students.

"I voted for Webb when he ran for mayor because he understood the diversity of the city," McNally said. "And being the city's first black mayor, this was important."

In Gary, most of my neighbors were black, but northeast Denver was different. Italian immigrants lived next door to my grandmother. I was always impressed when a son in that family, who worked for the post office, took his mother out to dinner every Sunday. A white family lived on the other side, and their daughter was elected by her peers as a top leader at Manual High School.

We had access to every necessity within walking distance from our front door. The Goodrich Grocery store was a couple of blocks from our home. A short distance from that was a drugstore, a dime store, a variety shop, and donut shop. If I walked a few more blocks, I found a barbershop, another donut shop, and another drugstore, where at one time my Aunt Vernadette worked.

Gem Market was also a popular place that hired many of the neighborhood's black and Hispanic kids and stocked items such as grits and collards that you couldn't find at the larger Miller grocery or Piggly Wiggly stores. (The owners of all three businesses were white.)

Although my neighborhood was diverse, there also were invisible dividing lines. If you grew up east of Broadway, you were referred to as an Eastsider. The Eastsiders who were politically active and came to political prominence in the 1970s included Rich Castro, Eloy Mares, Hiawatha Davis, King Trimble, Paul Sandoval, Don Sandoval, Wilma Webb, and me. And a few blocks away lived families of German and Polish ancestry who worked hard-labor jobs in the nearby industrial area.

During my lifetime, I watched the neighborhood change. Both of the drugstores became liquor stores. The donut shops closed. The dime store became a beer joint. The area went from comprising working families to people living on government assistance. Most recently, the neighborhood has become popular with young families because of Denver's strong housing market.

The alley where in my childhood the boys played basketball now has a mural of a young boy, Geronimo, who died during my tenure as mayor. The gang issue was part of my first term in 1993. The media tagged it as The Summer of Violence. As mayor, I fought to take the neighborhoods back to where kids, like me as a Cole Junior High School student, could feel safe playing in the parks or walking down the street.

Overall, my three years at Cole were basically uneventful. Some kids started out to be troublemakers, others were good students, and I was somewhere in the middle. I wasn't sure what group I wanted to belong to, and like many other kids, I would blossom late.

When I was fourteen, Grandmother Helen decided I was going to enter an oratorical contest for the American Woodman.

"Why? I don't want to do that," I told her.

"You're doing it. It will be good for you," she shot back.

She piqued my interest when she told me the winner would receive a $500 scholarship to college and qualify for the national competition in Austin, Texas. It was also an opportunity for her to do something with her grandson and take a trip.

She told me to practice, and my mother, who had moved to Denver by then with my brothers Joe and Ron, took it one step further. We went to Union Baptist Church and Reverend John Walker took me to the front of the church to speak. He taught me to speak from the diaphragm and to project. My mother walked to the rear of the church and told me to speak up, and that was my first speaking engagement.

I won the local contest and then headed to Texas, where I got my first experiences with blatant racism. We boarded a train in Denver and sat in the sixth row of seats. When we hit Amarillo, my grandmother grabbed her home-cooked chicken in a shoebox she had brought for our meal and began moving to the rear of the same car.

"Why do I have to get up?" I asked her.

"Because in the South, black people have to sit in the back of the train," she said in a matter-of-fact way.

I was fourteen years old, and I knew that was just plain wrong. I already didn't like the South.

The contest in Austin showed me that the kids from the South knew their black history and were great speakers. They spoke with passion that filled the whole building. I got more nervous the more I listened and was scared I wouldn't be able to speak. Then the girl before me forgot part of her speech, and I was able to give mine, but it wasn't nearly as good as the ones given by the kids from the South.

Losing the contest wasn't as disappointing as what happened next. We went downtown to a dime store, and while my grandmother was shopping, I wandered over to the lunch counter and sat down. I wanted some ice cream, but no one would serve me.

"You're not from here, are you?" a waitress finally asked.

I told her I was from Denver, Colorado.

"You know, I can't serve you anything here," she explained.

Before I could react to her comment, my grandmother jerked me out of my seat.

"Are you stupid?" she said. "You can't sit here. Negros can't eat at the counters here."

The feelings of having to get up and move to a rear seat in the train and not getting served at the lunch counter stayed with me a long time. Neither felt good, and I didn't like the fact that people did it just because they knew the rules and the consequences.

I learned as an adult why we were forced to go to the rear of the train. In 1890, Louisiana passed the Separate Car Law, which basically said that as long as the passenger comforts were "separate and equal," it was okay to segregate blacks into one section and whites into another.

A black man named Homer Plessy challenged the law in 1896 and sat in a white coach. The Supreme Court heard *Plessy v. Ferguson* and ruled in favor of segregation as opposed to seeing all of us as just Americans, not black or white. That law didn't change until 1954, with *Brown v. Board of Education*, which concerned segregated public schools in Topeka, Kansas. The court finally recognized that *separate but equal* really means separate *and* unequal.

Grandmother Helen tried to keep me on a positive path in other ways. She always went to the New Hope Baptist Church on Sunday, and her grandson went right along with her. The kids and adults went to Sunday school, but an electric, vertical, movable wall separated the two age groups. The wall would rise after the sessions, and the adults would automatically look over to make sure their kids were there and behaving. What the adults didn't know was that sometimes we would skip Sunday school, go to the creamery around the corner, and be back before the wall went up.

I also had a lot of fun with my two buddies in the neighborhood, Robert Williams and Donald Coleman. Coleman came from a very large family and liked to wear a leather jacket. He looked like The

Fonz on the television show *Happy Days* long before it aired. Williams and I thought it was a little cooler to wear sports coats and slacks.

"I was a little loose in those days," Coleman recalled. "I'd drink beer here or there, but he [Wellington] didn't care for beer, and I never saw him smoke."

Well, Coleman and some of my other classmates may be protecting me from the facts. I joined him and my other buddies in waiting outside liquor stores and getting older adults to buy us cheap wine. We'd drink the wine of the day, whether it was WPLJ (Wine, Port, and Lemon Juice), Ripple, or Mad Dog—all of which tasted good at the time and, more importantly, were cheap. After a few shared swigs from the wine bottle in a brown paper bag, we would end up on a street corner, singing the popular songs of the day.

Sometimes after a few drinks, we would stupidly get in someone's car and cruise. We were lucky we never got into an accident. Often, we ended up at all-night diners, or we would drive to Stapleton International Airport and stay up all night watching the planes land and take off.

One vice I didn't indulge in during my teenage years was smoking cigarettes, and that was because of my asthma. But I did, on occasion, put a pack of Parliament cigarettes in my rolled shirt sleeve. I thought it was fashionable. The Parliament box was blue and white and matched most of my shirts. Though as I got older and watched many of my friends die young from lung cancer, I was thankful my asthma kept me from that deadly habit.

Grandmother Helen was not ignorant of my teenage antics, and when I started Manual High School, she said it was time for me to get a job. She went to the Goodrich Grocery store near our house.

"Why are there no Negro kids working here?" she asked the owner. "Give my grandson a job."

For a kid in high school, $60 a week was a lot of money in 1957, so I was excited. But it was also a lot of work. My hours were from 8:00 A.M. to 8:30 P.M. on Saturday, 8:00 A.M. to 6:00 P.M. on Sunday, and two hours after school three days a week.

That job introduced me to the barrel of a gun. Late one Saturday evening, I was working the cash register and another guy was working behind the meat counter when a customer walked in shortly before we closed. He asked me for a pack of cigarettes. I got the cigarettes from behind a counter, and when I turned around, he was pointing a gun at me.

The robber's buddy pulled another gun on my colleague behind the meat counter.

I never knew a gun could look so big when someone has it pointed at you.

"Give me all the money out of the cash register," the robber demanded.

I gladly followed instructions. But when he asked me for my wallet, I hesitated—I had pictures inside of my girlfriend and classmates.

"Give it to me in the next ten seconds or I'm going to shoot you," he warned.

He grabbed my wallet and then shoved both of us grocery-store workers into the freezer. He warned us not to leave for at least five minutes. After ten minutes, I opened the door.

"Didn't I tell you to stay in that goddamn freezer!" he screamed. "I'm going to blow your damn brains out!"

My cohostage couldn't believe I opened the door either.

"Are you crazy? I'm putting meat up against the locker so they can't get in here!"

We got out safely about twenty minutes later.

Crime crossed my path again in high school. The neighborhood kids often played football in the streets. One of the players was an older guy and was dating a very attractive neighbor named Daisy. The teenage boys thought she was the most beautiful girl we had ever seen.

One Saturday, we were all sitting on the porch when we heard that Daisy had gone to her homecoming dance at Manual and someone had stabbed her to death. She was killed in the gymnasium by the same guy who had played football with us. He was insanely jealous and went crazy. We were outraged and started to look for the guy ourselves. He was eventually caught by the police.

I liked the social aspect of school, but was losing interest in class. I was seventeen, a year younger than most of my classmates because I had skipped one grade.

"Wellington always looked more serious than the other boys," recalled Manual classmate Connie Skillern Hall. "He wasn't like the other boys, who would just blurt out what was on their minds. He weighed what he was going to say before he said it. But he also had a sense of humor."

My grades were getting worse because I just didn't show up to class. I even signed up for all of the college prep classes and then just didn't go. It was the biggest waste of energy for the teachers as well as for me. The real problem was that we had no counselors who could guide us or try and get us back to class before we flunked. I never did have a good school counselor until I went to junior college.

"Webb was a quiet guy who couldn't get to class on time," McNally recalled. "He was at his locker or someplace else and was always late to class."

As my grades plummeted, it was questionable whether I would even graduate. Coleman told me he was quitting school and taking a full-time job with the city. He would make about $200 a month.

It crossed my mind to quit school too. I was so far behind in my classes that I didn't want to go because if a teacher called on me, I would be humiliated when I didn't know the answer.

The only class I attended was social studies, taught by Mary Pagano. She was a spinster who chose Manual because she wanted to help the kids in the neighborhood. Her class was about current events, something I was interested in, and she always called on the students. I got a B in her class. I think I did well in her class because I liked the subject and Pagano had high expectations of her students.

With only one decent grade, it would have been easy to drop out of school. But I decided instead to face summer school and get my diploma. I did make an attempt to avoid summer school by asking my English teacher to give me a D. I even sent my grandmother over to talk with her. She sided with the teacher.

"I never have forgotten how one weekend I asked him to borrow his grandfather's car and he told me he couldn't," Coleman recalled. "He said, 'I've got to hit the books. I can't run with you. I'm sorry.' At the time I thought, okay, whatever. He wanted to go to college and make something of himself."

I didn't quit school because I didn't want to fail. It was too easy to drop out. I didn't want to be part of that failure.

After I was elected mayor, my wife and family and a large group of supporters walked from City Park to the Civic Center. Near the park, I saw Coleman. We didn't really make eye contact because I wasn't sure how he would feel. We were high-school chums and he was still working for the city, in the custodial department, and I had just gotten elected the forty-second mayor. It crossed my mind how different my life would have been if I had dropped out of high school.

I didn't feel superior to him. I felt I was lucky and fortunate. Lucky enough to graduate, lucky enough to eventually finish college, and then fortunate enough to have people vote for me.

"I wasn't surprised when he ran for mayor," Coleman said. "He hit the books when we were kids, and I was running the streets. It paid off for him. He ended up as mayor and me as a custodian."

But my first run-in with the law as a naïve teenager could have changed history. While I was going to summer school, I decided to teach my girlfriend Vetha how to drive. I borrowed my grandfather's car. Grandmother met and married Bob Gamble in Denver, where he worked as a butler for a Denver bank president's family.

My buddy Tom Hall was in the backseat, and I told my girlfriend to back up the car. She didn't hit the gas, so I put my foot on the gas pedal. The 1949 Chrysler, which was made out of steel, not aluminum like the cars today, backed up all right—through the plate-glass window of a lamp shop that had an apartment in the rear. We took out the lamps and we took out the front part of the building. We were told that the man living in the apartment was in the bathroom at the time of the accident and barely got out of the building.

I was more worried about my grandmother than the police because of the damage to my grandfather's car.

Hall told me to get the girl out of the car and to get into the driver's seat. She left and two police officers arrived. They gave us the good cop/bad cop routine.

"This nigger drove the car through the building, and we just need to take his black ass to jail," the bad cop said.

Hall and I didn't say a word.

"Well, you know, I think it probably was an accident," the good cop said. "How could anyone end up crashing into a building like this?"

And then I made up the most outrageous lie. I said we were at a local restaurant called the Tamale Queen in the Points. We had been eating fried chicken, and I was not accustomed to driving a car. The lie came to mind because I had just finished eating some chicken and the sack was on the front seat. I told the cops that I was trying to back up to park the car and my hands, slippery from the chicken grease, fell off the steering wheel, and the steering wheel got out of control and backed into the building.

Instead of stopping there, I went on to say that I was trying to back into the adjacent alley and this was the first time I had driven this car.

"That's the most outrageous story I have ever heard," the good cop said. "But it's so funny and so peculiar, I don't think you made it up."

Then a little old black lady who was sitting on her porch and saw the whole accident walked over to the police car.

"Where's the girl that was driving the car?" she asked.

At that point, the bad cop said, "Nigger, you are going to jail."

They let Hall go home, and he did what we should have done in the first place: he called my grandmother and mother. My mother called a lawyer. This happened on a Friday night, and I didn't expect to be in the city jail for long. I had to be in summer school on Monday, so

I thought my grandmother would bail me out quickly.

That night in jail, one inmate kept yelling that it was cold in his cell. After the guards told him to shut up a few dozen times, I heard a loud pop, like a fist hitting something, and the inmate didn't say another word all night.

I waited and waited for my grandmother to show up, and then I finally fell asleep in a cell with two other guys. The guards woke me up to get my mug shot. My eyes were all bugged out of my head, my hair was uncombed, and my mouth was half stuck together when the photo was taken. No wonder people's mug shots look so bad. Then they took my fingerprints.

On Saturday morning, I was taken to a holding cell with about sixteen other guys.

"Kid, what are you in for?" an inmate in his thirties asked me.

I didn't want to tell him I let my girlfriend drive my car and she crashed through a building, so I told him I was in for an automobile investigation. He thought I stole a car, and I didn't argue with him.

The guards brought me a baloney sandwich, but I really didn't want to eat, even though I was hungry. I sat in that cell all day, and by evening, that baloney sandwich looked like a rib-eye steak. Finally, my grandmother and mother showed up and told me I wouldn't be arraigned until Monday. I told my grandmother I had to be in school on Monday.

"Well, you won't make school this Monday," she said.

I got charged with reckless driving, which was reduced to illegal parking and careless driving. I lost eight points on my license, was fined $250, and had to pay restitution to repair the building. I also knew I'd have to pay to repair my grandfather's car.

When I asked my grandmother how I was going to pay for everything, she said, "The way we always have done things. I'm going to pay for it, and every week you go to work, you'll give me two-thirds of your paycheck."

That was the most expensive date I had been on because, in addition to all of the payments, my grandmother charged me interest on the money she loaned me. She said it was only fair because a bank would do the same.

My grandmother supported me, but she also wanted to teach me a lesson. She was always the strong one in the family and had very high expectations of what was tolerated and what was appropriate. She was also the one who held my family together. No matter what happened in each of her children's or grandchildren's lives, she was always there for us. She had a big house with four bedrooms and only used one. If we needed a place to sleep after a marital quarrel or if we were in between jobs and couldn't pay rent, we went to my grandmother's house. She was the strong backbone of our family. And, like many black families, Grandmother was the matriarch.

As I grew older, I realized how her family became her life. Late in her life, she divorced her second husband and was alone. Her grandchildren became her joy and she was our rock. We respected her strength and wisdom.

Chapter Four

Mother, Brothers, Trips to Chicago

My brother Joe and I have always been close, despite the ten-year age gap and my leaving home to stay with my grandmother in Denver.

"Wellington was a buffer when my folks weren't getting along," Joe recalled. "I knew he was sick, but I was young and didn't quite know what was going on. When I think about it, my parents kind of brushed it over. It wasn't like what would happen today when the parents would sit a child down and give a long explanation. It was more like, 'This is necessary and don't worry about it.'"

When our parents split up, our father moved back to Chicago, and he was gone a lot on his railroad job.

"I don't really recall my mom being around a lot," Joe said. "I either repressed it or don't remember. She was working, and my dad's mother used to watch me."

While I was in Denver, Joe began moving frequently with our mother. She refused to move to Philadelphia, where her second husband, Samuel Crowell, worked. My brother Ronnie spent some time with his father in Philadelphia, but he also moved frequently with Joe and our mother. My brothers Charles and Michael were born in Denver but often relocated with our mother too. She took my brothers and lived in Moss Point, Mississippi, Detroit, and off and on in Denver with Grandmother Helen. Joe lived for a while with our father in Chicago.

"Wellington was not involved in all of that drama, because he was with our grandmother in Denver and later off to college," Joe said. "We bounced around from place to place. I later told my wife, Marilyn, there are two things that are horrible in life: dying and moving, and I'm not sure which one is worse."

The packing up and moving included several different homes in Denver and a short stint in public housing before Charles and Michael were born.

While I was in high school, my mother wanted me to live with her when she returned to Denver with Joe and Ronnie. We moved to the Globeville projects, located along the north-central edge of Denver in an industrial area. The housing authority built the project, which is isolated on a hill, during World War II. It was the only public housing project available for large families.

Globeville was not the typical Denver neighborhood. The housing facility was built on sand, and the wind seemed to blow all the time. The apartment was always dusty and dirty. The complex was also located near a smelter that put lead into the air and was later condemned.

I clearly remember the first night we were supposed to move into the projects. Joe and I were helping our mother move the furniture off a truck. Ronnie turned the light on in the bathroom and yelled out, "The dirt is moving!"

My reply: "How the hell can dirt move?"

Well, on closer inspection, we could see that there were so many roaches that they formed a solid mass that looked like dirt.

"Stop!" our mother said. "Put the furniture back on the truck."

This was before the Orkin man. Instead, the housing authority had what we called "the bomb" to get rid of pests. The chemicals were so strong that you couldn't live in the housing for five days, and if you had any clothes inside, the smell saturated them, and the fumigation often just moved the pests from one apartment to the next. Many kids knew who lived in the projects by the way their clothes smelled.

I really hated living there. It was isolated from the city. We had to walk down a hill to get to the only close grocery store. The owners, who were white, charged more for necessities such as bread or milk because they knew the families in the projects had limited transportation to the city. I once walked several miles back to my grandmother's house on a Sunday because the buses only ran once an hour and I didn't want to wait.

Living out there was like living in another country. You didn't tell anyone where you lived, because telling them was like having a scarlet letter placed on your chest. People who lived in these projects were considered the lowest of the low, because even the projects had a ranking system.

As mayor, I seldom spoke about my personal background because I didn't think it was necessary. However, when some issues came up—such as problems with public housing—I understood what people were talking about because of my own experiences.

It wasn't easy for my mother, who was single at this point, to raise three boys. To my mother's credit, she always kept her kids with her, even if my grandmother had more space in her home. My mother wanted to be independent.

That independence brought times when my mother struggled to feed us, especially after Charles and Michael arrived and after her third divorce. Our common "well-balanced meal" in her mind was lettuce-and-tomato salad with French dressing, cube steak, creamed corn, green peas, bread, and Kool-Aid. But this was her fantasy dinner. When she rattled off that menu, we all knew the cupboard was really empty. Those were the nights that dinner was a bowl of cereal because there was nothing in our refrigerator. Our diet was supplemented by welfare cheese and cans of Spam the government gave to the poor.

My mother's way to deal with three failed marriages and an unhappy personal life was to drink. Too often, we saw a liquor bottle on the kitchen table. In the beginning, it was for social cocktails for visitors, but later, more than one bottle was hidden for her personal use.

Some women focus on other things in their lives and don't need a husband. Many women of my mother's generation were housewives and that's what they knew. She had the skills to do more, but she saw herself as a failure and eased that pain with the bottle.

Joe usually got the brunt of the fallout from her drinking because he ended up, to some degree, being the father figure to our younger brothers.

"I was the oldest in the house, and she had a lot of problems," Joe said. "She was not a mean-spirited person, but she could be mean and it was related to drinking. She never overcame it. It caused all sorts of drama. There were a lot of episodes, and I tried to keep it together for the young ones so it would not go completely haywire."

Sometimes when all of the brothers are together, we laugh about the trying times, and our wives can't believe we see humor in the horror.

"Grandmother intervened on occasion," Joe recalled. "She once said, 'Mardina, you cannot treat these boys this way.' And she had us come live with her."

Grandmother also encouraged our mother to live with Aunt Frances in Mississippi.

"That didn't work," Joe said. "They were like oil and water."

She tried to reunite her family again by moving to Meeker, Colorado, where her third husband, Charles Frank Devereaux, had grown up and had a large extended family.

The Devereaux family members were the only African American residents in Rio Blanco County, a rural community about 225 miles northwest of Denver.

My cousin Victor Devereaux, a Denver city attorney who has a ranch in the San Luis Valley, researched how the family got established there. According to the 1870 Denver census, James Homer Devereaux came to Rio Blanco County from Texas after the Civil War and worked on the railroad. The Devereaux family members started a bulldozing and construction business. Their work included building roads and bridges, laying groundwork for the Denver Hotel in Glenwood Springs, and helping to lay out the town of Aspen. They also used their large construction trucks to transport uranium yellow cake between Craig, Meeker, Rifle, and Grand Junction.

I stayed with my mom and brothers for about three days in Meeker until I saw the sheep and other animals right outside Devereaux's home—which was a log cabin with a frame house built on top.

Joe stayed in Meeker longer than I did, because he was too young to come back to Denver with me. My mother and brothers drifted back to Denver, where they eventually settled, and my brothers all remain here.

Because my mother always believed in keeping her sons close to her, we never saw each other as stepbrothers or half brothers. We weren't raised that way, and it was always offensive to us to be stuck with labels. We were Mardina's boys who were her joy, her protectors, her everything. If a male friend happened to get out of line, it was not uncommon for her to say, "I can either call my sons or I can call the police. My sons are closer; they're downstairs."

One Thanksgiving, she got mad at a suitor, even after he had bought us a big turkey. She took the frozen turkey and threw it, and we watched it bounce along the floor like a basketball before the gentleman picked up the bird and left.

After his exit, my mother said our dinner that Thanksgiving would be lettuce and tomatoes with French dressing, cube steak, creamed corn, green peas, bread, and Kool-Aid. In other words, we had no dinner that Thanksgiving.

For several weeks each summer, Joe and I escaped the drama of our mother's drinking when we headed to Chicago to visit our father. We made the trips from the time we were old enough to travel alone and looked forward to our Summer with Dad program.

"But our mother's drinking often affected those plans," Joe said. "It was always a relief when we got on the bus or the train and it started moving. Because there was always a question of whether we would be going. Mother was very volatile, and at a drop of a hat she would say, 'You're not going anywhere.' This could happen when we got to the station."

Our father always had a routine for those visits. When Joe and

I arrived, he would pick us up at the station and we'd go to a juice shop for carrot juice or celery juice. He thought it was a big deal that they had a juice shop at the station. Then we'd take the L Train to a drugstore and get the best milkshakes in the world, which were served in frosty silver mixing tins.

Like many people in Chicago, my father didn't learn to drive until later in life. He was able to get anywhere by taking the L Train or the public bus.

We would spend one day at the Field Museum and the art museum. The next day, we would go to a Chicago White Sox or Chicago Cubs baseball game. My dad sometimes followed both teams, but you learn quite early in life that if you live on the south side, you're a White Sox fan, and if you live on the north side, you root for the Cubs.

I remember taking the L Train to Comiskey Park and watching the White Sox players: pitcher Billy Pierce, Nelly Fox on second base, George Kell at third, shortstop Luis Aparicio, outfielders Minnie Minoso and Jim Rivera, and catcher Sherm Lollar—the slowest runner on Earth!

We would always go see the Cubs when they played the Brooklyn Dodgers because we could watch a hero, Jackie Robinson, the first black player in Major League Baseball. We saw some great Dodgers: Gil Hodges at first base; Jackie Robinson at second; Pee Wee Reese at shortstop; Bill Cox at third; and in the outfield, Duke Snider at center, Carl Furillo at right, and Sandy Amoros at left. Every black in America was a Dodgers fan when the color barrier came down. We'd root for the Cubs and Mr. Cub, Ernie Banks. We also cheered for Jackie and the Dodgers. And I was a big fan of Larry Doby of the Cleveland Indians, the first black player in the American League.

Our father also took us to watch the Kansas City Monarchs, an all-black baseball team. They had this old man, Satchel Paige, pitching in their last season. He later went on to the Major League.

Sometimes we were still in Chicago when the football season began, and we sat in the stands to watch Chicago's two football teams at the time: the Chicago Bears and the Chicago Cardinals. We got to see the Cleveland Browns' great quarterback Otto Graham and fullback Marion Motley play the Chicago Cardinals. The Cardinals later moved to St. Louis, then Phoenix.

After spending a few days with our father, we then spent time with Grandmother Gertrude. She still lived in a kitchenette apartment on the second floor. We loved and respected our grandmother, but she was elderly, and the apartment was small. We really didn't like staying with her, and, as kids often do, we compared her to our Grandmother Helen.

Little things showed us the differences of living in a large city such as Chicago and being settled in Denver. On Saturdays, our father would take all of his newspapers from the week and lay them on the floor of Grandmother Gertrude's apartment. Then he would take my grandmother's bed apart and prop the mattresses against the wall over the newspaper. He'd spray DDT so the bedbugs would come out of the mattress and fall on the newspaper. The bugs hid in the crevices and corners of the mattress springs. We didn't know much about bedbugs until we got bitten one night and had little welts on us in the morning.

Between the DDT spray, the smell of my grandmother's liniment, and the heat of the summer, we didn't really enjoy our time there. During the week, our grandmother listened to her radio soap operas—*Stella Dallas*, *As the World Turns*, *General Hospital*—and we were longing to get outside.

She wasn't one to waste anything, and she made throw rugs out of stockings and scrap materials.

When we stayed with our father, there was another routine. We had to walk to a newspaper stand where a guy had a little trash can with a fire to keep warm in the early mornings. We had to buy the same four papers, the *Chicago Tribune*, the *Chicago Sun-Times*, and two national black newspapers: the *Chicago Defender* and *The Pittsburgh Courier*. I once asked him why he didn't have the newspapers delivered.

"Because those people need to have a job too," he said.

We loved Grandmother Gertrude, but we never really got to know her as well as Grandmother Helen. She was older when our father was born, and she was very strict. She was also pretty old-fashioned. She didn't keep money in a bank but wore it around her waist in a money belt. When she passed, her body was found without the money belt, which also was typical of a Chicago tenant building where an older woman lived by herself.

We spent more time with our father on those trips after Grandmother Gertrude passed. He had married Elizabeth Hawthorne, who stayed with him until his death.

"She was like a mother to me," Joe recalled. "She'd take us fishing at Lake Michigan and join our trips to the museum and Shed Aquarium. Wellington didn't have the patience for fishing."

Our father always tried the best he could to spend time with us. In our 1985 conversation, I asked him how he felt about his kids.

"Well, I'm a lucky man because my wife and myself had two sons and both of them turned out to be wonderful men. And they are devoted to their families, the same as I was devoted to my family. ... So as far as my kids, I love them madly. And when I was coming up, things were tough for me, but I did whatever I could to make ends meet."

My father came to Washington, D.C., for my swearing-in when I was appointed regional director of health and human services for President Jimmy Carter in 1977.

"He was busting buttons all over the city because he was so proud of his son," recalled Boots Flowers. "Just before Wellington died, he knew he was going, and he wanted to come see my husband, Henry. He and Elizabeth came for a visit, and we had a grand old time. I teased him that he was getting breasts from the chemotherapy. I'd go grab his breast, and he'd slap my hands away. I miss him so."

My father died shortly after I was elected auditor in 1987, and in a way, I lost my mother that year too. A few days after I had an argument with her about her drinking, she had a stroke. She was sipping her "ice water," and I could tell it was gin. It was our same discussion, the same refrain.

"Why don't you stop doing this before it kills you?" I pleaded with her.

"You got to die from something," she replied.

The doctors and nurses at Denver General Hospital were able to keep her alive, but the stroke paralyzed part of her body.

Parents teach their kids when they are young about how to get through school and the expectations of college, finding a spouse, and learning a career. Parents never teach their kids about getting old. Maybe because they are old, they never think about it. So when children find themselves with a mother or father who is unable to care for themselves or needs assistance, they don't know whether to keep them at home or put them in assisted living. Who makes that decision and how is it made? And if they aren't home, how often do you visit? Who takes care of the things that are important to that parent? If you have your own family, you get caught in a sandwich of taking care of the old and taking care of the young.

I was proud that we were able to dress my mother up, put her in a wheelchair, and allow her to watch me get sworn in as Denver's forty-second mayor.

Alcoholism is a sickness and an addiction. Anyone who has had a parent or child who has suffered from an addiction, whether it's alcohol or drugs or both, knows how defining that illness can be in terms of taking over the person. Everything else becomes subservient to the bottle or the drug.

"I know his mother's drinking was hard on Webb," lifelong friend Charles "Chuck" Williams said. "No one wants to see their mother drinking. Like most people, it wears and tears your body."

My mother never could admit she was an alcoholic, so treatment was not an option. When I was in the state legislature, I sponsored a bill that mandated group health coverage to include alcohol treatment. I didn't know it at the time, but several other legislators' families were dealing with the same problems with a loved one. They supported my bill because it was socially acceptable to get alcoholics help. They were not willing to fund drug-related programs at the time because of the stigma associated with drug addiction.

Sometimes I felt guilty that I was not present during my mother's outbursts. My brothers Michael and Charles remember my mother making a scene in Denver when tickets to see our cousin Ed Green, a classical violinist, were not at the box office. Green was the opening act for a Smokey Robinson concert. Mother didn't give a damn about Smokey Robinson, but she wanted to make sure everyone knew that Ed Green was her nephew and where were her tickets? It was an embarrassing moment for Charles and Michael in front of a crowd.

We loved our mother deeply, but we got caught in the dilemma of taking her out in public or keeping her at home. Sometimes we would go out and everything would be fine. Other times we wished we would have left her at home.

But whatever her shortcomings, my mother tried the best she could and made sure all of her sons felt like part of one family.

There was an age gap with my four brothers, but I tried to support them as they were growing up. Joe, Ronnie, Charles, and Michael were all good athletes, and I often attended their basketball or football games at Manual High School.

Ronnie was a star on the basketball team, and I consoled him when they lost the state championship. I was also proud when I watched him graduate from Fort Hayes State College in Kansas.

Charles had a natural gift of working well with his hands, whether fixing something electrical or plumbing. I often thought he wished he had been born a generation earlier and worked as a black cowboy on a ranch.

Michael earned degrees in biology and chemistry and became a medical researcher. He became politically active when I was auditor and mayor, and other campaigns hired him because of his good community-outreach programs.

Joe worked in the mental-health field, was a police officer, and got his law degree. He was part of my security detail when I was mayor and now owns a construction rebar business and is one of my partners in a development company.

My four brothers all graduated from Manual High School and eventually settled in Denver: (from left) Michael Devereaux, Joe Webb, me, Charles Devereaux, and Ron Crowell.

As brothers, we felt it was us against the world. I always believed that if the five of us are together, we are going to succeed, no matter the odds. At one time, I thought all of my brothers might run for public office, particularly Joe, yet their interests as adults never led them down that path.

Although we stuck together as brothers, sometimes I think my mother was always a little jealous of the close relationship I had with Grandmother Helen. When people asked my mother if she was proud of me, she always replied, "I'm proud of all of my sons."

When our mother died in 1993, we knew each of her sons would speak at her funeral, because that's the way she would have wanted things. No matter what one son accomplished, all of her sons were equal—even though I knew Joe and Michael were the apples of her eye.

Joe had a special place in her heart because he often acted as the oldest son in my absence; Michael because he was the baby of the family. My mother said she tried five times to have a daughter and after the fifth son, she said that was enough trying.

"It's not God's will," she said.

Chapter Five

The End of High School, the Filling Station, Sterling

Grandmother Helen kept a close eye on her five grandsons as we were growing up. She'd monitor my girlfriends as well.

"Who is her family?" she would ask me. "What college do they want her to attend?"

I guess my traits were more like my parents'—I just wanted to know if the girls were fun and I didn't care what anybody thought if I dated them.

When grandmother didn't like who I was dating, she'd make the girl's life miserable. One older girl used to have to walk past our home to get to the bus stop. My grandmother would perfectly time when her front yard needed to be watered. She'd turn on the hose exactly when my girlfriend walked by so she'd be a little wet catching the bus.

One day, I decided to tell my grandmother to butt out of my personal life. As I walked toward the front door, her silence surprised me, and I turned around just in time to miss an iron skillet that was thrown directly at my head. She was going to teach me a lesson for talking back to her and being sassy.

I ducked just in time. If that heavy iron skillet hadn't missed my head, I doubt I would be here today.

She treated all of her grandsons the same way. She had a curfew and expected us to abide by it. If we came home late, she'd turn on the porch light and look through the curtain on the door.

"Wellington, is that you?" she'd ask.

When she confirmed it was me, she laid down the law.

"Fine. I'm glad to see you're doing well," she said before turning off the porch light, not unlocking the front door, and going back to bed.

Those were the nights I either slept on the porch or in my car.

Joe, who was already getting the mind of a police officer, thought he'd outsmart our grandmother. He'd put gadgets in the door to keep it from locking. He came home, and the little matchbox cover and toothpicks he thought had jammed the lock were lying neatly clustered on the porch. The light went on, but the door did not open.

"Joseph, I'm glad to see you're home. Now go back to where you came from," she said.

Once Ronnie got to that age, I had my own apartment, so he'd come stay with me when he missed curfew.

"Helen would call me to come over and talk," recalled longtime friend Ruby Kirk Gray. "She'd say, 'These guys are driving me nuts.' Several times she just needed someone to help her clear her mind to get things off her chest so she wouldn't kill them."

Joe recalls that our grandmother demanded and commanded a lot of respect.

"We kind of say she was strict, but I would say she was firm," Joe said. "She knew the pitfalls lurking out there for black men by her experiences and living. She didn't want her grandsons to become anything she detested."

Drugs were not yet a major problem in the Denver neighborhoods, but there was bootlegging, gambling, and prostitution in the black community.

"She pushed and was strict because she knew the choices for black men could be very narrow," Joe said.

Black kids in Denver usually stuck to certain parts of the city for entertainment. There was a movie theater not far from my grandmother's home called the Alpine Theater. In those days, the telephone company had prefixes that had names to them, such as Alpine 343 or Main 333. They later changed the name to the Uptown Theater, and in the late 1950s and early 1960s, it developed a reputation that caused the owners to bring in police to watch the primarily black and Hispanic kids.

One time, a rookie cop tripped in the aisle and a kid took his gun. After a couple of shootings within the movie theater, it was shut down.

Another popular hangout was the Rainbow Music Hall. I'd wear a long coat and try to look older than my teenage years. One night, a fat woman grabbed me, pulled me to her chest, and made me dance with her.

My mother moved into a house next to my grandmother when I was in high school. That home became headquarters for me and some of the kids I ran with, Ben Wesley, Tom Hall, Frank Brown, Donald Coleman, and Jim Wagner.

Despite my poor grades and not playing basketball my senior year because I didn't like the basketball coach, I held out some hope that I could get into college on an athletic scholarship. A coach from Western State College in Gunnison, Colorado, talked to my grandmother about applying there.

"We think he has the ability to help our basketball team, and a different setting may help get his grades up," he told her.

My grandmother was so excited, and then I told her, "I'm not going to Gunnison. I don't even know where Gunnison is. I'm not going that far away from home."

She asked me what other options I had and I said, "I'm going to Regis College."

"Oh, that's real interesting," she said.

I played at Regis College, a Jesuit school in northwest Denver, one summer, and Coach Joe Hall said I looked good. My buddy Wesley was Manual's basketball star, as was Dennis Boone, whom I idolized. Boone was the biggest basketball star of our era and had attended Regis.

I applied to Regis and the reply dashed my hopes. "Because of your poor academic standing, we cannot accept you at Regis College," the rejection letter stated.

I was hurt, disillusioned, and disappointed. I had one short experience of going to the University of Colorado in Denver, walking in the front door of the admission's office, and turning around and leaving.

My grandmother had three options after high-school graduation for her grandsons: you went to college, which she preferred; you joined the army; or you got a job and paid her rent, paid her for food, and paid part of the utility bill. She was not ambivalent about being firm with me or my brothers.

Instead of looking into other colleges in 1958, I decided to go back to Gary, Indiana, and live with my Aunt Frances and her husband, Eddie. I would have more freedom than living with my grandmother, and I would also be close to Chicago and could spend time with my father.

"Helen and I would sit on our porches and talk from yard to yard," neighbor Ira Slack recalled. "When we worked on our gardens, we also visited. She would always say she was doing things to help Wellington. She wasn't happy when he didn't go directly to college after high school. But she was wise enough to leave it up to him, because eventually he did go to college."

I thought I was pretty independent, making this decision by myself. Little did I know that grandmother and Aunt Frances had a long-distance conversation about my move back to Indiana.

When I arrived, Aunt Frances showed me to my room, and I then met some kids my own age. We started hanging out. For one week, I had the life of leisure. I came back to her home to eat and sleep. Then one day when I came back from hanging out with my new friends, there was a filling station uniform on my bed.

Aunt Frances was the accountant for my Uncle Eddie's filling station, ran a beauty salon from her home, and was also studying to be a nurse.

"I gave you a week here to do what you wanted, but I thought you had enough sense to know you're not going to stay here for free," she informed me. "I'm not going to charge you for rent, but no one sleeps on me for free."

She said I would go to the filling station every morning by 8:00 A.M. and learn the business. I could keep my paycheck, which she wanted me to save for college, but she relented when I said I wanted to buy a car.

My first car turned out to be made from spare parts Uncle Eddie found in a junkyard, including an old engine. That vehicle allowed me to drive back to Denver on numerous visits.

Aunt Frances had talked to "Denver"—code word for "Grandmother Helen"—and it was all set up.

I joined my aunt and uncle on a trip to his hometown, Kinder, Louisiana, during the summer. Eddie still had family in the small community. There, I hung out with Eddie's niece, Letha DeVille, who has been like a sister to me. She often visited us in Gary.

When we got to Kinder, we turned down a road and I saw a scene right out of the movie *The Color Purple*. The houses were set back, and kids and folks were out there to greet us. I learned how much of a city folk I was. They decided to kill a hog, and I could hear the hog scream when they put it in hot water. They slit the hog's neck and hung it in the smokehouse. At night, we either had a jar under our bed or we had to go to the outhouse. Those rural kids also knew a lot more about sex. Being out on the farm alone, they were sexually engaged, and I was certainly shocked by that.

I was shocked again when we went into town. The county store didn't have any signs where blacks were supposed to enter, but everyone automatically went to the back door.

As I got older, I realized how automatically people did things just to avoid conflict. Some African Americans still feel the need to prove they are worthy to walk in the front door. There's an embedded feeling that we have to work twice as hard and be twice as good to keep a job or be accepted.

Maybe that's why as mayor, I made sure I never went in the back doors.

My press secretary Andrew Hudson got a quick lesson when we

were headed to an early-morning meeting at a television station.

"I called over to the station, and the producer told us to go to the back door, and she gave me the code to get in," Hudson recalled. "When I told the mayor, there was a giggle among his bodyguards, and then he laughed. He told me to call her back and tell the producer that his days of going in the back door were over."

I spent two years in Gary working at the filling station, meeting different girls, and having fun. I went through several hair phases, from the process to make my kinky hair straight to a quo vadis and a flattop.

When I came back to Denver for visits, I had money in my pocket and I had my car. Many of my friends had either joined the army, gone to college, or were lying around in Denver and not doing much with their lives.

My life was carefree, but it wasn't rewarding. In my heart, I knew I wanted to do more than pump gas. I didn't like being greasy and dirty. I liked wearing nice clothes. I wanted to be somebody. I wanted to give something back to the community, and all of that required getting an education. I also wanted to play basketball and hopefully achieve some success that I gave up when I quit the team in high school.

During one visit back to Denver, I decided I needed to go to college. I looked in the newspaper to see what Colorado colleges were located within a few hours of Denver and had basketball teams. I narrowed down my choices to Mesa College in Grand Junction, Pueblo Junior College, and Northeastern Junior in Sterling.

Sterling is about 125 miles northeast of Denver, and I knew if I ran out of food or wanted to see my friends, I had only to take a two-hour trip to get back home.

The rural community was primarily white but had a good reputation for treating black students well.

I convinced my high-school buddy Frank Brown to go with me to Sterling and see if we both could get basketball scholarships.

We met with basketball coach Roy Edwards, who told us we

could get scholarships, but in order to see if we were serious about college, the financial aid wouldn't kick in until January. We were on our own for tuition money the first semester.

Coach Edwards took me under his wing, and we remained life-long friends.

The day I told my grandmother I was going to college was one of the happiest days in her life. She knew if her oldest grandson went to college, my brothers likely would follow, and three of the four did.

Coach Edwards was excited because Manual High School had a reputation for producing talented basketball players and he had a chance to get not one, but two players. But when we came back to Denver to get ready to move to Sterling, Brown told me he was joining the army. His family couldn't help him financially, and the army was his only option to get out of the neighborhood.

Many black families struggled at that time to send their kids to college, and it seemed as though the girls got preference in that area. Black males usually got to college in one of two ways: either with an athletic scholarship or by being funded by their middle-class parents. Few black men got scholarships based on their grades.

I drove up to Sterling with my grandmother and mother. The dormitories were full, so I had to find a place to live. We pulled up to one hotel that rented rooms by the month. They charged approximately $500, which we thought was outrageous until we realized that three or four students lived together in the rooms. I finally ended up at the Albany Hotel, where many of the customers were men who worked on the railroad.

This was a Sunday, and I remember being scared that I was one of the few black students at the college. Then I heard chatter in the hallway and knew there were other black men in the hotel. My first roommate was Wendell Tyree of the Bronx, New York. We walked over to the dormitories and met the football players. I was baffled how these guys from states back East ended up in Sterling.

A few guys came from New York and the communities of Mount Vernon, New Rochelle, White Plains, and Hempstead. Others were from Pittsburgh, Pennsylvania, and the cities of Youngstown, Massilon, and Canton, Ohio.

I later found out that Northeastern was going to be a feeder school to the University of Colorado's (CU) football team in Boulder. These guys were encouraged to come to Sterling to get their grades up and then transfer to CU.

During college holidays and spring breaks, I would travel with some of these guys to their homes because I was curious about other cities. I'd spend weekends in Ohio, New York, and Pennsylvania. I was twenty-one years old, and freedom was in the air.

After meeting the football players on my first day at Northeastern, we decided to go over to the gym where two kids from Texas, Raymond "The Gun" Maxey and Roy "Snake" Williams, were playing a pickup basketball game with two familiar faces, Charles "Buddy" Caldwell and Robert Ennis, both of Denver. I knew that I had to establish my reputation early, and I played quite aggressively in that practice game.

We went to the Cactus Restaurant, and I told the waitress I wanted pork chops, grits, and eggs. She told me in a friendly voice that they had no pork chops or grits. Instead, she brought me my very first meal of chicken-fried steak and hash brown potatoes. At home in Denver, we usually ate rice or mashed potatoes.

Other black kids from Denver attended Northeastern that same semester.

"I liked Northeastern College, but it was in an isolated rural area," recalled Carl Pipkin, a childhood friend whose family owns a large African American mortuary in Denver. "We couldn't wait to get home on the weekends and back to Denver."

I also looked forward to our weekends in Denver, but I genuinely liked the community of Sterling, and that baffles some people: I was a black urban kid raised in a strong Democratic district in Denver. Sterling was an urban, Republican, conservative, and primarily white community.

I have good memories of Sterling for a couple of reasons. It wasn't my first time living away from Denver, but it was the first time I was completely independent of my family, and that's a thrill for any college student. I always felt welcomed in Sterling. I knew there was bigotry there, but in two years at Northeastern, I never had anyone call me a derogatory name. The locals supported the black students, especially if they were athletes and the teams were winning. As happens in so many small towns, athletes are kings of the hill—the local newspapers were not shy about running large photographs of the athletes and doing feature stories on our backgrounds.

The white students, many from nearby farm communities, probably didn't see a black person until they went to Northeastern. But many embraced us, and we used to joke about what was harder: working in the city or working on a farm. One spring, a group of us black students worked on a farm throwing hay. It quickly became apparent that the farm kids worked a lot harder than us city folks.

Northeastern, unlike larger colleges, also had coaches who cared about the athletes. Coach Edwards served as my academic counselor, the first time any teacher had really given me direction with my classes. The classes were small, with about twenty-five students, so the instruction was more individualized.

Coach Edwards encouraged us to stay two years and graduate, not only so our credits would transfer to a four-year college, but also so he could have a good basketball team.

He was like everyone's father away from home. Coach Edwards often had his athletes over for spaghetti dinners with his family, and on one occasion, he helped keep me out of jail.

I stayed at the Albany Hotel for a quarter before moving into a house I rented with my buddy Leo Willingham, a football player from Pittsburgh. I felt like a big shot. We had a two-bedroom house in Sterling and no longer would have the forty-five-minute walk from the Albany Hotel to campus or have to carpool with friends.

Grandmother Helen also fulfilled her promise of buying me a car when I went to college. It was a green-and-white four-door Oldsmobile and only about four years old. I was finally driving a real vehicle instead of the one pieced together by my Uncle Eddie.

The police came to our house on our first Saturday night and told me there was a theft at the Albany Hotel.

"You must be kidding," I told them. "I'm not going to be taking nothing from a hotel."

The police knew Coach Edwards and his brother, who was the district attorney. The officers were polite but persistent.

"You seem to be a good kid, but you and your roommate were the only students at the Albany, and they told us to check everyone out," one officer said.

I asked what was missing, and they said sheets and pillowcases.

"You think I would be stupid enough to steal sheets and pillowcases?" I told the officers.

Then Willingham said in a soft voice, "You know those sheets I said I got from home? I didn't really get them from home."

His eyes told me he was guilty. Willingham didn't just take a pair of sheets and pillowcases, he took every sheet and pillowcase for the whole hotel. The hotel didn't have any linen for their guests. Willingham could have appeared on those television shows about dumb crooks.

Willingham was still my buddy, but I could not believe he stole all of the linen and never expected to get caught.

The police marched us down to the Sterling city jail, where I immediately called Coach Edwards. Willingham was expelled from Northeastern Junior College. We would meet again about twenty years later in Washington, D.C.

We bumped into each other while Willingham was driving a taxicab and I was in D.C. for a Congressional Black Caucus event. I told Willingham to get a tuxedo and I took him to a party that evening. He had a female admirer at the event who jumped to the conclusion that he owned the taxi company. She disappeared when he made it clear he just drove a taxi.

Other black students struggled at Sterling. Kids had to drop out because they didn't have enough money for tuition, and some left to join the army. Others were avoiding Vietnam by playing sports, which gave us a lower military draft number.

Boredom also got us into trouble. There were about twenty-two black athletes at Northeastern and only two black girls. That was not a time for interracial dating with the white girls whose hometowns were Burlington or Julesburg. If there was any interracial dating, it was done quietly, and the white girls usually were from the East.

Usually, we headed to Denver for the weekends, but one Friday night, we were stuck in Sterling and restless. Sterling was dry at the time, and you couldn't buy liquor or beer. But nearby Merino had a bar, and Ennis and Raymond Roundtree had cars. We had the option of driving two hours to Denver or a few minutes to Merino. We piled into the cars and sensed we were heading toward trouble from the get-go.

We walked into the 3.2-beer joint and there must have been a couple hundred white kids dancing to country-western music. Some Latino kids were there as well. After about ten minutes, one of my buddies asked a white girl to dance and we heard someone say, "Nigger." A fight broke out between six-foot-two Donald Hardiman, who was 260 pounds, and a Hispanic guy who was about the same size.

They fought inside the bar, outside the bar, through the next business's front glass window, back through the broken glass, and into the street. They both were bleeding.

A crowd started forming around the fight, and one of the kids from Texas, nicknamed "Snake," pulled out a knife. Later, I asked why he stabbed the Hispanic guy in his buttocks, and he said he knew from anatomy class that he couldn't really hurt him badly, and the stabbing would likely break up the fight.

Everyone froze for a moment after the stabbing. We jumped back into our cars and headed back to Sterling, where we took Hardiman to the hospital to get the glass out of his butt.

The next day, we had a basketball game and at least twenty-five Colorado State Patrol officers were stationed around the gymnasium. Fifty Hispanic kids walked into the gym about the same time Caldwell was on a fast break. He missed an easy layup when he saw those Hispanic kids ready to fight before they spotted the patrolmen. The ball flew over the backboard.

We were lucky the holiday break started the next day and the hard feelings were gone once we returned to school.

"Snake" was also legendary for another confrontation in the lunchroom that permanently scarred Wendell Tyree. He picked up a fork, jammed it into Tyree's forehead, and dragged it down his cheek. You can imagine how that story still makes the rounds.

Sterling, for me, was a second chance. I screwed up high school and I was not going to screw up college. Sterling was my time to grow up into an adult. It was my time to blossom. I liked Sterling, and Sterling liked me.

Playing basketball was a dream I gave up in high school. I reached some important milestones at Northeastern that I never achieved at Manual High School. I made the starting five as the team's forward and was the second-leading scorer on the team and the top rebounder my freshman year. I also was named to the all-conference squad for junior colleges.

It was fun to play with fellow Denverites Caldwell and Mickey Marsh. Buddy was part of the starting five along with me, Jerry Menke, Alan Morrow, and Steve Kelling.

Marsh came off the bench along with Jim Weikel, Jack Amen, and Dan McKienan. McKienan later coached several Colorado high-school teams to prominence.

At the end of my freshman year, I had a B average and felt like the whole world was in front of me.

Chapter Six

College, First Marriage, Twins, Greeley

Sterling was a dream come true for me, and after my first year, I looked forward to coming back, finishing another year, and then transferring to a four-year college. I spent my summer in Denver working and playing basketball.

I arrived in Sterling for my sophomore year with great anticipation for our basketball season. Our goal was to win the junior college championship in our league and compete at the national junior college championship. We fell one game short that season, but I had a good year. I was named to the all-tournament team and was the second-leading scorer, eight points behind good friend Joe Folda.

The team had to travel throughout the state to compete with other junior colleges, and our mode of transportation was driving. In two large station wagons, we drove to Trinidad, La Junta, Lamar, Grand Junction, and Pueblo. Those station wagons also took us to colleges in Scottsbluff and Cook in Nebraska and Casper and Sheridan in Wyoming.

As a sophomore, I was allowed to drive one of the station wagons. We were headed to Casper, Wyoming. Coach Roy Edwards was never known for driving the speed limit, and I was following him, trying to keep up. I hit a patch of black ice, and while I was trying to regain control of the station wagon, it hit an embankment. The car flipped into the air, hit the ground, and rolled about five times.

The windshield popped out and everyone was afraid the car might catch on fire, so we piled out through the empty windshield. I

I was able to live my dream of being an accomplished basketball player when I went to Northeastern Junior College in Sterling, Colorado. Coach Roy Edwards took me under his wing, and we became lifelong friends.

was the last one out because I was on the bottom.

At the time, Wyoming allowed motorists to leave abandoned vehicles along the highway. Some passing motorists didn't even recognize that we had been in an accident, and they drove right by. Finally, a truck driver saw us and took us to the Wheatland hospital. There, one of my teammates hatched a plan to get rid of a suit his parents had sent him: he didn't like it, so he tore it up, thinking it would be replaced by insurance from the accident.

The insurance guy didn't buy his story.

The only person who got hurt was Dave Cromwell, a basketball player from Mount Vernon, New York. He had to get several stitches in his head.

We made it to Casper in time for the game but lost 60–59.

I sometimes faced my childhood friends from Denver on opposing teams. Chuck Williams and Sam Batey played for Pueblo Junior College. Pueblo was considered one of the elite teams, and they were favored to beat us in the division championship, held in Sterling.

We won a close game, but shortly after the buzzer went off, a player—we weren't sure from which team—threw a punch, and we had a melee in Sterling. Batey told me to get out of the way, and an older lady in the stands started hitting him on the head with her big purse.

"With Webb and me knowing each other, we just moved to the side and watched," Batey recalled. "The Pueblo players got escorted out of town by the Colorado State Patrol. They didn't want us to stay overnight because of the fear that someone might come to our hotel."

Then we faced Trinidad in the regional division championship. Trinidad Junior College, located in southern Colorado, beat us 73–64 (and later went on to national prominence).

A couple of years later, the Trinidad coaches took a chance on a kid named Spencer Haywood who had had trouble in high school. Haywood became the only junior college player on the U.S. Olympic team and later played for the American Basketball Association Denver Rockets.

The best junior college player I faced was a kid named Flynn

Robinson out of Wyoming who also went on to play professional basketball.

Coach Edwards later used me as an example to recruit more black athletes to Northeastern. In many cases, the young men were similar to me—they struggled in high school and they needed a smaller college with a caring staff in order to succeed.

I went back for several reunions when Coach Edwards was still alive. It still gives me a sense of pride that Northeastern Junior College considers me one of their most famous alumni.

College basketball helped give me a new lease on my education and also introduced me to my first wife, ShirLyee "Lyee" Martin. She was a cheerleader at Northeastern, and we sort of had this storybook romance of the jock and the cheerleader getting together. Before the end of my second year of college, we got married.

It was quite obvious to me shortly after the marriage that we both were too young for that kind of commitment. But it also wasn't too long before Lyee was at St. Anthony Hospital in Denver giving birth to our first child.

I was sitting with my mother-in-law in the father's waiting room, because in those days the men couldn't go into the birthing room. After the doctor told me Lyee had given birth to our son, Tony, I pulled out the cigars. About twenty-two minutes later, doctors and nurses started rushing down the hall: they said a woman was giving birth to a second child. All of the men looked around wondering which woman was having twins.

"We better check on Lyee, because her father is a twin," my mother-in-law informed me.

I thought to myself, *God wouldn't wish twins on me, because I'm a college student. I can barely afford one child, let alone two.*

And sure enough, Allen Webb arrived twenty-two minutes after his brother. He was four pounds, ten ounces, and Tony was four pounds, eight ounces.

I worked two jobs that summer and almost juggled a third to pay the bills. I vacuumed the carpet at the Hilton Hotel downtown, now the Adam's Mark, and cleared and washed dishes as a busboy in a local restaurant. I was trained as an orderly at University of Colorado Hospital to care for patients but only lasted through one week and one bedpan.

Tony and Allen were on different formulas, so Lyee and I were very busy that summer, and it was tough working two jobs and raising two kids.

Now that I was married and had two babies, I needed to find a four-year college close to Denver, where both of our families lived. I enrolled at Colorado State College in Greeley, about an hour north of the city. (They later changed the name to the University of Northern Colorado.)

I applied for married-student housing, which turned out to be full, but I found a nice apartment near the campus. My neighbors were professors and graduate students. This is where Allen got a scar on his forehead; he was sitting in a baby seat, and we had forgotten to tie him down. He jumped out and hit his head on three heating pipes on the floor. We rushed him to the hospital, where he got seven stitches.

Later on, we moved to married-student housing that was really like a World War II Quonset hut—in other words, small and not real comfortable. It was a difficult time of balancing marriage and college. Lyee worked part-time at a factory that made blue jeans. I was gone a lot at class and basketball practice.

Greeley was not as friendly as Sterling was to black students, and some of my friends left the college.

"Even though I was playing basketball and leading the team in scoring, I couldn't deal with the city," recalled Williams. "The only time I had someone call me a 'nigger' was in Greeley."

I couldn't afford to keep Lyee in Greeley, so she returned with the boys to Denver to live with family. Robert Ennis occasionally was my roommate, along with Chuck DeMorst. A frequent visitor was our good friend Ken Morman.

Although I was married to Lyee, I was also a college student, and that meant occasional parties at our apartment complex. We were having a good time at the downstairs apartment that was occupied by twin girls from Florida. More than forty years later, Ennis didn't hesitate to remember the girls' names: Birdie and Ruthie. Ennis also recalled that the girls were famous for making southern sweet tea and sweet Kool-Aid, both of which had mounds of extra sugar.

At one of our parties, an unexpected guest showed up.

"I saw his grandmother drive up," Williams said. "I ran into the house and told him, and he thought I was joking. He was dancing and having fun, and in walks his grandmother."

Once I saw my grandmother's shoes and her black coat coming down the stairs to our party in a basement apartment, I quickly ran up the stairs to greet her. She made it clear her visit was to remind me I was in Greeley to study, not party. I got the message.

I graduated in December 1964 with a degree in sociology and did my student teaching in Adams County to become certified to teach. I ended up in Adams County because Colorado State College, which produced the most teachers, was in a disagreement with the superintendent of Denver Public Schools, so the student teachers went to other counties until the issue was resolved.

I liked student teaching at Adams City High School, located just outside of the Denver city limits. I taught social studies and history and helped coach the basketball team, the Adams City Eagles. Yet I still wanted a full-time job with the Denver schools.

I had dreams of getting a teaching job at Manual High School and earning the going salary of $5,000 a year. I wanted to take the Manual basketball team to a state championship. I wanted to live in a house with a white picket fence with my young wife and sons. I thought I had it all figured out.

When I didn't get a job in the Denver schools, I signed up to be a substitute teacher in Adams County. I had to wait for a 6:00 A.M. call and then jump in my car and drive to a school often located across town. The work was not steady, and I only got paid once a month. That didn't jibe well with the daily need for food, diapers, and formula.

Fortunately, I was able to fill in for a social-studies teacher in Adams County who had gotten elected to the state legislature and would be gone from January to June. I never dreamed I'd be serving with state representative Wayne Knox when I joined the legislature in 1972.

When that teaching job ended, I did what a lot of teachers did during the summer break: I looked for work outside the field. Someone had told me that there were jobs at the local Frito Lay potato-chip factory. I put on my suit and applied for a job. Once I got the job, I turned in my suit for blue jeans, a light shirt, and boots. It was very hot, wet, and sticky inside the factory. It was a menial job, and I didn't tell my coworkers I had a college degree. I can't remember the pay, but I do know I got a check every Friday.

Batey was also looking for a job while he waited for a teaching position in Denver.

"The problem for a lot of African American men was that we had to substitute teach before we could get a full-time job," Batey said. "I guess they saw it as a way to prove ourselves."

Batey hoped his job at Frito Lay would be temporary.

"Webb recommended me so he could move up and move on to driving a forklift," Batey said. "The big joke is that I showed up in a suit and ended up in a potato line, peeling potatoes."

Batey found a full-time teaching job that fall. He spent thirty years in the Denver Public Schools as a teacher, basketball coach, principal, and administrator.

While working for Frito Lay, I was looking for other ways to supplement my income. The University of Denver had put together a program called Neighborhood Youth Training with Model Cities money. They were looking for minorities to train as coordinators. Bernie Hyman taught the class for the coordinators that focused on politics, economics, budget, helping the poor, and learning how to empower people.

I probably was the only person in the program who had a college degree, but I didn't tell anyone. The program paid $2.50 an hour, and the money came in handy. Each of the graduates was also promised a job at one of the city's two neighborhood health centers in the medical-records department, but I didn't take the job. I still wanted to be a full-time teacher.

I met several community activists during this time and sought their guidance in how I could get a teaching job. Colorado Civil Rights Division director Jim Reynolds and deputy director Warren Alexander were amused that I assumed I could get a teaching job right out of college.

"Being from the West, you thought by getting a degree in education that automatically qualified you for something," Reynolds said at the time. "It doesn't qualify you for a damn thing other than now you have a degree. If you grew up in the South, where black people have it harder, you would understand you have to be more aggressive in seeking employment."

I went to the labor unions and met Herrick Roth, the head of the local American Federation of Labor and Congress of Industrial Organizations. He was chairman of a program called Job Opportunities Center. I told him about the difficulty I was having finding a teaching job, and he informed me that he helped the Denver Public Schools' teachers form a union. Then he showed me what having power is like: he picked up the phone and called James Galvin, a psychiatrist and director of the Job Opportunities Center who was hiring counselors to work with the poor. Roth told Galvin that he wanted me to start work on Monday. Some people talk about having power but never make anything happen. They'll give you a calling card and referral but not much else. Others really have power and it shows in how they get things done.

I became a counselor for the poor, which reflected my financial status as well. The staff was a mixture of black, whites, and Hispanics. We helped individuals find jobs. The U.S. Department of Labor funded the program; it was the forerunner for the Neighborhood Youth Corp.

But the program wasn't perfect. The government supplemented

the families by paying them based on the number of children they had, which was unlimited. Someone finally figured out that we were subsidizing the number of kids people were having and it probably was not a good policy. In some cases, the clients were making more money than the counselors who were training the clients to find jobs. A cap was placed on the amount each family could receive, despite the number of children they had.

I also watched while some female clients gave their checks to their boyfriends who would go directly to the liquor store. The women's children would be without food for a week. I got fed up once and confronted a client's boyfriend. He told me, "This is my woman and if she wants to give me her check, she will." I later discovered that the woman was giving the man the money to avoid getting beaten.

I felt so bad for another woman that I took food out of my kitchen and went to give it to her family.

"Just set it on the table," she told me about the bag of groceries.

To be polite, I opened her kitchen cabinets and discovered that she had more food in her home than my wife and I had for our two kids. I felt like a fool.

The majority of the clients were honest people just trying to survive, but a lot of people knew how to work the system.

We coached clients about how to dress and be prepared for questions on job interviews. We worked with the transportation district to improve public transit for the working poor. We made sure our clients were aware of federal programs such as the U.S. Department of Agriculture's program to provide surplus cheese and other items to the poor.

As part of the program, I began going to neighborhood meetings with Latino activist Corky Gonzalez. Our staff often hung out at Joe's Buffet on Santa Fe Boulevard, where I had my first Mexican hamburger and jalapeño peppers.

I liked the job, but I still yearned to be a teacher. Reverend Leon Sullivan, based in Philadelphia, started the National Opportunity Industrialized Center to train African Americans for jobs and wanted a satellite office in Denver. The Denver program was to be operated out of Reverend Acen Phillips's church. It was going to take place at night, so I thought I could squeeze it into my schedule. Several people said they would teach typing classes. Dorothy Rose Riggins, one of the best teachers from Denver Public Schools, who was retired at the time, said she would teach writing skills to the clients, many of whom didn't even have a high-school diploma.

Reverend Phillips then said he needed someone to teach black history. I raised my hand for that job. I liked history; it was my minor field of study in college.

"I think this is how Wellington really got into politics," Phillips said of the program, which helped at least 150 African Americans get jobs. "I liked his personality, his honesty, and sincere commitment to see people succeed—and that was people of all creeds and colors."

I had about six weeks before the program started, and I headed to the Denver Public Library. I planned to check out every book on black history so that I was prepared for the class. I looked through the card catalog and asked the librarians, but there were no history books on African Americans. The only books that discussed black Americans were located in the sociology section or talked about marriage and family issues. I took those books and headed to black bookstores.

In the black bookstores, I discovered several authors and started reading books by Frantz Fanon, E. Franklin Frazier, John Hope Franklin, Lerone Bennett, Jesse Billingsley, Ralph Ellison, and Richard Wright. Black activists were saying we should not use the word *Negro* because it does not signify a place where our race originated. My mind started drinking in these concepts.

I still had my history books from classes I took at Colorado State College. I was horrified that those books talked about how happy the slaves were on the plantations. What a contradiction of terms.

The Vietnam War was raging, and I started raging about the injustices that black Americans faced. My clothing began to change. I wore a black medallion around my neck when I taught the black-history class. I started discussions with my students about Jeffersonian

Democracy and the hypocrisy of the history books that said slaves were happy.

My students learned about the contributions of African Americans, including Garrett Morgan, who invented the traffic light, Dr. Charles Drew, who developed blood plasma, and the famous open-heart surgeon Daniel Hale. These were black men and experts in their fields.

Outside the classroom, I got involved in projects that helped people in the black community and tried to improve life for the poor in Denver.

Politics was growing in my soul, but my wife, Lyee, had no interest in my newfound passion. That was another sign that our troubled marriage would not survive.

Chapter Seven

Mayor Tom Currigan, Fort Logan

My self-education as a black-history teacher helped me use my degree, but the road to finally getting a full-time teaching job hit a few potholes.

I went to see Leonard Stezler, the director of personnel in 1965 for the Denver Public Schools. In hindsight, when I recall my interview, it's no wonder he didn't hire me: I answered every question honestly and candidly, and that was exactly the wrong tactic. I told him I wanted to be a history and social-studies teacher at the high-school level and coach a high-school basketball team.

What I didn't understand was that the district was putting most new male teachers in the elementary schools to help enforce discipline, and those males worked their way up to the high school. He also informed me that some men waited twenty years to coach high-school athletics.

"I may not want to continue teaching after twenty years," I boldly told him. "Why would you not give me that kind of a job when I am young and alert? I have all of this energy, and the things I've learned, I want to share with the students."

I didn't get a job and was even more disillusioned when I heard two other men, including Fred Applewhite of Texas, had just been hired by the Denver schools. Applewhite and I later became friends.

"They tell you to graduate from high school and then go to college," said friend Chuck Williams, who worked for the Colorado Association of Public Employees for thirty years. "But even with a college degree, it was tough to find a job."

I told my grandmother I didn't understand how even though I grew up in Denver and have roots here, I still couldn't get a teaching job in the local public schools.

She had campaigned for Denver mayor Tom Currigan in the black community, and even though as mayor he had nothing to do with the Denver schools, my grandmother thought he might be able to help me.

I told her I didn't want to ask for the mayor's help, and then questioned whether she could even get him to see me.

"I'm a committeewoman. He'll take my call," she said.

She was right, and I quickly had an appointment with the mayor. I went down to the Denver City and County Building and met Mayor Currigan. I explained that as a Denver resident with a teaching degree, I should be able to get a teaching job in Denver. I told him I had a wife and two kids. He listened and told me he appreciated my situation, but there was nothing he could do.

"This is humiliating," I replied. "I don't even know you and I'm asking you for help. I now understand why some people go out and rob stores. I have kids at home who are hungry and crying. I did what people told me to do—get an education—yet the system has failed in doing anything reciprocal for me."

Our meeting was on a Wednesday. Two days later, I had a contract to teach in the Denver Public Schools at Smiley Junior High School. I called Herrick Roth, and he informed me that the district put all the potential troublemaker teachers at Smiley.

I had a job, yet it just didn't feel right. That same week, Henry Morgan, a college friend of mine, told me they were hiring teachers at the Colorado Mental Health Institute at Fort Logan. It was a new school for emotionally disturbed children. The state was taking a new direction and separating those children from retarded kids (who are now referred to as developmentally disabled) who lived in a facility in the suburb of Wheat Ridge.

The Fort Logan job paid about $517 a month, which was less

than what I could get teaching at Smiley. I also would get only two weeks of vacation at Fort Logan, compared to almost three months as a Denver Public Schools teacher.

I contacted Fort Logan principal George Buttles of Park Hill, who took me around the school on my interview. He had sandy, curly hair and spectacles and looked disheveled.

But the day of my interview didn't start out very well. I couldn't find Fort Logan. It is located in the southwest corner of Denver in an area then primarily undeveloped. When I finally arrived at the complex, I wasn't sure where to go. I entered one cottage and interrupted several social workers during a private discussion about the confidential status of each child.

Once I got situated, I was sitting in a classroom, observing, when a student about twelve years old tried to hit his teacher. She restrained him, and he hit her on the shoulder. I forgot I was an observer, got up, and made the kid sit in his chair. She explained that the kid didn't mean to hurt her; he was just trying to get our attention. I felt kind of silly, but that response would help me understand the kids down the road.

I ended the interview with psychologist Jay Benedict and social worker Tom Little. I accepted the job at Fort Logan, and the principal at Smiley was stunned when I called him.

"You know how valuable these jobs are. You can get a job in the Denver Public Schools and stay here for the rest of your life," he told me.

I wasn't swayed. The experience of applying for a teaching job at the Denver schools was humiliating. I would get less money and a shorter vacation at Fort Logan, but I kept my pride.

"What would have happened if Webb took the teaching job in Denver?" asked friend Sam Batey. "He probably would have had forty years in education, but we would not have had him as our mayor."

I spent most of my time as a gym teacher, but I also learned to do therapy with the students. One of my most unforgettable colleagues was social worker Harold Parker. He was loud, boisterous, and the best clinician I ever met. He was great with the kids and dealt with his colleagues with a sense of humor. He had the right balance of professionalism and common sense, which he shared with me.

I used to say that being the mayor of Denver was easy because at Fort Logan, I saw every psychological behavior known to man while working in the children's division. The kids would test my patience, and usually they were working together as a team. One time I tried to play softball with them, and when I hit the ball, they all dropped their gloves and ran and hid. One boy organized the kids to throw dirt clods at the principal and his wife when he brought his family from Maryland to see the school. The same boy also convinced a kid to throw a pool table ball at a blackboard, which cracked on impact. I told him if anyone attempted to throw a pool ball at me, I was going to hit him. The boy then cited the Colorado Revised Statute that said it was illegal for a staff member or a teacher to hit the kids because they were emotionally disturbed.

"You don't understand," I told him. "I had to be emotionally disturbed to take this job!"

Another time, a group of kids bolted from me during a hike. They discovered a canal and waded to an island. I took off my shoes and started to go after them, until I realized that they were laughing because my new pants were getting ruined. When I turned to leave, they yelled that I couldn't abandon them, but I kept walking. I sent the Fort Logan security guards to retrieve them.

I got some extra money in my budget, so we converted a small area outside for the kids to play handball, tennis, and volleyball and planted some trees and grass. The kids dubbed the area Webb Park.

Some children faced long recoveries from horrendous abuse or trauma. The physical stimulation was geared to help the kids overcome their emotional problems.

One girl had been repeatedly raped by her parents. She thought she was pregnant, and every day she would come to class holding an invisible baby in her arms. Every day I asked her to put the baby down so she could participate in activities.

89

An autistic farm boy from Nebraska had watched his parents die in a barn fire, and all he wanted to do was swing from a rope tied to a tree.

Another kid went around with his coat tied around his neck like Superman. He jumped out of a second-story window and never got a scratch. The staff struggled even more after that to convince the kid that he could not fly.

Many of the children stayed for short periods of time and got their lives back in order after counseling. They went on to be productive adults. But other kids never recovered from the abuse or trauma. They often ended up back at Fort Logan at the hospital that treated adults.

The job was challenging and exhausting. By the time I got home from long days, I had no energy for my own young family.

Fort Logan's location, about fourteen miles from my home, was also an issue. As a state employee, I got paid once a month. One time, I ran out of gas and had to walk home because I had no cash. The next day, I carpooled to Fort Logan and borrowed money for gas.

I enjoyed my time at Fort Logan, but I also longed for new challenges. When my students sensed I was leaving, they got upset. One kid stole my car keys. When I went to look for my keys in the gym, I saw that someone had defecated in center court. The kids had suffered a lot of loss in their young lives and they didn't want to have to get used to a new teacher.

I worked at Fort Logan from 1966 to 1969. For me, it was a good time to start a new career because my first marriage was near the end.

We tried to make the marriage work and find our niche as a young couple in Denver. I helped start the Esquire Club as a social outlet for us and other young black families. The club allowed us to spend time together and socialize with longtime friends. The club included a basketball team so us old jocks could play against other club teams across the state.

"There wasn't much going on in Denver for young black males," recalled charter member Williams.

The original members of the Esquire Club were Williams, Sam Batey, Robert Ennis, Henry Morgan, Ron Cox, James Gordon, Reggie Scott, Frank Brown, and me. Our friendships dated back to high school and college.

"We were always together, constantly doing something," Batey said. "If we had a party, we'd bring the kids. None of us could afford babysitters, so the adults were upstairs having a party and the kids were downstairs."

The Esquire was a brotherhood. The members went through marriage, divorce, remarriage, the birth and loss of children, and struggles to get their jobs. About ten members were allowed at a time.

"Membership was by invitation only, and some people weren't allowed to join," Williams recalled. "We wanted to make sure the person would fit in. But people didn't always get along, and that's when Webb was always the peacemaker. He would try and see everyone else's side. I'm more direct and would just tell someone to chill. Webb has a more diplomatic way."

The Esquire Club was active in community projects and raised money for nonprofit groups. We extended a hand during the 1965 South Platte River flood.

"Here we were, young blacks helping the white community whose homes were flooded," Williams said. "The middle-class white-owned homes are the ones that got hit by the flood, not the black neighborhoods."

We lived in the Park Hill neighborhood at this time, and our neighbor was the Democratic committeeman of the area. I knew what his job entailed because this is what my grandmother did. He invited me and Lyee to participate with the Democrats in the area. This went by the wayside because Lyee was not interested. Less than four years later, I would be elected to the Colorado General Assembly.

Lyee and I had been slowly drifting apart for years. The tidal wave that helped drown our marriage was the sudden death of our daughter.

To this day, it's hard to believe that I had a daughter one day who got sick and died in less than twenty-four hours. No job, no election victory, no amount of time heals the lingering pain a parent feels when he buries his child.

Chapter Eight

Felicia, Black Studies, Wilma

I have a black shoe box with a red top that contains the sympathy cards mailed from family and friends after my daughter's death. Under the mounds of yellowed envelopes and cards is her tarnished silver baby spoon. A Polaroid photograph shows her tombstone: "Our Darling Felicia V. Webb" is inscribed on gray granite.

Felicia was born on July 20, 1965. She was a sweet little girl. We have photographs of her sitting under a tree near our home. We buried her under a tree at Fairmount Cemetery.

We named her Felicia just because we liked the name. Her middle name was Vernadette, for my aunt.

Tony and Allen were six years old when their two-and-a-half-year-old baby sister suddenly got ill on February 20, 1968. We took her to Rose Memorial Hospital. Her pediatrician was out of town, so we called our family doctor who prescribed some medicine. After taking the prescription, she got a little better, and Lyee and I took our daughter home.

In the middle of the night, Felicia started having convulsions. We rushed her to Mercy Hospital at about 1:00 A.M. on February 21, and we stayed with her until about 5:00 A.M. The nurses, who were Catholic nuns, told us to go home and get some sleep. They had our little girl resting in an oxygen tent, and she seemed to be okay. They told us to come back in a few hours.

We were home when the phone rang at about 9:30 A.M.

"You need to get back here right away," a nurse told me.

I didn't like the sound of her voice. The trip to the hospital was a blur. We got off the elevator and were walking toward Felicia's room when a nurse stopped us.

"I just want to tell you that your baby passed," she said.

It was unbelievable. Felicia got sick on February 20 and she was dead on February 21.

We walked into her hospital room and saw her lying in her bed. They had cleaned her up, and I could tell her body was starting to cool down. Lyee became hysterical, and they gave her something to calm her.

I sat there in disbelief that God would do this and that my baby would die so young. I was angry at the hospital. I was angry at the doctor. I was angry at my life. My good friend Chuck Williams came by the hospital to sit with me. We both were angry at God.

"Felicia was my favorite girl," Williams recalled.

My brother Joe also helped me grieve that day, and years later, we shared a bottle of booze in another hospital when his daughter was born with spina bifida. The doctors told Joe she was born with a hole in her spine and that she might not live long.

I remember him bravely telling the doctors, "My daughter may be handicapped, but we're going to fight to give her as good of a life as possible."

His daughter, Ciara, grew into an independent woman. Oh, how I wish Felicia had gotten that same chance.

My baby girl, who posed in photographs with her grandparents and shared holidays with her brothers and uncles, was suddenly no longer a part of our lives after February 21, 1968.

The day Felicia died, I was driving in the car with Tony and Allen when I told them, "Your sister is gone."

They both said, "No, she isn't. She's sitting right next to us."

I just about had a car wreck and pulled over. I don't know what they saw or what they felt. She obviously was not there … but maybe she was.

Then we had to face going to the mortuary and picking out a

casket that was the size for a large doll. Felicia's hair had never been pressed, and I remember looking at her at the funeral and it was so clear that this was only a shell of a body and not my baby girl.

"Another friend and myself went to the store to get pink ribbon because that's what Lyee wanted for the funeral," Eula Patton Mills, Williams's first wife, recalled. "No one even knew the baby was sick. Then she died. Lyee wanted everything in pink."

The letters of condolences flooded in. A note from Allen and Tony's elementary-school principal offered the family help. A long letter from a friend quoted scripture. Another friend wrote, "She was such a beautiful little girl, and every time I saw her, I thought how cute she was."

My bosses at Fort Logan sent a letter. The kids at Fort Logan also sent a card with their signatures printed in large block letters or scribbled.

Auntie Frances sent a card. She was pained that she could not be at the funeral.

Lyee's colleagues at Chevron Oil Company sent a long office envelope with memorial donations from 104 people who had also signed their names.

Our doctor called the day after Felicia died to say how sorry he was. I wondered if the prescription he gave Felicia played a role in her death. I also wondered what happened after we left the hospital. Did the nuns miss something? I had a doctor in the children's division at Fort Logan look over the autopsy.

I still have the typed autopsy report, which was mailed to us in August 1968. The doctor who wrote the autopsy referred to Felicia as a "colored girl." His report states that after a few hours of being admitted to Mercy Hospital, Felicia's temperature rose to 104 degrees, she developed convulsive seizures and apnea, and died.

"None of us really knows what always transpires in medical circumstances," my friend at Fort Logan told me, "because what is written here is basically [that] she died because her lungs were saturated with fluid."

We never would find out what caused the fluid to fill her tiny lungs.

What I did was to continue to live my life because I had two other children. But that doesn't mean the anger disappears. I wanted to know what exactly had happened. I wanted to know how a baby could be living, thriving one day, and the next day, she could be gone, that quickly. I didn't understand why then and I still don't.

I promised myself that if I ever had a chance to help others get through the morass and bureaucracy to answer important questions, I would do it.

I quit my job at Fort Logan several months after Felicia's death and wanted to leave that part of my life behind—the loss of my daughter and the breakup of a failed marriage.

During that time, it was pretty unusual for a father to get full custody of his children after a divorce, but Lyee and I agreed that I could provide more stability for Tony and Allen.

What was not unusual in the black community was for me and the boys to move in with my Grandmother Helen. The extended family was the cornerstone for black families throughout America.

Then, as a single man, I did what single men do: I dated.

I had free time and was independent and making money. I eventually rented an apartment, and my buddies would come over in the afternoons and play bid whist, which was black bridge. My friends kept me company: Williams, Bob Pickford, Len Jones, and Jeroba Wright. Wright's real name was Milton Wright, but he changed his name to sound more like a black activist. Thirty years later, he died in the Denver County Jail. We had lost touch over the years, and I'm still not sure the exact circumstances of his death.

I had dated several women during that time, yet there still was something missing. Eventually, I asked Wilma Jean Gerdine Thomas, a young woman I had admired from a distance, to have lunch with me.

She would soon become my wife, Wilma J. Webb.

I had known about Wilma since we both attended Manual High School. She is two years younger than me, and we didn't have anything to do with each other as teenagers. In fact, at the time I resented her name because of a high-school yearbook mistake. Under one of my basketball photographs, instead of identifying me as Wellington Webb, it read "Wilma Webb." I guess we both should have taken that as some sort of a good sign.

Unlike me, Wilma was a motivated and excellent student who was active in student-council leadership and was an honorary cadet, a highly coveted core of girls in high school, whose membership was limited to the top students. We were such opposites in high school, with me being a slacker and her being a school leader, that we never would have dated. But as young adults, we discovered we enjoyed each other, we had a lot in common, and we had several mutual friends. This is still true today.

Wilma, who was not only pretty, but also smart, had become politically active before me while working with an organization called Committee on Greater Opportunity, as well as being active in other civic groups. The group worked closely with Denver Public Schools board member Rachel Noel on a resolution to integrate the schools. They also helped provide calm in northeast Denver following the assassination of Dr. Martin Luther King Jr.

We both were young divorced parents with two children. We fell in love with each other, and I asked her to marry me.

We were both involved with our community and concerned about political issues. As our relationship grew, we thought the idea of raising our four children together was possible. We would be similar to the weekly television show *The Brady Bunch*. But we learned the successful blending of a family with two sets of children was more challenging in real life than it was on a TV show.

Wilma and I also related to the fact that we often felt displaced in time from our friends. Even though we were in the same age group as our friends, Wilma and I felt older, which had to do with becoming parents at an early age. When our children were in high school, our friends' children were in elementary school. There was always that gap in what we could relate to with our friends.

97

"Wilma is kind of like Webb: low key and caring," said our friend Carl Pipkin. "They match up pretty good, and that's why they've been together for so long."

Wilma was supportive when I started the first job I had after Fort Logan: teaching an African American history course at the University of Colorado at Denver (CU). There weren't many teachers at that time who were qualified to teach the new course, but I had my previous experience with Reverend Acen Phillips's program.

I was excited to teach at CU and met with Black Studies director of counseling Cecil Glenn. The Black Studies Department at CU was typical of the 1960s: it was radical left-leaning in politics, anti–President Nixon, anti–Vietnam War, and heavy on black culture and black pride.

My grandmother was still sewing and made me the most beautiful African top, called a dashiki, with blue and silver trim. She always wanted to make sure I had something more exquisite to wear than anyone else.

"Helen would tell me, 'Ruby, I'm going to make a politician out of Wellington.' It took a lot of doing, but she did it," Ruby Kirk Gray said. "But at times, she got frustrated with him. He used to wear his hair in a big Afro, which was popular in the late 1960s and 1970s. Helen told me if she could get him down, she'd cut it off."

My father was also making me socially aware of problems when, on trips to Chicago, he would show me the dilapidated schools for the city's black students. In 1985, I asked him what he thought about Chicago, having lived there since he was nine years old.

"See, well, I've been in Chicago for sixty years, and the changes that have happened are remarkable," he told me. "But after all that time, Chicago is still one of the most prejudiced and segregated cities in the country."

He talked about how it took black politicians years to get elected. He also gave me some advice that I would later use in my political career.

"The thing is, you have to be prepared and be ready," he

explained. "If you're lucky enough to be in the right place at the right time, you're all right."

When I took Wilma to Chicago to visit my family on the south side, she had a natural reaction as a black woman who grew up in predominantly white Denver.

"Where are all the white people?" she asked.

Chicago's black population was on every street corner and every block. Wilma was not used to seeing black people in such large numbers. She was amazed.

Before I started my job at CU, I was scheduled to meet with Black Studies Department director Roosevelt Hill after he returned from Cañon City, where he had taken some college students to the state penitentiary to meet with black inmates. They stopped in Colorado Springs at a Mobil Oil Gas Station to fill up their car with gas. Hill tried to pay for the gas with his state credit card, but the young station attendant wasn't familiar with the credit card and demanded cash.

When the attendant again refused to take the credit card, Hill attempted to get back into the car and leave. The kid ran into the station, got a shotgun, and killed Hill in the driveway.

Wilma was working for Mobil Oil Corporation at the time. A young black man named King Harris who worked for United Banks of Denver helped organized a protest against Mobil.

Wilma participated in some of the mediating process between Harris and Mobil.

That tragedy opened up the director of black studies job, which went to Cecil Glenn. I took over as the interim counseling director part-time, as well as teaching classes. The only thing I requested was that the course give the students three hours of credit toward their major instead of being an elective class. Wilma helped me put together a syllabus for the course.

A couple of history teachers questioned whether the class should count as credits toward the students' liberal arts or history degrees. I challenged them to debate me on the subject in the student union with students present. I told the professors that I would show up on any day and at any time. They never took the challenge.

I won the battle, and the class did count toward the liberal arts and history degrees instead of being an elective.

At this time, I also started working at the Colorado State University (CSU) Manpower Laboratory, a program started by CSU psychology professors Gene Etting and Charlie Cole. This was another U.S. Department of Labor program.

Despite my workload, I decided to go back to college in Greeley and get my master's degree in sociology. This required me to drive back and forth from Denver to Greeley several times during the week. Some days, I had to drive to Greeley for a morning class at the University of Northern Colorado, drive back to Denver for work, and then back to Greeley for a night class.

The schedule was brutal, but I knew in my heart that if I didn't complete my master's then, I probably never would.

So at one time I was involved with three colleges: the University of Colorado at Denver, Colorado State University, and the University of Northern Colorado.

I even had to get a hotel room toward the end of my classes in Greeley to give me adequate time to study. Staying at the hotel wasn't all bad. Wilma joined me there during our engagement to be married. We enjoyed each other's company while I studied. We were compatible because of our similar interests, and I admired her as a committed mother and as a woman who was dedicated to her community.

The professor gave the students taking the comprehensive exam one question, an essay that required us to write all afternoon. I graduated with a master's in sociology from the University of Northern Colorado in August 1971.

Three months before Wilma and I got married, we both gave up our individual rented homes to save money to buy our own home. Wilma, Stephanie, and Keith moved in with her parents. Tony, Allen, and I stayed with my grandmother.

Wilma found a house through a newspaper advertisement that

read "Old house for sale; needs handyman." It was located at 2329 Gaylord Street in northeast Denver.

Well, I'm not a handyman; never have been. But I was impressed because the house had four bedrooms, was sturdy, and had potential for becoming a home. We also liked the house because it was close to both of our childhood neighborhoods.

Wilma and I spoke many times about moving out of the area when the children were getting ready to go to high school. But we decided they would receive a decent education at East High and staying in a predominantly black neighborhood would benefit them. The neighborhood also gave me a strong political base that would help me in each of my elections. Keith is the oldest, so he was the first from our family to attend East High School. Stephanie, Tony, and Allen, all near the same age, entered East High School together.

Wilma and I had a small wedding in her parents' home. Our pastor, Reverend W. T. Liggins, presided. Afterwards, we had a party at a friend's home. It was a second marriage for both of us, so we downplayed the reception, including telling our friends not to bring presents—and boy was that dumb.

Shortly after we moved into our new home, I announced my candidacy for the Colorado House of Representatives for District Eight. I had started laying the groundwork to join the state legislature a couple of years before. The city had a political program called Residential Participation Denver, Incorporated, or RPDI. The program required interested people to run for a seat based on geographic districts. The elected group voted on such things as how to spend Community Development Block Grant money from the federal government.

I ran for the position, although I was not completely dedicated to the political process. Wilma campaigned for me, going door to door in the rain. Meanwhile, the same weekend of the election, I had a basketball game with my semiprofessional team. We played on weekends, primarily for money, throughout the Rocky Mountain region. This was before the NBA created minor leagues throughout the country. Businesses and communities would sponsor teams and

Wilma and I both graduated from Manual
High School in Denver, but it wasn't until we
were young adults that we met, fell in love,
and got married in her parents' home.

put up prize money. Our sponsor was the Maddox Ice Company, whose owners loved basketball. We also traveled to play other members of other privately sponsored teams in Washington, Kentucky, and Montana. The day of the election, I was in Pueblo at a game, but I had learned from my grandmother to organize well, and I ended up being the top vote-getter in my district.

I also was getting more involved in social issues. I joined Black Panther organizer Lauren Watson's protest of the Denver Police Department over a brutality charge. We took over the mayor's office for the day. To Mayor Bill McNichols's credit, he heard we were coming to protest and, instead of a confrontation, he gave us his office for a press conference and he went and played golf.

That was the first time I sat in a mayor's chair.

This was not the first time the black community questioned the tactics of the Denver Police Department. Officer brutality and claims of unjustified shootings were common themes year after year, including during my three terms as mayor.

Denver city councilman Elvin Caldwell, the first African American elected to a council seat, became a target of the Black Panthers. Watson brought in some members from California, and they held a mock trial of Caldwell at a community center. They claimed that Caldwell was not doing enough for the black community. I remember sitting there while they called Caldwell every derogatory name under the sun.

"Thank you very much for the compliments," Caldwell said calmly.

He never lost his edge. He never lost his decorum. I thought at the time that I would never let someone talk to me like that. I later realized that Caldwell knew who he was and he was comfortable with himself. The longer I stayed in public life, the more I respected Caldwell as a politician. He knew that most of the Black Panther protesters were from California and they never voted in a Denver City Council election. The mock trial was probably the last time Caldwell would have to calmly take their insults or even see their faces.

At the time, my political advisers were a small group of friends who began meeting regularly. I came to know a young attorney named Dan Muse when I was working at the Jobs Opportunities Center. Muse would join me at Saturday morning meetings with attorneys Raymond Jones, King Trimble, and Norm Early.

We all had high aspirations. Jones wanted to be a judge; he became a state district court judge and went on to the Colorado Court of Appeals. Trimble was good at organizing and mentioned one day that he wanted to run for Congress; instead, he had stints at the state legislature and on the Denver City Council. Early wanted to be Denver's district attorney; he achieved that goal when Dale Tooley died in office and Governor Roy Romer appointed Early, who was an assistant district attorney, to the top job. Early later won election and served for more than ten years.

It's ironic how life works, because at the time we began our political meetings, Early and I never dreamed that in 1991 we would be running against each other to be Denver's first black mayor.

Muse said he was a behind-the-scenes kind of guy because he said his personality wouldn't allow him to be elected. I introduced Muse to my grandmother at a political event.

"Shortly after I met Mrs. Gamble, she asked me to come to tea at her home," Muse recalled. "She was dressed up, wearing a hat and gloves. She told me, 'I've been watching you, and I think you have a lot of potential and my grandson has a lot of potential. My grandson is going places, and I really think it would be good for you to be with him because he is going to make a difference for this city.'"

Muse had already heard about my grandmother's reputation.

"She didn't take anything from anyone," he said. "She would command the floor at political meetings, and she had a good temper at times. She could bless you out without swearing at you. She had no tolerance for foolish people."

My focused interest in politics in 1971 led me to run to be a delegate at the national Congressional Black Caucus convention in Gary, Indiana. This was during a time when I was questioning authority, questioning whether Caldwell had been in office too long and if the same were true of George Brown, who served as Colorado's only black state senator and later as lieutenant governor. McKinnely Harris, president of the Five Points Business Association, worked closely with Caldwell to control old politics in Denver. I, along with members of my political group, was a typical thirty-year-old who thought the old-timers were out of touch with the younger generation. It was our time to grab some power.

We thought many of the longtime black politicians were of the "get-along-to-go-along" philosophy. "They did not want a lot of other people at the table," Muse recalled. "They wanted to shoo us away, but Mrs. Gamble was quite the deal maker. She worked behind the scenes to make sure they didn't go after us in a vicious way."

The national convention in Gary inspired and fueled what would be my life's purpose: helping others through politics.

If you were an elected official, you might be poor, but you could be at the table dealing with such issues as realtors who were keeping minorities out of certain neighborhoods or bankers who refused to give loans to low-income people.

If I was an elected official, I would have clout to talk to public-school officials about why minority students were failing or dropping out of school. They could not ignore me as the average Joe citizen. If I held the title of state representative, a snub could result in consequences.

So when I came back from Gary, I was ready to run for the Colorado House of Representatives.

When I told Wilma, her initial reaction was that we had been married for less than a year, just bought a new home, and were raising four quite different children. Now I wanted to run for political office?

She also reflected on our earlier conversation when she tagged me the "people's politician."

When I told her we would find a way to work it out, she told me we would do it together.

Chapter Nine

The Legislature

Paul Hamilton decided not to seek reelection for District Eight in 1972. I was the first to announce my candidacy. I was thirty-one years old.

"I'm tired of seeing the same kind of candidates year after year making the same kind of promises that aren't kept," I said in my announcement speech. "Black people don't need that kind of representation."

At the time, I had a goatee and an Afro and wore a black medallion around my neck. My campaign literature sounded similar to John F. Kennedy: "The torch has now passed to a new generation, and we of that generation must strive for excellence." Another brochure read "We have been divided too long. We need community action through political power. United, we have that power."

A fund-raiser dance on July 15, 1972, asked for a $2.50 cover as a donation for my campaign. That same year, Pat Schroeder, referred to as Mrs. Pat Schroeder in newspaper articles, ran for a U.S. House of Representatives seat for Colorado that she would hold for twenty-four years. I thought that Schroeder was a breath of fresh air in Congress. She had a way of grabbing center stage and bringing attention to important issues.

This was kind of a glorious age for politics in Colorado. It was the changing of the guard and a time for many young people to get involved, including Gary Hart and Tim Wirth, who would be elected U.S. senators, and Richard Lamm, who served in the state legislature before being elected governor.

We brought populism, youth, energy, and grassroots politics to the Democrats and to Colorado. As young adults, we thought the older politicians were not aggressive enough, and we wanted change and progress in our communities. We also wanted the power of elected office to be part of the decision making.

As I mounted my campaign for the Colorado House of Representatives, I knew that Josh Stewart was the first African American to be elected to the state legislature, in 1892.

Eighty years later, in 1972, there were three blacks, including myself, Ralph George, and Terry Paige, and one white man, Gary Mundt, an anti–Vietnam War activist, running as Democratic candidates for District Eight.

Sometimes campaigning is more fun than being elected. I like the camaraderie of meeting new people and voters. I enjoyed going into the neighborhoods and learning the issues. To some degree, politics is like sports. You have two teams: the Democrats and the Republicans. Third-party teams are an afterthought. You have star players, role players, and bench players. The media follows us, and the championship in politics is the election in November or May, in the case of city elections.

A House candidate needed at least 20 percent of the Democratic delegate votes to get to a primary. My goal was to be the only candidate, which meant I had to get a large percentage of the delegate votes.

I continued to get involved in community issues by protesting the shooting of nineteen-year-old Harvey Watts by a jeans-store owner who claimed that Watts was trying to rob the store.

I was also part of a group of black leaders who charged Hollywood with stereotyping African Americans as black studs and hustlers in such movies as *Super Fly*, *Shaft*, and *The Legend of Nigger Charley*.

Norm Early was the district captain, so we knew we had a friendly person in the chair. King Trimble was working half of the delegates and Dan Muse was working the other half, whereas Raymond Jones was working the delegates who were lawyers. Community activist Chuck Mitchell went after other community activists to support me. My grandmother and her group of seniors called all of the delegates and said it was time for a new, young leader. Wilma advised me and helped me personally call each delegate.

My first speech at George Washington Carver Day Nursery was better than anyone anticipated. The quiet boy who sat in the back of the classroom in high school was suddenly commanding respect from this speech.

I didn't get 90 percent of the delegate votes, but I got 82 percent, so I didn't have a primary. The lack of a primary in a Democratic-controlled district is an automatic victory, but I mounted a campaign anyway.

My experience teaching a college black-studies class and being a former counselor meant I had young people willing to pass out campaign literature and knock on voters' doors for me. Several established politicians were wondering how, "out of the blue," I was getting support from all these young voters.

My campaign literature, with a five-by-seven photograph and signature on one side and a biography on the back, touched on several issues. I campaigned about the need for Denver Public School Board of Education members to be elected based on districts and not just elected at-large. I spoke about the need to increase the minimum wage and provide better housing for the working poor. I opposed additional tax increases. I also spoke about issues unknown to most Denver residents: apartheid in South Africa and freedom movements in Mozambique and Angola.

Six months before the election, I went to the Colorado state capitol building because I had never set foot inside before.

Denver city councilman Elvin Caldwell hosted my first fundraiser in his backyard, even though I had been critical of him. My grandmother had always been a big supporter of Caldwell. She had my younger brothers and my children pass out literature when Caldwell ran for reelection. Plus, I think Caldwell was relieved I was running for state office and not against him for his city council seat.

I remember introducing Wilma and other political candidates

at the fund-raiser. I forgot to mention my grandmother. As I drove her home that night, I felt smaller than a peanut.

"Don't you ever forget to introduce your entire family, and specifically me," she scolded.

That never happened again.

In my neighboring District Seven, there were about six candidates in the race that same year. The only District Seven candidate my grandmother told me to get support from was Arie Taylor, a black woman who drove a taxicab and worked at the city's Election Commission. Taylor was a character who could cuss and drink like a sailor and turn around and give a stranger the shirt off her back. We became fast friends.

Former San Francisco mayor Willie Brown, who was then a state legislator in California, campaigned for both of us. We walked in as a team after Taylor and I won our elections.

I won with 5,997 votes. My opponents Tom Crowe, an independent, got 801 votes and Emilia Alvarado, a La Raza candidate, garnered 503 votes.

"I remember one time shortly after the 1972 election, Wellington, myself, and David Gaon were walking together at the state capitol," recalled former legislator Ruben Valdez. "Someone said, 'Well, boy, you guys pretty much represent the Democratic Party. Ruben, a Hispanic; Wellington, an African American; and David Gaon, a Jew."

The swearing-in was a grand day. My mother was very proud, my father came from Chicago, and my grandmother just beamed next to Wilma and our children and my in-laws, Frank and Faye Gerdine.

I wanted to do something special for my grandmother, so I took her to lunch at a restaurant called the Profile, an upscale place near the state capitol where lobbyists wined and dined legislators. She looked at the menu and then the prices.

"My stomach will not digest this food because it costs so much," she said. "It's outrageous, people spending this much money for lunch. I wonder what dinner costs?"

I told her she earned her right to a pricey lunch, to order anything

My first day as a state legislator following the 1972
election began with a prayer in the House chambers.

she liked, and to sit back and pretend she was one of the rich folks.

"Have a leisurely lunch with me, your grandson, who is very proud that he's an elected official," I told my grandmother. "This is something I want to be special for you."

I soon found out that politics is a rich man's game. The pay was only $7,600 a year, not nearly enough on which to raise four children. The salary was why many rookie legislators quit after one term. The established longtime politicians were wealthy or worked at large corporations. I remember someone asking me how I was going to survive, and I replied, "Well, my wife works."

Wilma worked at Mobil Oil Corporation because there was no way a family of four could survive on $7,600 in 1972. I remembered she had said, "We'll do it together."

On my first day as a state legislator, Colorado's only black state senator, George Brown, stopped me in a hallway and pulled me over to a corner.

"Fuck you. Fuck you. Fuck you," he told me. "I want to get you ready for what's going to happen to you for the next two years and for you to get into the proper perspective."

I didn't appreciate his advice at the time, because I really didn't understand what had just happened. After the first day or two, it was crystal clear though that because the Democrats were not in the House majority, we were literally just keeping seats warm. I was so young and ambitious, and I was not prepared to sit there and do nothing because the Republicans controlled the House and Senate. I would learn to be patient and find a way to be heard when the time was right.

"Wellington's first year in the legislature was pretty quiet," recalled former lobbyist Maria Garcia Berry, who worked for Governor Richard Lamm. "He would go to the mike when he had to, but he usually sat in the second row and listened intensely."

Democratic colleague Gerald Kopel remembered my first year more from my appearance than what I said.

"Wellington was tall enough, but with his big Afro, he looked even taller," Kopel recalled. "He didn't talk a lot. He was not a strutter. He was quiet and laid back."

I was a liberal Democrat, but I also got along with the Republicans.

"I liked Wellington personally and thought he was honest," recalled former Republican speaker of the House Carl "Bev" Bledsoe. "My philosophy was much more conservative than his, but that doesn't mean I didn't like him. He was honest and worked hard, and I respected him."

Republican Carl Gustafson was the majority leader my first term, and the Democrats always knew when Gustafson was getting ready to pass Republican-proposed bills without debate. He'd put on his tennis shoes and, without breaking a sweat, he and the Republicans would approve up to forty bills despite the Democrats' objections or questions.

But unlike today, where Democrats and Republicans barely speak to each other outside the state capitol, we usually left the politics in the chambers and socialized after work. We'd go to a bar called Nick's on East Colfax, and Democrats and Republicans would play cards or have a drink together. On any given night, the police chief, district attorney, state attorney general, and a slew of legislators were in the bar until 3:00 A.M.—even though the bar was supposed to close at 2:00 A.M. We didn't talk politics much. It was just a good way to get to know each other as people and not only as politicians. We didn't take ourselves too seriously back then.

And going back to the analogy that politics is like sports, the legislators played an annual basketball game against the lobbyists. Some of the legislators would take out their aggression on the basketball court against the lobbyist who had gotten their bill killed. Democrat Eldon Cooper, a good friend and a cowboy, would throw a ball near a lobbyist so he could "accidentally" knock the guy into the stands while trying to recover the ball.

Wilma sometimes brought the kids to visit me at the capitol. Three of our children showed up in the newspaper getting an autograph from then governor John Love. Tony and Allen were ten at the time and Stephanie was eleven.

One of the first things leaders in the legislature do is assign their colleagues to committees. I learned a long time ago that you have to have a specialty in order to get ahead. When you are a technical expert or have an area of expertise, people will look to you for advice and consultation. That rarely happens if you are a generalist.

I wanted to find a way to be seen as a legislator who made a difference, and I knew I could do this by finding the right committee. Being a minority, I knew people would call me about civil rights, housing, and employment issues. I needed a broad-based subject area of expertise beyond the important civil-rights issues.

Initially, I thought I would ask for a committee that focused on education because of my teaching background. I quickly learned that discussions about education in the legislature are not about students in the classroom, but about financing school districts.

My second choice was water, which is an important issue in Colorado because the state faces a shortage of water resources. This committee had interest statewide.

The House minority leader, Tom Farley, asked me to defer to legislator Lamm, who also wanted to be on the Natural Resources Committee. Farley gave me my next choice: health.

I chose the Health Committee because health is a subject that touches everyone's life. I was pleased to have an area of expertise to focus on and then began formulating which bills I would sponsor.

The first bill I introduced was a proposal to get rid of IQ tests in Colorado schools. I thought that IQ tests were culturally biased. That proposal died. My second bill, which passed, required school districts to get accident insurance covering the medical expenses of students injured on buses. This allowed school-bus drivers to take children to the nearest hospital in case of an accident instead of the former requirement to go to a public county hospital. Another bill passed, concerning property tax refunds, but several of my other proposals died. I could not get enough votes to support bills for prescription benefits, food-tax refunds, or to give senior citizens use of school buses for free transportation. Still, some of those failures didn't go unnoticed.

"We felt there were a lot of issues with the elderly and wanted to have a hearing," recalled former legislator Morgan Smith, who sponsored several bills with me. "We thought the hearing might attract a few people. It ended up lasting two days. The Republicans weren't happy with us, because we packed the committee rooms."

I did something unusual my first term that now is commonplace for elected officials: I opened a community office in my district. The idea was to have a place where constituents could meet with me if they didn't have the ability to get to the capitol or had to work during the day. We opened the neighborhood office two nights a week. This became a financial nightmare because I had to raise money to pay the rent, utilities, and telephone bill.

"In the past when politicians got elected to office, they just ran off and you didn't see them again until the next election," I told *Denver Post* reporter Sandra Dillard, who did an article about the community office. "I want to have the power to make positive directions for the community, and one way is to be in the community."

We tried to keep the office running with a small committee that eventually consisted of Wilma and me. The financial burden became too much, and we had to close the office. Elected officials now have money annually in their budgets to run the community offices.

I also made my first attempt to get a bill passed that endorsed the federal holiday for Dr. Martin Luther King Jr.'s birthday. Later, I would unsuccessfully try to get support for a state holiday recognizing Dr. King. That battle would be taken up by Wilma when she was elected to the state legislature.

Dr. King had made memorable visits to Denver. One of the most famous photographs of the civil-rights leader—with his hands resting on a chair and wearing an Urban League pin on his lapel—was taken in Feingold's Studio in downtown Denver.

During my teen years, my grandmother was the Women's Day chair at New Hope Baptist and invited Coretta Scott King to deliver

I often had community meetings following my election to the Colorado
House of Representatives in 1972. I was the first legislator to open a
neighborhood office with my own money.

a speech. At the time, the flyer said Mrs. Martin Luther King Jr. because women were usually identified by their husband's name. Reverend M. C. Williams of New Hope was a great orator, much like Dr. King. His wife, Anna Lee Williams, was a great classical soprano, much like Coretta Scott King. Unbeknownst to me, the organist at the church was Wilma Jean Gerdine, my future wife. I didn't hear Coretta Scott King that day, nor did I see Wilma playing the organ. I skipped the event to play basketball with my buddies.

One of the songs of the era that Anna Lee sang often was "Then My Living Shall Not Be in Vain," a signature spiritual of Dr. King.

"After Dr. King was assassinated, there was a real uproar and a lot of tension and rebellion among blacks in Denver," recalled Reverend Acen Phillips.

Reverend Phillips and several other religious groups—including Catholic nuns, Jewish rabbis, and Christian ministers—came up with an idea to empower young blacks and avoid riots that took place in other large cities. The group, with the help of a $500,000 grant from Presbyterian churches, bought the Dahlia Shopping Center in the heart of the black community. We tried to honor Dr. King by our actions to empower people through economic programs.

The group kept the anchor grocery store from moving for several years and attracted many black entrepreneurs. But the uphill battle to get the area redeveloped was still under way when I left the mayor's office in 2003.

In late 2005, my brother Joe, former Denver economic development director Ron Bernstein, and I formed a development partnership called the Alliance Group. One of the projects we went after was Dahlia, with the help of successful developer Jim Sullivan and attorney Steve Farber.

I wasn't the first to introduce a resolution recognizing Dr. King's civil-rights work. Senator George Brown had made an unsuccessful attempt prior to 1972.

"I like your resolution," Speaker of the House Gustafson told me. "I just want you to take out this one paragraph that says we go on record supporting the national holiday for Dr. King."

"What if I don't take it out?" I asked him.

"Then we'll kill it," he informed me.

My first big decision as a freshman legislator was to keep the paragraph, otherwise it was a resolution with no real meaning.

"If you're going to kill it, kill it," I told Gustafson before making my first speech in the general assembly asking for support for a resolution supporting the federal King holiday.

I felt it was a good speech, a passionate speech about why Dr. King should be honored. James Chappell, an older black Democratic committeeman, came to the capitol on his day off to listen to that speech. He was in his seventies, underemployed and overeducated. We often heard symphony music coming from his home.

"That was a great speech, Wellington," he told me. "It was off the cuff, extemporaneous. Yes, a great speech for your neighborhood, but not a great speech on the floor of the House of Representatives."

I felt like two cents after his comment. I had spoken about how the appendages of racism had reached into the hearts and souls of people who were voting against a resolution in support of Dr. King. Oh, it was a fiery speech. But then I read the words again and I knew Chappell was right. It was a great neighborhood speech, but I was not going to get any votes by calling legislators racists. I knew I would have to refine my methods. I was grateful that Chappell not only took the time to listen to me, but he gave me some heartfelt criticism. I had to tone down some of my anger and control my impatience without compromising my integrity or values.

But if nothing else, I am persistent. Because it was so hard to get a resolution passed just recognizing Dr. King's work, I was challenged to bring up another bill each year. I unsuccessfully sponsored a Dr. King bill for a state holiday every year I was in office. Wilma successfully took up the cause in 1980 when she began her long tenure in the legislature.

The only other time I made a big speech that session was in opposition to the death penalty. I got a big write-up in the newspaper, and I learned the human behavior of some legislators. Some of my colleagues complimented me on the article. Others, whom I thought were my friends, were jealous because I grabbed the spotlight for a day.

I also got some press when I supported a woman who claimed she was discriminated against by Frontier Airlines for hiring too many black stewardesses. Wilma and I brought our brothers, sisters, and our four children to picket the airlines because several black women dropped out of the protest when they saw the woman's husband was white.

I didn't care that she was married to a white man. My thought was that we had to support this woman if she was wronged. Turning our backs on her because her husband was white would be adding to the injustice.

The president of Frontier invited me and Reverend John Morris into his office. When the president started giving excuses that as a private business, Frontier could hire and fire anyone, Reverend Morris dropped to his knees and grabbed my hand.

"We're going to pray for this president that God will give him the wisdom to be able to judge people fairly," Reverend Morris said as we both got down on our knees. "He should look for redemption and purify his soul."

The woman didn't get her job back.

But in the statehouse, I was relatively quiet my first term. What most people didn't know is that I was part of the group that set out to change the legislature. My colleagues Valdez, Smith, Gaon, and myself were some of the ringleaders. The Democrats were determined to take back the majority of the House, as well as to get a Democratic governor elected.

We achieved both goals. Lamm was elected governor in 1974, and the Democrats succeeded at regaining the House majority.

I wasn't fully engaged in partisan politics for the U.S. Senate seat race in 1974 and didn't know much about Hart and his involvement with George McGovern's failed presidential bid. I was set to support another Democrat, Herrick Roth, who was facing Hart in

118

a primary. I never forgot that Roth had gotten me a job and showed me the difference between real power and perceived power.

But then Roth made a statement that doomed his campaign: he said there was too much big money in campaigns and he would not accept more than $19.74 from each individual for his campaign. Hart went on to win, and the rest is history.

This was also the year I saw a political split in the black community. Taylor was a colorful legislator and popular with the press because she was quick to give a quote. She was running for reelection, and Regis Groff, an African American and a teacher, decided to challenge her. They both made the primary ballot, and the black community was split down the middle in their support.

Groff's campaign theme was A Chance to Share, and Taylor was running on her record. The contrast between the two candidates was obvious. Taylor was categorized as big, black, loud, and boisterous and drank a lot. Groff was an educator, refined, and articulate.

"There weren't enough African Americans in Denver to really call it a schism," said black activist John Bailey. "It was really just nonsense."

Yet that so-called nonsense resurfaced in 1991 during the mayoral election. In 1974, I supported Taylor and Early sided with Groff. The split would grow over the years as Taylor successfully faced another reelection challenge, this time by Groff's colleague Gloria Tanner. By 1991, the crack between the two factions became a canyon when Early and I faced each other in the mayoral election.

Taylor won the election, but Groff ended up getting the promotion. Senator George Brown was elected lieutenant governor, and that opened his Senate seat. I was unopposed for my reelection in District Eight, and I briefly thought about seeking the open Senate seat, but Democrats were still in the minority there. I decided to stay in the House, where the Democrats had the majority and could make things happen.

I told Speaker of the House Valdez that I planned to run as the chair of the Democratic Caucus and I also wanted to chair the

Health, Environment, Welfare and Institutions Committee. Valdez was a little hesitant because a single legislator had never held both positions before. My thought was if I lost the caucus vote, I'd still have a committee to chair. He agreed to the proposal. I won the caucus election and had my committee to chair as well.

"This guy who barely spoke his first term wanted to be the caucus leader, and he became caucus leader," Maria Garcia Berry recalled. "He told me the best advice he got about being a legislator was to first listen and see what's going on. Wellington had phenomenal gut knowledge of how to push people and when to push."

Garcia Berry was working for the Lamm administration, and her job required her to report to me and Valdez, the state's first and only Hispanic speaker of the House.

"Wellington taught me patience," Garcia Berry said. "I was a twenty-one-year-old smart-ass out to conquer the world and in the middle of everything. He told me there was a time and place and that I was going to burn myself out."

I thought the time and place to make a statement was Lamm's first inauguration. Several black legislators urged Lamm to appoint an African American to his cabinet. We raised about $2,500 to take out an advertisement in the local newspapers explaining our position. Taylor issued a press release that she was going to walk out of the inauguration and other black elected officials would follow her. George Brown told us it would embarrass him if we walked out on Lamm.

We tried to convince Lamm and his lobbyist Roy Romer that the black community was a big reason Lamm won the election. If the state could elect George Brown as the first black lieutenant governor, then the state was ready for Lamm to appoint a black cabinet member.

"Lamm told us something like 'Don't burn your bridges' when we talked about walking out on his inauguration," recalled former Denver city councilman Bill Roberts. "It was a little agonizing. We were all Democrats and we liked Lamm, but the greater issue is that we thought African Americans should be represented in state government."

Roberts later put pressure on the city and state to divest all investments in South Africa when the country supported apartheid, and Wilma did the same in state government.

"I sponsored a bill in council every single year to divest in the Krugerrand [gold coins] and not to do business with South Africa," Roberts said. "Both Wellington and Wilma came down and spoke in support of the resolution."

The Sunday before Lamm's inauguration, some of the black ministers castigated Lamm. The older black politicians were proud of our brashness, but some were embarrassed at the same time.

After Brown was sworn in, several of us left in protest before Lamm was given the oath of office.

Leaving the area with television and newspaper cameras pointed at us were me, Taylor, Groff, Paul Sandoval, Rich Castro, Leo Lucero, Odell Barry, Muse, Wilma, and City Councilmen Roberts and Caldwell. Penfield Tate Sr., the mayor of Boulder, and Omar Blair, president of the Denver Public Schools Board of Education, signed our newspaper advertisement but did not walk out on the event.

Tate Sr. later would be recalled for supporting gay rights in Boulder. The election took place when the University of Colorado was not in session, and Tate Sr. lost his position as mayor.

The group of black leaders felt we had no choice but to make a statement against Lamm, but others thought our move was wrong.

"It was a big snub and it didn't accomplish anything," Garcia Berry said. "I understood they felt they needed to get Dick Lamm's attention, but I disagreed [with] how they did it."

But some young black activists supported the protest.

"My deciding moment about Wellington came when I was watching TV and he walked out of Governor Lamm's inauguration," said Charlotte Stephens, who ended up working in my mayoral administration. "I thought, *This is the person for me.* Denver definitely needed some changes, and it wasn't going to happen without someone willing to stand up for what he believed in."

My grandmother was not thrilled with my actions and said I was a little over the edge.

Evelyn Davidson, the new chief clerk of the House, also was not impressed.

"Wellington you're going to be a great politician, but you've got to read your audience, and I don't know which audience you were trying to get to," she told me.

I told her the statement was that if the governor was going to embarrass us by not having a black in his cabinet, we were going to embarrass him by walking out.

"Yes, and you probably improved his poll ratings, because most whites in the state like what he did, standing up to the black community," she said.

Lamm's ratings did go up, but he never held a grudge. Lamm eventually appointed blacks to his cabinet, including me, and he worked harder for me than any elected official in the 1991 mayoral race.

Chapter Ten

Second Term, Georgia Peanut Farmer

In 1975, the Democrats were the majority in the House for the first time in seven years, and we were not going to let this opportunity go to waste. I tried to right every wrong, and there wasn't any limit to the amount of bills I could introduce.

The Senate was still controlled by the Republicans, and Senate President Ted Strickland was a conservative. Strickland and I met and agreed on the following: we looked at all of the bureaucracy bills that kept the government going and we both agreed to let them pass. Other bills that we disagreed about would be put to the side for discussion and a vote. Unlike previous years, bills would not automatically die because of majority opposition. Because of this agreement, we were able to get a large number of bills approved that benefited Coloradans.

"It was great fun being in the majority; that's the only way to fly," recalled former Democratic representative Doug Wayland. "I always felt Wellington was a person who was there and had a sense of purpose; it was more to him than just having the title of state representative."

I sponsored a bill concerning improving care in nursing homes. At the time, all of the patients were clustered together, including the young and old mental patients, seniors, and retired people who were mobile or disabled. It was my view that the disabled youth should have a different wing. They were not senile and should be among themselves. A young nursing aide, Wade Blank, brought some young patients to a hearing on the issue. He was fired for bringing the patients to the capitol, but he later founded Atlantis Community, Incorporated. This group gained a national reputation as an advocate for the disabled; their efforts included forcing public buses to have lifts for wheelchairs.

Arie Taylor also got a few of her pet peeves resolved. She introduced a bill to do away with pay toilets at the airport, and she also passed a bill to get a women's restroom closer to the House chambers. She actually counted the number of steps and found that women had to go much farther than men to relieve themselves.

Someone had the audacity to question if the pay-toilet issue was frivolous.

"Well, when you are a big fat lady like me, it means something when you get off a plane and have to go to the restroom, but because you don't have a dime, you have to crawl under the stall," she said.

I was feeling pretty confident and decided to tackle some important discrimination issues. At the time, banks would only grant credit cards and financial services to women's husbands; the first bill would no longer allow them such discrimination. I was successful with that bill and teamed up with legislator Jack McCroskey on other discrimination bills based on sexual orientation. It was 1975, and we were way ahead of our time.

I introduced two bills prohibiting discrimination against gays and lesbians in matters of housing and employment. McCroskey addressed public accommodations for and granting credit to gays and lesbians. I didn't realize what a raw nerve I had hit until the gay bills came up in committee for discussion: Democrats wanted nothing to do with them. Members of the black community were shocked that I'd propose such a civil-rights issue. Some black men went so far as to call the proposal the "faggots'" bill or "sissies'" bill.

"You are a strong black man. You're supposed to fight for us, and you shouldn't even have it on your record, supporting something like this," one black man told me.

I supported antidiscrimination laws for gays and lesbians because it was the right thing to do. I did it instinctively. Some people in the black community feared I would lose support from minorities. Yet for me, these were civil-rights issues, and I had to stand up for civil rights for everyone. I couldn't pick and choose who deserved to be treated equally.

In 2004, Democrats finally regained the majority in the House and Senate. They approved an antidiscrimination law for gays and lesbians during the 2005 session that would have protected them from discrimination in the workplace; however, Republican governor Bill Owens vetoed the bill, saying it would cost small businesses too much money in possible litigation costs, and the proposal died.

As a legislator, I also tackled two other issues that turned out to be controversial, one that would also resurface thirty years later. The first would have allowed adopted adults to locate their birth parents, and the second would financially compensate a man who had been unjustly jailed. Initially, I didn't want to carry the adoption bill.

"Well, I don't know if I had a kid I put up for adoption if I would want to get a knock on my door twenty years later," I told a woman who headed the group Adoptees in Search.

"You're just like everyone else," she told me. "You keep talking to us like we're children. I'm fifty-five years old. I would at least like a chance to ask my parents if they want to see me, and if they don't, they can tell me they don't through the Department of Social Services and then I'll go away."

More than 300 people showed up for one hearing on the adoption bill, and the majority of the speakers accused me of trying to destroy families. I got my first death threat because of that bill, which was also opposed by the newspapers and died quickly. Thirty years later, representative Fran Coleman, herself adopted, introduced a bill during the 2005 session to allow adopted children access to their parents' medical records. The bill was approved with limitations.

I had more success helping a man falsely imprisoned for robbery. Kenneth Lee wrote to me that he was cleared by the Colorado Supreme Court of a robbery charge that kept him in the state penitentiary for thirty-four months. He wanted to be compensated for his time. I introduced a bill that would award him $15,000, or approximately what he would have earned with a minimum-wage job. During the first reading, legislators assumed the guy was black and was probably released from prison on a technicality.

For the second reading, I decided to bring Lee and his family into the chambers to meet the legislators. They were shocked to see a short white man with his wife and two children standing beside him. It was clear this man just wanted to be compensated for the time he had unfairly spent in prison.

I had also initially thought the man was African American. Passing the bill proved an important point: that it doesn't matter if a person is white, brown, red, yellow, or black—injustice is injustice, and when possible, wrong should be rectified.

I didn't give up on the injustice of the state ignoring Dr. Martin Luther King Jr.'s accomplishments for civil rights. During my second term, the bill passed through the House for the first time. Some Republicans even voted for it because they knew it would die in the Senate. But if Ruben Valdez had not been the speaker, it would have died in the House.

Valdez left the voting machines open long enough for me to beg House Democrats to support the bill. We needed thirty-three votes, and I had thirty-two. I walked up and down the aisle, and finally Chuck Howe of Boulder agreed to support it. Once again, the Republicans killed the proposal.

House Democrats supported Governor Richard Lamm; he called on several minority legislators to help him with a prison riot at Cañon City. Taylor wanted to go, but there was the issue of her being a woman, because the prison guards would be strip-searching the prisoners. So a group of men that included me, Rich Castro, Paul Sandoval, and Valdez joined the governor and Lieutenant Governor George Brown on a plane trip down to the prison.

The inmates complained about their items being destroyed by the guards, who were looking for handmade weapons. They wanted to save things such as birdhouses they had made out of matchsticks. We worked to get funding to allow inmates to have shelves in their cells that could be used to display their personal items but not hide contraband. Before they got the shelves, the inmates were strip-searched and the cells were cleaned out of any contraband.

Castro and I both saw former classmates in the prison that day who had told their friends they were in California on "vacation." We knew not to say something stupid, such as, "How have you been?"

The presence of the governor and the legislators did help calm things down at the prison.

I also started to listen and learn from my more conservative Democratic colleagues in the legislature. Walt Waldo of the rural community of Olathe was a farmer whom I respected. After I had passed several bills, I asked Waldo how he expected to win reelection if he didn't start proposing more laws.

Waldo explained to me that his rural constituents aren't fond of any new laws.

"In my part of the country, they try and take laws off the books and not put new ones on," Waldo said.

About this same time, Reverend Jesse Jackson began a PUSH (People United to Save Humanity) satellite in Denver after his split with the Southern Christian Leadership Conference. Jackson asked Ruby Kirk Gray to help fund the program and find a satellite president.

"Wellington and Wilma were married then and they were doing just fine," Kirk Gray recalled. "I needed a president for the local PUSH, and I decided I didn't need an election. I just asked Wellington if he would do it. I picked him because I knew his grandmother so well and I knew how stable she was and how she raised him. He needed a chance and he was willing to work to make it a success. He made a dandy president."

That group became an advocate for the poor and took on such issues as the Public Service Company shutting off electricity to elderly residents who were behind on their bills. We objected to the company's policy of allowing service to be shut off on Fridays, meaning these elderly people would have no way to cook and no heat for an entire weekend.

We also worked with Denver-area black leaders Chuck Leali and Edna Mosley to raise money for the United Negro College Fund. We brought in world-renowned jazz and baritone vocalist Billy Eckstein for one fund-raiser. I remember going to the airport to pick up Eckstein and seeing him sashaying in front of the baggage handler, who was dragging five or six pieces of his designer luggage, including a standing trunk. Eckstein had on a cashmere camel-hair coat, white scarf, and leather gloves. We took him to a suite near the Merchandise Mart instead of to a first-class hotel downtown because that's all we could afford. He never complained and instead spent dinner with our group telling us stories about working with Dinah Washington and Sara Vaughn. He recalled the days of entertaining mostly white audiences and then having to eat in the kitchen because blacks were not allowed in the main dining room.

He epitomized class and refinement. Spending one evening with Eckstein taught me more about refinement and the history of the big-band circuit than I learned in more than four years of college.

I balanced my community work with trying to make a living in the legislature. In the second term, I was part of a group of legislators who supported giving us a raise from $7,600 to $12,000. They asked the minorities who faced little opposition for reelection to take the heat for this one, even though we all needed the raise. (It always bothered me that the legislators who voted against the raise by saying it was against the voters' wishes still took the money. That kind of hypocrisy stinks.) Still, the money was tight, and both Wilma and I were scrambling to make ends meet with two full-time jobs.

Our children all had their own individual interests and needs. Our oldest son, Keith, was interested in electronics and computers. Stephanie, Tony, and Allen were all about the same age, so our expenses always tripled to accommodate their needs in school and individual activities.

I needed another job when the legislature was not in session, and

City Councilman Elvin Caldwell decided to help me. He took me to a Denver Broncos game, and we sat in the city's box with the mayor and other council members. Mayor Bill McNichols, who was a big fan of my grandmother's and appreciated her help in his campaigns, said he would give me a contract with the city, but first I had to go speak with Minoru Yasui, who was head of community relations.

I didn't know Yasui's background and made a foolish comment when we met.

"Why aren't you more aggressive as the head of community relations?" I asked him. "We've got to be doing more."

He looked at me and must have thought, *What an ignorant man.* I didn't take the time to learn his background before our meeting. Yasui was a national leader among Japanese Americans who were trying to get reparations for being sent to internment camps during World War II. There were camps in several states, including Colorado. I didn't know Yasui had gone to prison for trying to join the army and refusing to be relocated with other Japanese Americans. I always felt bad for not giving him the proper respect when I met him. When I was mayor, I named a city building in his honor. I wanted generations to see the name, be curious, and learn more about his life. The Asian community was thrilled with the recognition because not many public buildings were named for Asian Americans.

After that meeting with Yasui, the city gave me a six-month contract to work with the Public Works Department. I reviewed minority compliance on contracts.

My inexperience would catch up with me again when I later snubbed my nose at Mayor McNichols. I conveniently ignored the fact that he helped me get the city contract and decided to support District Attorney Dale Tooley, the candidate who was perceived as being more liberal, when he challenged McNichols in the 1975 election. Ben Bezhoff, McNichols's go-to guy in his administration, was disgusted with me.

"McNichols gave you the job and fed you and now you went out there and endorsed Tooley?" Bezhoff quizzed me.

My grandmother had no intention of dropping her loyalty to Mayor McNichols.

"I don't know what you're doing, but I'm endorsing Bill McNichols and that's who I'm working for," she said.

My grandmother never cussed or swore, but when her grandsons started getting too full of themselves, she used to chastise us in her own way.

"You started smelling yourself," she'd say, implying we were getting too big for our britches.

McNichols won reelection, and my contract with the city was not renewed.

Still in search of extra income for my family, I met with John Rice Jr., who was an assistant dean at the University of Denver (DU) and taught a class called "The Black Experience in America." He arranged for me to get a part-time job teaching classes at DU, and we became friends. He also introduced me to his daughter, Condoleezza.

Rice never called his daughter Condi or Leezza; it was always Condoleezza. I saw her again shortly after President George W. Bush named Condoleezza as the country's first African American female national security advisor, and she later became the first female black U.S. secretary of state.

Although my choice of Tooley for mayor went nowhere, I made a better decision to endorse a U.S. presidential candidate in 1976. I was asked to come to the Executive Tower Hotel downtown to meet with the governor of Georgia. I told Wilma I was just going to meet the guy, nothing more. It was the beginning of his presidential campaign, and I met with just Jimmy Carter and one staff person.

I visited with Carter for about thirty minutes. In the course of that meeting, Carter spoke about what values were important to him and the importance of restoring the people's trust in the federal government. There was an aura about him of calm confidence. He had a strong moral character. He was someone who had a clear vision of where he wanted to go. I did not automatically endorse Carter after our meeting, but I was impressed.

I went back home and told Wilma, "I think I have just met the next president of the United States."

She reminded me that Carter was an unknown candidate.

"I didn't even know him before, but I just have a hunch," I told Wilma. "He just seems honest, comfortable, and, yes, presidential. I think he's going to win."

After Wilma met Carter, she agreed with me.

A few days later, I took out my checkbook and wrote my little contribution of $15 to the Jimmy Carter campaign. Fifteen dollars was $15, and I'm sure we could have used that money for our household expenses. I later found out that I was the first Coloradan to make a contribution to his campaign. My God, how far that $15 took me.

There were lots of skeptics among my Democratic friends about Carter's candidacy.

"We used to give him a hard time and say, 'Jimmy who?'" recalled former Democratic representative Gerald Kopel. "Carter at the time was a long shot to win. But Wellington Webb was basically with Carter from the beginning."

Many liberals thought Carter had no chance at winning the nomination against popular Arizona congressman Mo Udall. The liberals thought I was nutty for endorsing the more conservative Carter. But what many people didn't understand is that many African Americans are conservative, especially when it comes to religion and family issues.

I got a little less heat from my friends when notable African Americans, including Martin Luther King Sr. and black elected officials in Georgia, endorsed Carter. That said volumes—that people in his home state, which did not have a good record in race relations, supported Carter's candidacy.

Political activist John Bailey said the Carter people also unsuccessfully tried to get Regis Groff interested in the campaign.

"Regis knew white guys who didn't think Carter would win," Bailey said, "so they let 'Mikey' handle the Carter campaign, like that popular cereal commercial. 'Mikey' was Wellington Webb."

I joined former Colorado lieutenant governor Mark Hogan on the Colorado campaign for Carter along with Art Requena, who was managing the Colorado campaign at the time. I was also launching my bid for a third term in the state legislature.

I highlighted my record in campaign literature. On state and national issues, I endorsed the lettuce boycott to protest the working conditions of Latinos in California that was headed by César Chávez of the United Farm Workers and also supported by Colorado legislators Castro, Wayne Knox, and Sandoval. I endorsed doing away with the sales tax on food because poor people spent a larger percentage of their income on food and the tax was regressive. (Never did I imagine how much revenue the cities lost without that tax on food, something I would have put to good use as mayor.)

The black community had another police brutality issue to protest. Carl Newland, a middle-class black man, was jailed on April 9, 1976, on a robbery investigation. The robbery victim would later clear Newland of the charge, but it was too late. Newland, a forty-eight-year-old retired air force sergeant with no criminal record, died April 13, 1976, from a stroke caused by a blow to his neck. Another inmate claimed the jail guards beat Newland to death.

Several minority elected officials called a press conference. I didn't want the police investigating Newland's death, because those reviews usually ended up with the officers being cleared no matter what the evidence showed.

"If it had not been for the investigative work of one reporter, Carl Newland would have been just another dead nigger, buried and put in the ground with no questions asked," I told the Denver media.

We urged Mayor McNichols to appoint a citizens' panel to investigate the death and for Tooley to call for a grand jury. It was clear the administration and district attorney were too close to the police to be objective. They both denied our request.

Then, less than a month later, Stanley Muniz claimed he was beaten by police following a drunk-driving charge. Castro, Reverend

J. Langston Boyd, and the American Civil Liberties Union organized a rally outside of the Denver City and County Building.

During the same time, I also supported my friend Lucius Ashby, a CPA, who was running for Denver auditor. I thought he would give Auditor Johnny Dee a good race. The auditor position is supposed to keep a close eye on city finances and act as a watchdog over the mayor and city council. City Councilwoman Cathy Donohue also supported Ashby, but for another reason: she knew Ashby was going to campaign that the auditor's position should be eliminated as an elected position and replaced by a hired professional, which Donohue also strongly supported.

Most cities the size of Denver have a professional auditor—such as a finance director—and not an elected position.

Denver had various forms of territorial government until 1902, when voters approved "home rule" for the city. This amendment to the state constitution created a combined city and county of Denver, a self-governing community with both municipal and county powers. Denver residents in 1904 approved the city charter, which gave Denver a "strong mayor" form of government. Because of the mayor's power, the charter also included an independently elected auditor. The auditor acts as a check and balance between the mayor and city council to ensure no single person or group dominates city government. Denver's charter requires the auditor to be the general accountant and to sign all of the city's checks, including payroll. Critics of the office often ask, "Who is auditing the auditor?"

Denver's position of elected auditor is similar to New York's elected comptroller. But most cities that had elected auditors have since replaced the position with hired financial directors.

I knew that Ashby's campaigning against the need for an elected auditor would hurt his chances; even my kids questioned his platform.

"Why are we passing out literature for him if he doesn't want the job?" the wise children asked.

This issue would come up again when I ran for Denver auditor in 1987.

The Carter campaign was gaining momentum in 1976 when, at a speech in Indiana, Carter said that government shouldn't deliberately try to destroy the "ethnic purity" of a neighborhood by injecting members of another race. He also said he was against building low-cost high-rise housing in wealthy suburban neighborhoods. After hearing this, I put out a statement that I wasn't sure if I was going to continue supporting his candidacy.

Carter quickly apologized for his choice of words but not the content. He said he should have chosen the phrase "neighborhoods with ethnic character and ethnic heritage" instead of "ethnic purity."

I felt comfortable that Carter did care about the poor and minorities. He kept my endorsement and started to pick up other supporters, including Colorado attorney general J. D. McFarlane.

I thought Carter was the right person to be president at the right time because of his honesty and integrity, especially after President Richard Nixon. I became close to his campaign staff, primarily Tim Kraft, who is out of New Mexico. He is one of the best political field organizers in the country.

I was elected a Colorado delegate for the Democratic National Convention in 1976. Wilma and I were not thrilled that the Colorado group was put in a hotel far from the convention events at Madison Square Garden in New York City, but it was exciting to be there. We attended the Democratic committee meetings during the day and then enjoyed Harlem at night.

It was heartwarming when Carter got the nomination and we were able to see him take the stage in person. I was among a group of delegates who got their photograph in *The New York Times* while watching Carter make his acceptance speech.

When we got back to Colorado, Kraft told me that they were sending someone from South Dakota to run the Colorado campaign until Election Day.

"We don't want anyone coming from South Dakota to run the campaign," I told Kraft. "They don't even know Colorado. We should use someone from here."

He told me it was a done deal.

"The only way you will get someone from Colorado is if you do it," Kraft said.

I was terrified. I had never run a campaign this large, but Kraft assured me I could get the job done.

"Well, this is really going to shake up the establishment in the Democratic Party, because I'm the youngest person you could choose," I said.

"They'll learn to live with it," Kraft told me.

Carter had all of his state coordinators meet in Georgia. The poor bus driver got lost trying to find Carter's home in Plains. The press would have had a field day with that tidbit of information, but thankfully we eventually got to the Carter's home and no one was the wiser.

All of the state coordinators were armed with campaign brochures and a small peanut lapel pin. That pin prompted a lot of discussion among voters about Carter. Throughout my political career, I have always worn a lapel pin that signified my elected job, whether in the state legislature, as Denver's auditor, or mayor.

While I focused on Carter's Colorado campaign, I asked my brother Joe to run my reelection bid to the legislature. I was running unopposed for a third term, but we still had to make an effort to campaign in the district and distribute my literature.

Joe had already been through a lot in his young life. In high school, his girlfriend became pregnant with his oldest daughter.

"My grandmother was beside herself that I could be so stupid," Joe recalled. "But she told me, 'You will do the right thing.' Mother wouldn't dare cross grandmother's desires of what to do or what not to do."

Even though he was married, our grandmother still hoped Joe would go to college. The University of Colorado (CU) was having problems because of its low minority enrollment and set a goal of recruiting 250 black students. Joe sought a football scholarship, but that didn't work out. He didn't play football, but he did get some scholarship help from the university.

As a freshman, Joe was also required to live in the dorms, so his wife and daughter stayed in Denver.

"I got the shock of my life that first day at CU," Joe said. "Manual was integrated but still predominantly black. I go to my first class in Boulder, an introduction to sociology, and there are about 500 kids and I am the only black student. I thought to myself, 'What am I doing here?'"

Joe didn't know anything about *Cliffs Notes* to help with his studies, and he quickly fell behind.

"I went home one weekend and told my grandmother I was in way over my head," Joe said. "I told her I don't have a clue what I'm doing. And she said, 'Joseph, you have a lot of responsibilities and you have a lot to carry. Don't you dare let them know you don't know what you're doing. Find a way.' I was not allowed to bow out."

Joe later left CU after clashing with the university president while serving as the president of the Black Student Alliance. He stayed in Boulder, worked, and got a divorce. Later, he worked in the mental health field, became a Denver police officer, and studied in night school for his law degree.

He took on my 1976 reelection campaign with the help of two campaign supporters, Annie Slaughter and Myrna Durley Crawford.

"Wellington and I had the same philosophy of working for progress and the rights of blacks in Denver," Slaughter said.

Slaughter asked her friend Durley Crawford to help with the campaign.

"I've known Wellington for years. He used to play basketball with my brother, Jerry, but because I was the little sister, I couldn't hang around," Durley Crawford recalled.

She helped knock on doors and answer phones throughout most of my political campaigns.

"I'm not politically inclined, but Annie said for me to come do this," Durley Crawford said. "I usually don't get involved, but it was for Wellington, and his friends wanted me to help him. Once I got to know him, I believed in him and believed he would do the right thing, not necessarily only for his own people, but for the people of Denver and Colorado."

Earnest Patterson, a political-science professor at CU who became my political adviser, also helped with the campaign. He worked with a young CU student, Wayne Cauthen, who would later become my mayoral chief of staff.

They crunched numbers in each of my campaigns to see which precincts we needed to target. Our operation was as sophisticated as anyone's, because it helped us identify voters we needed to focus on.

So the roots of my political life were seeds in the 1970s that grew deep by the 1991 mayoral race. And the strength of those roots, which did not break or wilt under pressure, would surprise many.

Chapter Eleven

President Jimmy Carter, Department
of Health and Human Services

With my brother Joe running my reelection bid, I had time to concentrate on Jimmy Carter's campaign.

Carter's aunt Sissy came to Colorado to campaign, and she decided to stay with Wilma and me at our humble home on Gaylord Street. A newspaper article described Sissy watching a debate on television between Carter and President Gerald Ford in our "dimly lit living room in our modest Denver home."

We were proud to have her as a guest, and we thought her decision to stay with us was one reason voters related to Carter. The Carters didn't always have to go into the homes of the rich and famous or the most powerful. They acknowledged all classes of people.

I remembered this when in 1991 we decided to bring the mayoral campaign into the homes of Denver residents.

But Sissy's visit also raised sensitive issues that would plague Wilma and me throughout our political careers. Sissy watched the debate with me, Wilma, my grandmother, and a couple of other people in our home, yet the photograph that showed up in the local newspapers the next day was just Sissy and me.

"Boy, the newspapers really worked hard to get me cut out of the photograph, as the three of us were sitting on the same couch," Wilma commented.

Wilma would experience this type of treatment throughout my mayoral terms. She often was either cropped out of the photographs or shuttled to the side during interviews.

The newspapers wanted to show the contrast of the two campaigns, and the photograph of me and Sissy spoke volumes. In one photograph was a tall black man with a large Afro sitting next to a white woman from the South. The newspapers showed another photograph of a bunch of white middle-class Republicans in an upscale home watching the debate in support of President Ford.

On November 3, 1976, Carter was elected president and began helping the country heal after the Watergate scandal. I also won reelection for a third term to the state legislature, but the Democrats lost the majority in the House.

Then I began the waiting game: would I serve my third term or would I join President Carter's administration? I sat around the house expecting to hear from President Carter's transition team. Instead of getting calls from Washington, D.C., other campaign workers started calling me and asking me if I had heard anything about possible jobs in the administration.

Wilma suggested I better get to Washington, D.C., to see firsthand what was going on. I used our last dollar in our savings account for the airplane ticket, and that turned out to be a very smart investment. Half of President Carter's volunteers in America were in the nation's capital, job hunting. There were thousands of people sleeping in the halls of federal buildings wanting to go to work.

I found out that most of the resumes and applications would be shifted to storage somewhere, so I went in search of President Carter's transition team members: Tim Kraft and Hamilton Jordan. They asked me if I wanted to come to Washington or stay in Denver. I told them I wanted to stay in Denver. They also asked if I would want a job in Housing and Urban Development or Health, Education and Welfare (HEW).

My background in education and health made a good fit in HEW. I've taken a lot of risks in my life—from working at Fort Logan instead of the Denver schools, to teaching a black-studies college class before the subject matter was popular, to supporting

President Jimmy Carter appointed me as Region Eight director for the U.S. Department of Health and Human Services.

Carter for president. But my risks are not without calculations. I was prepared to do a good job in HEW through my work in the state legislature as chair of the Health Committee. I would not be taken off guard by learning a new subject matter.

I flew back to Denver knowing quite clearly then that if you want to be a player in national politics, you have to go where the action is. I called President Carter's campaign managers in Utah and Wyoming and urged them to go to Washington, D.C., or else they would get lost in the transition.

They didn't go to D.C. and they didn't get a job. Other campaigners who only had political skills also did not get jobs with the Carter administration.

Little did I know that it would be almost a year before I would get and start my desired job. Wilma and I went to President Carter's inauguration. We came back to Denver and I started working on other issues, such as submitting the name of a lawyer from Boulder, Jim Carrigan, to the U.S. Senate to become a federal district judge.

While I was waiting to hear from President Carter's people, I began my third term in the state legislature. In 1977, the Democrats no longer controlled the House and the Republicans took the opportunity to make our lives miserable as payback for our two years as the majority.

But whenever we Democrats could stick it to the Republicans, we did. Our tactics were a little showmanship-like, but for a day or two we got some attention on important issues and we felt good that we were going to be heard.

In one instance, the Republicans wanted to make it more difficult for people to get welfare. New laws would also stigmatize those applying for assistance. I got all fired up and said the only difference between the Republicans' proposal and Nazi Germany was that they didn't have boxcars ready to ship the welfare people out of the state or tattoo their arms.

In an effort to stop the proposed bill, I thought I would try my own filibuster and began reading from one of the state statutes for several hours until the committee would adjourn. At the same time, Representative Doug Whalen realized that if I left the meeting, the committee couldn't vote.

"We were passing notes back and forth, and Wellington got up and left, so the Republicans didn't have a quorum," Whalen said.

One headline the next day said, "Representative Webb Stomps out of Welfare Meeting." Another headline said the Democrats put the kibosh on the committee's quorum.

My one-man walkout held up the bill for a few days, but it did eventually pass.

Wilma ran for Colorado Democratic Party secretary that same year.

"It's easy to be in the shadows when you are standing behind someone who is six-four," she told *Denver Magazine*. "He casts a pretty long shadow."

Months passed, and I was still waiting to hear about the federal job. I was having mixed feelings about leaving the legislature. I loved being a state legislator and missed the activity when the session was adjourned.

Wilma said the decision was mine, so I sought some advice from legislator Arie Taylor.

"Well, how much are you getting paid as a legislator?" Taylor asked, knowing full well we got $12,000.

When I told her the new job would pay $42,500, she told me I would be stupid not to leave the legislature.

I felt that by virtue of me leaving the legislature, I would also be giving up my dream of running for U.S. Congress. Many people think I always wanted to be Denver's mayor. I didn't. I wanted to run for Congress because that's where I thought all the action was and that's where elected officials could really make a difference.

When Schroeder was elected in 1972, she said she would serve for ten years. Ten years turned into twenty-four years, and a lot of minority elected officials who would have pursued that position fell by the wayside, including me, King Trimble, Regis Groff, Ruben Valdez, Rich Castro, and others.

President Carter offered me a job as regional director for HEW. I oversaw Region Eight, which included the states of Colorado, Montana, North Dakota, South Dakota, Utah, and Wyoming. Geographically, the region encompasses more than 574,000 square miles and had some 6 million people at that time.

I managed a payroll of more than $34 million, and about 2,000 people were employed by HEW in my region. More than $3 billion was disbursed annually to the region for a variety of federal programs, including Social Security, welfare, Medicaid, Head Start, and student loans.

President Carter appointed other Coloradans to federal jobs. Valdez went to work for the Department of Transportation. Sam Brown served as director of Action and Barbara Kelly was general counsel of Action, which oversaw the Peace Corps and Volunteers in Service to America. Lynn Allen, who worked for the Colorado Department of Social Services, went to the Washington office of Health and Human Services. (He died a few years later when a United Airlines flight leaving Denver crashed in an Iowa cornfield and all of the passengers were killed.)

On October 3, 1977, I submitted my letter of resignation to the speaker of the House, and my good friend Trimble was appointed as my replacement by a Democratic vacancy committee.

Before Trimble agreed to take the position, there were some discussions that Wilma should have taken my seat. Dr. Earnest Patterson came to our house and urged Wilma to consider representing District Eight, but Wilma was adamantly against the idea.

My political group—Dan Muse, Trimble, Norm Early, Ray Jones, and me—met at Muse's house. Muse, Early, and Jones had other aspirations, so the only ones that it seemed practical to submit for my seat were Wilma or Trimble.

"I can't do it," Trimble told us. "I don't want to be in the legislature. I'm more interested in the city council."

We wouldn't give up.

"You're always talking about politics," I told him. "You talked about running for Congress. You talked about taking on Pat Schroeder. Now you're afraid to run for state representative?"

He said he had to discuss it with his wife, Dixie.

"You have to go home and tell Dixie you are running," we implored.

His name was submitted, and Trimble was elected by Democratic committee people.

Meanwhile, I went to meet my new boss, HEW Secretary Joseph Califano. Califano had no choice in my appointment because it was pushed on him by the White House. However, I fit his criteria of what he was looking for in the regional directors: he wanted people who were engaged politically, primarily in state and local politics. Eddie Bernice Johnson was in the Texas state legislature and was the representative of Dallas; Cecil Morales of New York was an outstanding attorney and actively involved in politics; Jack Bean of Boston was a neighbor and a good friend of Tip O'Neil's—need I say more?; Chris Cohen was a member of the Chicago City Council and his father was former U.S. HEW secretary Wilber Cohen; Sarah Craig of Atlanta was a friend of the Carter family; Tom Higgins served as a Kansas City legislator. Califano was smart and also retained some HEW career people, such as Buck Kelly of Seattle. Buck worked with Democrats and Republicans and was well liked. Ben Jeffers, who was active in Louisiana politics, later replaced Johnson in Dallas when she was elected to Congress.

"Wellington and I became fast friends," recalled Jeffers. "We were the only two African Americans in a group of ten regional directors, and we immediately bonded. Even though we both are self-starters, we need people who we know we can talk to about anything."

My family members traveled from throughout the country to be at my swearing-in ceremony in Washington, D.C., including my father from Chicago and my Aunt Frances from Mississippi. Wilma was on my right, holding the family Bible, when Undersecretary Hale Champion gave me and other regional directors the oath of office.

The one person missing that day was Grandmother Helen. She

had a feeling I would get the job, but she had died a few weeks before it happened.

I clearly remember the night my phone rang in our Gaylord Street home. It was my grandmother, and she sensed she did not have long to live. She told me to come to her house right away. I found her in bed reading her Bible. She said she wanted to start giving her family her personal items. I couldn't emotionally handle what she was telling me.

"You're going to live a long time," I told her. "This isn't the way to talk."

Then she started telling me about her family. The last thing we talked about that night was her asking me to get Muse to help her write a will.

About two months later, I got a call at my office that my grandmother had passed.

My brother Charles was living with my grandmother at the time. She had turned a downstairs study into her bedroom because climbing the stairs had become difficult. Charles found that grandmother had fallen during the night in her sewing room, surrounded by her Singer sewing machine and the patterns she still had from fashion magazines. Charles picked her up off the floor, got her to her bed, and called 911. The firefighters got to the house, but she had passed in the night. I gave a statement to the coroner and they removed her body.

In the process of setting up the funeral, I saw the best and worst of my family. We argued about whether to sell or keep her house. There was no will, so who was the executor of her estate? Once Aunt Frances arrived, there was no question about who was in charge.

The material things really didn't matter, although I was pleased to get her old rocking chair that had hand-carved lion heads in the arms. As a young boy, I used to put my small fingers in the mouths of the carved lions.

I also got a magnificent green vase that a wealthy family had given my grandmother and she in turn gave it to Wilma. It was

Wilma's favorite vase and got broken into several pieces when it was being delivered to our home. Wilma glued that vase back together piece by piece. Today, like my grandmother in my memory, the vase stands tall and remains a fixture in our home.

The greatest gift my grandmother gave me was her love and her wisdom.

The condolence cards and letters that came after my grandmother's death filled a large box.

"I hope the love and prayers of your family and friends will console you in this loss," wrote President Carter.

"She was a great lady and I loved her very much," wrote *Denver Post* society columnist Olga Curtis, who had employed my grandmother to make some of her clothes.

"Your dear grandmother was truly an aristocrat, a woman of gentility and refinement. It was a privilege to know her," wrote friend Frances Kent.

Other cards were from her first husband and my grandfather George Williams; Mayor McNichols; Governor Richard Lamm; District Attorney Dale Tooley; and U.S. Senators Gary Hart and Floyd Haskell.

Charles fought to keep the house, but Aunt Frances decided to sell it and divvy up the proceeds. Charles was right, but Aunt Frances had issues of her own back in Mississippi. By this time, our mother's drinking was totally out of control, and the money that my mother received from the estate was gone within three months.

I missed my grandmother greatly at the swearing-in ceremony in Washington, D.C. I think she would have agreed with me that the event ended abruptly and in what I considered a very tasteless manner. Instead of a reception for us to visit with our loved ones, we were told to say good-bye and headed to a two-day retreat. I thought the retreat could have started the next day.

We were off to a monastery in Maryland that had no phones and no television. Our boss, Califano, a staunch Catholic, wanted to get us accustomed to his style. He required monthly reports about the issues going on in each regional director's six states. If you didn't send a report, he would critique you on what you weren't seeing in the districts. If we did send in a report, he would critique us on what we were doing wrong or could improve in our reports.

I used the same management tool when I was regulatory agency director, auditor, and mayor. It kept the staff on their toes. If they brought up a problem, I expected they also try and find options or a solution.

The Department of Health, Education and Welfare was created to deal with health issues for the states, and we were also the state's bank to stabilize the poor population. One of Carter's campaign promises was to spin off the Department of Education, which was a trade-off to garner the endorsement of the National Education Association.

When he spun off education, my department became the Department of Health and Human Services (HHS). It made political sense for President Carter to do this, but I still believe that if a child has health issues or human needs at home, he cannot learn properly at school. Therefore, I think the U.S. Department of Education should have taken Health and Human Services as a subset. This would have allowed Social Security to stand on its own, which is what President Clinton did twenty years later.

Making education a separate department was one of the first riffs between U.S. Senator Ted Kennedy and President Carter. Califano worked for President Carter, but his loyalty was more to the Kennedys, and that eventually got him fired.

It was my belief that President Carter gave away too much authority to his cabinet after he became president. He let the cabinet set too much of their own policies instead of the White House, and in some instances, it seemed like the government was in chaos.

President Carter also just about sank the career of the youngest governor in the nation. The Carter White House placed thousands of Cuban refugees in Arkansas against the wishes of Governor Clinton. The refugees and subsequent riots were a political mess for both men.

We were now the HHS, but we used to joke that we should have been part of the Social Security Administration because two-thirds of our budget and two-thirds of the employees dealt with Social Security.

The national budget for HHS at the time was $197 billion, the largest federal establishment.

Califano changed our titles with the department's new name. Instead of regional directors, we were principal regional officials.

During my tenure at HHS, I met several interesting people. Frank Ishida was the finance administer for thirty years and worked well with regional directors. He died shortly after his retirement. Hillary Connor ran the Public Health Service office and was a commissioned officer in the navy. He occasionally wore his naval uniform in the office. Social Security was administered by Sandy Crank, an African American expert on Social Security.

"I like Wellington Webb, but Wellington Webb often doesn't listen," Crank used to like to tell people about me.

It wasn't that I didn't listen; I just thought I had a better way to do things.

Crank was transferred to headquarters in Baltimore, and the division was then headed by Leeza Gooden, who had been deputy regional commissioner for Social Security in Chicago.

Most of the HHS workers were longtime bureaucrats who worked for Democrat and Republican administrations. I had just two people whom I could recommend for appointment. My deputy was Grace Mickelson, a former teacher and Democratic activist from Rapid City, South Dakota. My press person was Norma Jones, a broadcast journalist who formerly worked at Channel 2 in Denver.

My philosophy with any job is to do the best I can, and that means taking some risks. I was determined to get out into the states and listen to people's concerns.

I knew I would get an earful, because my office covered such issues as child support, Social Security, the rights of the handicapped, and the Office for Civil Rights. We also hit some controversial topics of the times, including a universal comprehensive health plan for the nation—still under debate—and in vitro fertilization, which was opposed by the Catholic Church.

Region Eight covered twenty-five different Native American tribes—about 100,000 Indians—living on twenty-three different reservations. I wanted to do something no other regional director had accomplished by visiting every reservation, but I had no idea of the scope of that ambition. I made it to about nineteen of the reservations, including Rosebud, Pine Ridge, Turtle Mountain, Standing Rock, and the Mountain Ute Reservation.

I wanted to see firsthand what it was like to live on a reservation and the problems the people faced. I did not want to read about it or have someone tell me about it. Most people have no idea about the poverty Native Americans face and how this often leads to other problems, such as alcoholism. As a country, we should be embarrassed and ashamed that these conditions still exist.

I took a four-seat plane to most of the reservations, and we often landed on grass because there were no airports or highways near the reservations.

The Indians were often unsure of outside visitors, but at Standing Rock, a resident named Al White Lightning introduced me to the culture. He took me to a powwow and we ate the Indian staples of fry bread and stew while watching a rodeo of Indians riding bucking horses bareback under the lights from a circle of pickup trucks.

If I had an early morning meeting with tribal officials, I was never sure if they would show up. If it was a good day to go fishing or hunting, the meetings would never take place. If they liked you, they sent someone to cancel the meeting; if they didn't like you, the official would sit there and figure it out himself.

In addition to my trips to the reservations, I held public meetings in each of the region's six states, battling freezing temperatures in the Dakotas during the winter and taking trips in small commuter planes to other isolated areas in Montana and Wyoming.

It was a big deal for the regional administrator from Denver to land in Kenner, Wyoming. I listened to people talk about the coal trains that were going through town every day and kids dropping out of school to work in the coal mines.

I also held information meetings to allow the public to understand how the department worked. The meetings focused on a different topic each time. One week, I would bring in experts to talk about programs for senior citizens; the next week, we would focus on programs for the mentally ill.

It's always been my belief that good public policy is good politics. This also built up the constituency that would support me when I ran for other elected positions.

I also knew it was important to resolve a $2.3 million audit against Colorado that had been filed by the federal government. Governor Lamm disputed that the state misspent the money from HEW between 1971 and 1974. Governor Lamm's letter, which was delivered with the $2.3 million check from the state, said the settlement was a "good-faith effort to cooperate" with HHS.

HHS headquarters in Denver was a lightning rod for social issues in the region. Sioux Indians wanted to have a sit-in at my office to protest federal policies. HHS officials wanted to call in federal guards to remove the Indians, but I remembered Mayor McNichols's smart move of not confronting us when we protested police brutality in the mayor's office.

"This is a free country," I told them. "They're Americans, and, hell, they helped pay for this office."

I gave them my office and went home for the weekend.

I was learning the difference between state and federal governments. As director of the largest federal agency in the state, I thought I could make a decision about closing the office when we had a large snowstorm. Soon after I had announced that the office on 1800 Stout Street was closed, I received a call from a federal judge. The courts were also housed in the building, and the judge informed me that he would make a decision about when to close the courts.

A more controversial issue was being able to fire federal employees. I turned to my friend John Mosley, a retired Tuskegee airman and longtime HEW employee, for advice.

"The arrangement was, I knew the politics and where all the rats were," Mosley recalled. "I had some tough recommendations for him. He said he couldn't fire everyone, but there were a lot of people there who should have been fired."

I tried to fire one person and learned that incompetent people in the federal government are usually transferred to other departments instead of losing their job. An employee initiated a complaint against me, and by the time we were done with the process, I felt like I was on trial.

I also tried to move one employee to a different office and, in turn, had another grievance filed against me. I didn't know people at certain pay levels were to have a certain number of windows in their offices. I thought this was silly. When I was in the state legislature, I had an office with no windows in the basement of the capitol.

The silliness turned into petty juvenile paybacks when unhappy federal employees started sending notes to Wilma.

One said, "You husband's trench coat is dirty. Why don't you have him take it to the cleaners?" Another note, "Tell your husband he needs to polish his shoes."

Although the notes were a nuisance, the juvenile tactics escalated. I had to keep my travel schedule private after someone canceled my plane reservations home after a visit with Califano in Washington, D.C. It was the Christmas holiday, and by the grace of God and my Denver staff, I got rebooked on another flight home.

"There were people looking for ways to sabotage Wellington and make him look bad," Mosley said. "My relationship was to cover his back, if you know what I mean. I recognized that not all of the people were behind him 100 percent. I knew Wellington before he came to the job, and we continued our friendship after he left. Our job was pretty much putting out fires all of the time."

Chapter Twelve

1980 Presidential Campaign, Wilma's Election

I was wrapped up starting a new job in 1977 while Wilma was dealing primarily with raising our four children. I wanted to run the house as if it were a military campaign, where all of the children were forced to do the same thing at the same time. Wilma wanted the children to have their own personalities.

The kids were all very different individuals. Tony and Allen were always on the aggressive side; whereas Keith, the oldest, was very smart. Keith was interested in chemistry sets and building little spaceships. Tony and Allen were interested in knocking the hell out of each other in basketball or football games. Stephanie excelled in her classes, the arts, and athletics. Keith had fish. Tony and Allen wanted a dog. One thing they all had in common was that they liked fireworks, which were legal back then.

One day, our children were counting their fireworks on the bunk beds, and the next thing we knew, it sounded like D-day at 2329 Gaylord Street. Someone had lit one of the bottle rockets, and they began shooting from one wall of the bedroom to another, setting the mattress on fire. Wilma ran to get water from the bathroom and then resorted to dipping into Keith's aquarium for water to douse the fire. Keith's goldfish were flopping among the fireworks.

The kids also had their own way of fitting in. This was evident in the way they handled their lunch money. Stephanie was a responsible student at East High School who always paid for her lunch. Tony sometimes paid for his lunch, and Allen somehow got a welfare card and ate for free. This was interesting, because I told the principal that I always gave all of the children money for lunch. Until the principal alerted us, we didn't know Allen got the welfare card from a friend whose family legitimately was on welfare.

I wasn't sure what Tony was doing with his lunch money until one morning our Catholic nun neighbors stopped Wilma and me as we were leaving our house.

"Tony had a really good night last night," a nun told us. "What is he going to do with all of his money?"

It turned out that Tony was playing bingo at the church. He took his allowance, meant partially for lunch money, and won $200 in blackout bingo.

I kept busy at the Department of Health and Human Services, and, I think luckily, I dodged a chance to get fired. Joseph Califano was a stickler for getting things done right. He also was Catholic and pro-life, so he went everywhere with a bodyguard because of protestors.

On a trip to Denver, Califano told me to get a staffer to pick him up at the airport and take him to his speech in downtown Denver. My employee was supposed to stay with a nine-passenger van in which Califano would always sit next to the door—for safety reasons. The staffer left the van and went to listen to Califano's speech. Califano got back to the van before the staffer, so Califano ended up flagging down a taxi to go to dinner.

The next day, I had an 8:00 A.M. meeting with Califano and thought the best defense was an offense: I said I was sorry about last night before he brought it up.

Califano told me always to get a former military person to be the driver because they never leave their post. I told him I would heed his advice in the future, but I felt I barely missed a possible dismissal.

"We timed everything in advance to get as much done [as possible] in a short period of time," Califano recalled. "He never would have gotten fired over that. Wellington was impressive. He was young, ambitious, and energetic."

Califano worked all of the time. He had two different groups of

It wasn't always easy on my children that I was Denver's mayor. Wilma and I gathered them for a family photograph: (from left), sons Allen, Keith, and Anthony, and daughter Stephanie.

secretaries, one for the morning and one for the afternoon, because he was burning them out. Everyone at HHS worked a minimum of six days a week to keep up with the boss.

When Califano was fired by President Jimmy Carter, his assistant Sue Foster said HHS employees would resign in protest. But the jobs paid too well and were too secure to walk away. Foster, to her credit, still works for Califano in his efforts to educate the public about the hazards of drugs, alcohol, and tobacco.

In Colorado politics, King Trimble hated the legislature and still wanted to be on the Denver City Council. There were rumors that Elvin Caldwell was going to seek reelection and then resign to take a position in Mayor Bill McNichols's cabinet. Mayor McNichols, in turn, would appoint Caldwell's seat to Caldwell's aide Hiawatha Davis. I liked Davis, but he wasn't part of my political circle, and I thought Trimble should get a shot at the council seat.

There were also rumors that Wilma was going to challenge Caldwell if he ran for reelection. We all gathered at Pierre's Supper Club, where black politicians used to meet every Friday afternoon.

I was at HHS and not supposed to be involved in local politics, but I set up the meeting between Wilma and Caldwell.

We told Caldwell that Wilma was being pushed to run for his council seat. At the time, if there was a vacancy on the council, the mayor would appoint a replacement. We asked Caldwell to get Mayor McNichols to change the charter to require a special election where the race would be open to all interested candidates.

Caldwell had just gotten out of the hospital from a hip replacement and didn't want to deal with another political battle. He got the message that if he didn't push for the charter change, he would face tough competition in the election.

Caldwell carried the ordinance to change the charter. The amended charter was good government, but the issue came back to haunt me as mayor. I could have appointed several council replacements over my twelve years if we had never forced Caldwell to seek the charter amendment.

Wilma did not challenge Caldwell, and wouldn't have anyway, because she thought of him as a beloved and wise uncle. He won reelection and, as expected, he resigned his seat and was appointed to McNichols's cabinet. Caldwell had already set up Davis to run for the special election, and because of the charter change, he had to face Trimble.

Trimble didn't want to stay in the legislature, because it was a full-time six-month job and it was killing his law practice. We campaigned for Trimble by going door to door. He won the council seat by a narrow victory over Davis, who would later be elected to the same council seat.

I was ecstatic. Trimble joined Bill Roberts as the second black member on the council. Then Dr. Earnest Patterson was back on our doorstep urging Wilma to seek the open legislative seat left vacant by Trimble's departure.

Wilma wasn't sure she would run for the seat. She had heard negative comments in the community. Some people were saying that one politician in our family was enough. Others were saying that she was "just Wellington's wife."

After much consideration, Wilma decided to seek the seat. She planned to serve for just one term.

Wilma was elected to the House of Representatives for District Eight by Democratic committee members in July 1980 and ran for the election in November 1980. It was fitting that Judge Ray Jones, part of our original political circle, administered Wilma's first oath of office. She was reelected five more times before deciding not to run again in 1993, two years after I was elected mayor.

I enjoyed my work at HHS but was getting a little bored. Even though I oversaw six states, all of the action came out of Washington, D.C. I couldn't send out a press release without Washington's approval, let alone make any independent decisions for the states.

One idea lost in the bureaucracy was my proposal to directly fund the Standing Rock Sioux Indian Reservation. The reservation covered North Dakota and South Dakota, and the welfare payments were higher on one side of the reservation than on the other. I wanted to let the tribe equally administer the payments instead of having the states distribute the money, which was the policy nationwide.

My proposal was met with the criticism that the federal money should be distributed by the states. I believe there also was fear that if we changed the rules for one Indian tribe, the other tribes would want the money to go directly to them too, instead of to the states.

The only news out of the regional offices was usually when an employee filed a grievance.

On a day-to-day basis, I was restless, and I jumped at the request to help run President Carter's reelection campaign in Illinois.

Wilma was running for reelection in the House while I headed to Chicago to help President Carter. We knew we had a tough opponent in Ronald Reagan, and the campaign needed seasoned workers.

My main stipulation was that because I had to resign my job to work on the campaign, HHS would agree to give me back my position even if President Carter lost. I wanted the agreement in writing.

If Carter won, I could make a decision if I wanted to stay at HHS or go to another job in Washington, D.C. If Carter lost, I would have a job from after the November election until January 20, 1981, when the new president would be sworn in and all of Carter's appointments would be unemployed.

My philosophy is that it's easier to get another job if you are already employed.

"I remember when Wellington Webb negotiated to get his job back if Carter didn't win reelection," recalled Jean Mason, who worked with Health, Education and Welfare and HHS from 1966 under President Johnson to 1997 with President Clinton's administration. "It was the right thing to do, because it worked. I believe he may have been the only one who ever did that."

Mason saw a lot of regional directors come and go. Her job was to oversee everything from special management to budget operations, travel, and personnel evaluations.

"I appreciated Wellington Webb's calm under pressure," Mason said. "No matter what the emergency—and we always had tons of emergencies—he was a very controlled and thoughtful person. I was comfortable he could handle a crisis without getting overly excited."

Mason also was impressed that I was able to work well with state officials.

"The regional directors were political appointees and had to be able to pick up the phone and get in contact with a governor or another state office at a moment's notice," Mason said. "They had to be able to go up and down the ladder of command. Wellington had the personality to get it done."

Before I joined President Carter's reelection campaign, I asked Rosalyn Carter to call Wilma and explain why I was needed in Chicago. It wasn't an easy time for me to be away from home, with Wilma mounting her own campaign and raising the kids.

In addition, I asked the Carter campaign to announce my appointment in Illinois newspapers so that the community knew I was legitimate. Some people thought I was just a bagman bringing campaign money. Some of the locals figured they would run me off in a few weeks.

But I had every intention of staying the duration and making sure people knew I was serious about the job. Campaign manager Mike Casey helped introduce me to Mike Holowinski, a Chicago City Council member who educated me about Chicago politics and what precincts to target.

Maggie Williams also worked on the Illinois campaign. She went on to serve as chief of staff for First Lady Hillary Clinton. A friend of mine from Denver, Marge Price, was the press secretary for the Illinois campaign. Judy Byrd, a recent law-school graduate at the time who went on to be an investment banker, coordinated some of the campaign outreach.

I worked with other Chicagoans: Reverend Jesse Jackson; Harold Washington, who was in the Illinois state legislature; Jane Byrne, Chicago's mayor at the time; and Wallace D. Muhammad, head of the Black Muslims.

Harold Washington was candid with me that we faced an uphill battle to get President Carter reelected.

"The true reality is we don't give a damn who the president is," explained Harold, who would be elected the first black mayor of the Windy City in 1983. "The president for Chicago is whoever is mayor. That's where all of the jobs come from and where all the money comes from. The president is secondary."

Despite his lack of interest in the presidential race, Washington didn't dismiss me, because we had known each other as legislators. Washington assigned his employee Sam Patch to work with me. Illinois State Comptroller Roland Burris asked Norris Washington to assist me. Norris Washington was helping Burris prepare a run for governor.

We started training volunteers to work the phones, and I was dismayed to discover how many adults who applied for phone-bank jobs did not know how to read. We also had to find enough bilingual volunteers to reach the growing Latino population, most of whom were from South America.

I started bringing in important African Americans to help us campaign, including Coretta Scott King, Coleman Young, and Muhammad Ali.

Young was the mayor of Detroit, and I was impressed with his style. He sent his people, including Detroit police, to Chicago early to check out his campaign-appearance locations. I spoke to Coleman for quite a while, and that was the first time I ever said, "You know, this being mayor might not be a bad idea."

I suggested that President Carter visit a black church in Morgan Park. Vice President Walter Mondale filled in for Carter at the church because the president was tied up with the Iran hostage crisis.

Being in Chicago was also great because I got to see my father. He initially let me use his car, and my brother Ronnie helped me campaign. We shuttled several people back and forth to campaign events in my father's car.

"You know, I've been around these people for ten days, and they talk about needing a million dollars for this and a million for that, yet ain't nobody offered to buy gas for my car," my father said. "I'm an old retired railroad porter, and I think you just ought to move downtown to campaign headquarters and give up my car. I have never seen so many important cheap people in all of my life."

Ronnie was driving my dad's car because I had let my driver's license expire. When my dad took back his car, we had to find a rental. The rental place required a credit card, which I had, and a driver's license, which I had let expire. Ronnie had a driver's license but no credit card, so we were stuck.

But God had a way of smiling on us that day. The same time I was trying to convince the rental agent to let us have a car, the television in her office showed me with Muhammad Ali campaigning for President Carter in Chicago.

"Vote for Jimmy Carter because he's the right white," Ali said.

Only Ali could say that and get away with it.

"Hey, that's you with Ali!" the rental agent said.

For the cost of four tickets to Ali's reception that evening, we got to rent a car.

When working in the Chicago suburbs, I met my cousin Bill Brazley, whom I hadn't seen since I was a kid. He was working his way up to being a top architect in Chicago. He and his wife, Peggy, helped us campaign in the suburbs.

On our final push toward Election Day, I made sure some of the campaign money went to the ministers and community activists who showed their ability to get people out to vote.

On the night of the election, Ronnie and I got on a plane to Denver. Before we landed, the pilot announced that Reagan had defeated Carter and would be our next president.

The good news was that we arrived in time to walk into Wilma's campaign headquarters and celebrate her victory. It was a total surprise to her that we made it back to Denver on election night.

Chapter Thirteen

After Carter, Colorado Department
of Regulatory Agencies

After President Jimmy Carter lost reelection, I waited to hear when I was going to return to my job at the Department of Health and Human Services (HHS).

President Carter was a unique politician in that he thanked his appointees for their work. He has always been gracious when our paths crossed, including when we met in 2003 at a unity rally for Democrats. The Democratic Party has not always embraced Carter, but he always has remembered that I was one of the first in Colorado to support him.

The man who was put in my HHS job temporarily didn't think I was serious about coming back, even though I had a written agreement that the job was mine until President Reagan's inauguration.

"He's taking all of your plaques off the wall," my press secretary Norma Jones warned me shortly after I went to Illinois to campaign for President Carter. "He's taking all of your pictures down. I don't think he thinks you're coming back."

The Republicans had no problem with cleaning house. The political appointees under President Carter knew their jobs were over January 20, 1981, when President Ronald Reagan took office. I called the guy who had replaced me and said I would be returning in a couple of weeks. I knew the Republicans would clean house of all the remaining Democratic appointees immediately.

I agreed to let him tell the staff that I was coming back, but I was also upset that he was trying to position himself to block my return.

My return was not exciting. Unlike when I was first hired, I wasn't getting a lot of calls. Matter of fact, one day Wilma was the only person who called me. Working under a Republican administration in transition put a damper on the job.

I began to think about my future after HHS. I started meeting with longtime Colorado politicians. One of the most interesting men was former governor Steve McNichols. After he lost his reelection bid, he took a minimal position with the federal government as a regional administrator for the Department of Commerce.

I asked him why he took the job.

"I need the money," he frankly told me.

Governor McNichols then explained an important lesson in politics. He said he made a tragic mistake when he took out a personal loan in his unsuccessful reelection bid against John Love; when he lost, there was no money to pay off the loan.

I did not adequately learn the lesson, and I once took out a loan for a campaign. If you win a campaign, you can pay your debts off pretty quickly because the money starts rolling in. But if you lose, you end up having a long-term debt and a lot of explaining to give a spouse who was not consulted in a timely manner about the personal loan in the first place.

I also learned it is an indication of a campaign's support if you can't raise money for an election. Usually, the candidate with the empty campaign war chest loses. I was one of the unique elected officials in 1991 who went against that conventional wisdom and beat a candidate who raised more than $1 million.

Governor McNichols's story also was tragic because he faded quickly from the public's radar. He was elected in 1957 and served until 1963.

"I was governor of the state and half the people hardly remember me at all," he told me. "And if they do remember me, they don't have much to do with me."

His brother, Bill McNichols, the former Denver mayor, served in office from 1968 to 1983 and also had a sad future after politics. He ended up working as a greeter in a downtown Denver bank. I thought it was demeaning to see the former mayor of Denver welcoming people at a bank. It reminded me of former heavyweight boxing champion Joe Louis ending up as a greeter in Las Vegas casinos to pay his bills.

That's one reason I made sure that when Bill McNichols died in May 1997, he received a funeral fit for a former mayor. He had a full police escort, and I attended the service along with many elected officials. His family thanked me for respecting Mayor McNichols for his decades as a loyal city servant.

I also made sure that we named a city building for the McNichols family when McNichols Arena, where the NBA Denver Nuggets and professional hockey team Colorado Avalanche played, was torn down and replaced by the Pepsi Center. The McNichols family—including Bill and Steve's father, William, who served as the city's auditor from 1931 to 1955—had given a lot to Denver and deserved the recognition.

Combined, this one family spent forty-five years of their lives in public office.

While I was at HHS, Ruben Valdez left the federal Department of Transportation and had taken a job in Governor Richard Lamm's cabinet. Valdez in state government was like a duck in water. Valdez knew my job with HHS was coming to an end in January 1981, and he asked if I would consider coming back to state government.

"I would, but I would be surprised if Dick wanted me," I told Valdez.

In addition to walking out of Governor Lamm's first inauguration, I boycotted the second inauguration because of Governor Lamm's stormy relationship with Lieutenant Governor George Brown.

Colorado's constitution in 1974 allowed the voters to elect a governor and lieutenant governor separately. The law had since been changed to allow the governor candidate to pick a running mate. Brown helped Governor Lamm get the support of the black community during

Lamm's victory in 1974. Brown was the first black elected lieutenant governor of a state since 1871, when P. B. S. Pinchback served as the lieutenant governor of Louisiana. Brown also balanced Governor Lamm somewhat because Lamm was for zero population growth and was campaigning against the Winter Olympics coming to Colorado. I supported Governor Lamm's position because we saw how Lake Placid, New York, which had hosted the Winter Olympics in 1980, poured millions into facilities and was then stuck with the debt after the Olympics concluded. I thought that kind of money should be spent on my core values—education, training programs for the poor, and business to stimulate the local economy.

In 1979, after some public clashes with Governor Lamm, Brown was urged not to run for reelection.

Valdez challenged representative Nancy Dick of Aspen for the lieutenant governor spot, but Dick won. George left Denver and went on to be a vice president of the Grumman Aircraft Company in New York. As a former Tuskegee airman, Brown found a niche lobbying Congress for the aircraft company.

I was not hopeful that Governor Lamm would want me to join his staff because of our history. I also learned that some of Governor Lamm's cabinet members were not thrilled with me joining his administration because of the continued political rift in the black community, which began with Regis Groff's challenge of Arie Taylor's representative seat.

I went to Governor Lamm's third inauguration, and about a week later, he called our home and asked if I was interested in joining his cabinet. He wanted to gauge my interest and asked me on a scale of one to ten, how interested was I in a job? I told him a six.

"Well, that's a fairly low number to give him when you have no idea where you'll be working," Wilma told me. "After all, he called you; you did not call him."

I called him back and gave him a seven.

He offered me the job of director of personnel because he was having problems with Rudy Livingston. Livingston was my fraternity brother and a longtime career service employee who knew the state's personnel rules very well. But he and Governor Lamm did not get along philosophically, and Governor Lamm wanted to make a change.

I discussed the job offer with Wilma and my political group and then called Governor Lamm back.

"I would really like to join your cabinet, but I need to do something that is meaningful for me," I told Governor Lamm. "Frankly, I'd like to move out of the social-service area and move into something that will help me grow intellectually and in a new area of responsibility."

Governor Lamm agreed, and when he called back, he offered me the job as executive director of the Department of Regulatory Agencies. Unbeknownst to me at the time, he had the difficult decision of moving the current director, Gail Klapper, to the personnel job. Klapper was not thrilled about the decision, but she was a good soldier and she moved.

I thought it would be pretty perfunctory to get confirmation from the general assembly for my new job. But it seems like nothing I do is perfunctory. Wilma was making her own name in the legislature, but there was opposition to my appointment. My confirmation went before a legislative committee and stalled on a 3–3 vote.

The senators who supported my confirmation were Dick Soash of Steamboat Springs, Martin Hatcher of Gunnison, and Sam Zakhem, who was the chairman of the Business Affairs and Labor Committee. In opposition were Republicans Joel Hefley, Ken Clark, and Maynard Yost.

Two committee people who were missing from the meeting were Democratic senator Don Sandoval and Republican senator Les Fowler, so Zakhem took the vote off the table for a few days.

I was able to get confirmation by a 5–2 vote. Hefley and Yost said because I had not worked in the private sector, I shouldn't have a position that oversaw the licensing and regulation of many private-sector jobs.

Under my jurisdiction, we had business committees monitoring the testing and licensing process for real estate, banking, savings and loan, horse and dog racing, civil rights, and the Public Utilities Commission. In addition, under Division Director Bruce Douglas, the state oversaw the professional occupation boards of psychology, social work, nursing, passenger tramways, engineering, plumbing, electrical engineering, and barber and cosmetology.

As executive director of the Department of Regulatory Agencies, now my name graced every license granted to people pursuing these professions.

One of the first things I discovered in my new job was that a bill I had passed as a legislator had never been implemented by the state. The bill that mandated that group-insurance policies provide coverage for alcohol-abuse treatment had been held up by the insurance commissioner, Richard Barnes. I made sure the law went into affect immediately. It was a lesson that you need both legislative and executive branches to get the job done.

The Department of Regulatory Agencies was involved in a lot of tough issues, including the savings-and-loan solvency and penny-stock scandals, business deregulation, and ski-lift safety following a gondola accident.

I really liked working for Governor Lamm because his cabinet meetings turned into debates that were better than anything debated on the floor of Congress.

Governor Lamm's legacy is that he hired some of the brightest people, many of whom are still involved in politics and public policy.

"Lamm's cabinet was very fun," recalled Paula Herzmark, who worked as a lobbyist for Governor Lamm and with the government watchdog group Common Cause. "It was full of talented people who laughed a lot and worked very hard. As colleagues, we had some turf wars, but it still felt like family. It was a unique group. We were all young and had ideals and weren't jaded—yet."

I got a kick out of Governor Lamm because he was so focused on water, growth, and the environment that he, by and large, let me run my department as I saw fit. I always kept him abreast of what was going on, but he never micromanaged me.

Governor Lamm wanted his cabinet to reflect his environmental views. He was unhappy when his cabinet members drove a couple of blocks from the capitol to the governor's mansion instead of walking. I didn't say a word until he called on me.

"Intellectual white people are always changing the rules," I said. "First, us black folks had to walk everywhere, whereas you had cars. Now, we have cars, and you tell us to walk? I'll drive to take out the trash if I can."

It took him a few seconds to burst out with his great laugh.

I seldom was such a smart aleck with my remarks to the governor, because I knew how the system worked.

"Wellington's MO, as I used to tell people, is that he is always low-keyed and reserved," Herzmark said. "But you would wake up one morning and discover that a project was no longer in your department and now in his department. He was—is—very skilled at being a back-channel operator. He is very skilled at maneuvering the political sea."

Some of Governor Lamm's cabinet didn't hold back at staff meetings.

"Some of us would be whining to the governor while Wellington just quietly did his thing," Herzmark said. "He may be quiet and reserved, but I tell people to never underestimate Wellington Webb. Anyone who ever did underestimate him paid the price."

Bruce Douglas did an outstanding job as my division director, and he also had a sense of humor. Once, Douglas, with the help of Joan Ringel, found a mannequin in a storage room and put it under the desk of Byron White, who oversaw the Department of Administration. When White turned on his office light, he saw the mannequin's legs, thought it was a human, and just about had a heart attack.

The Office of Regulatory Reform was started under former director Klapper, and I pushed for real changes. Senator Hefley, who voted against my confirmation, had set up the office. Ringel oversaw the office and was doing such things as trying to cut down on the enormous amount of state paperwork required for businesses. She also put together start-up kits to make it easier for small businesses to understand state rules.

"My job was to set up a lunch between Wellington and Joel," Ringel said. "I was walking down the street between two six-foot-four men who were polar opposites but who worked well together because they both believed in regulatory reform."

Understanding how the legislature operated was a benefit in my new job.

"Clearly, Wellington's political skill made a big difference," Ringel said.

She remembers me calling up legislators and getting their support on issues.

"Gail was smart and competent, but she was naïve to politics," Ringel said. "Wellington also knew if he wanted to get anything passed, he had to work with Republicans."

My goal as director of Regulatory Agencies was not to sit back, but to be aggressive in terms of deregulation and also aggressive in protecting agencies that needed protecting. When the Joint Budget Committee (JBC) said it was going to cut the Civil Rights Division, I took members on a statewide hearing to understand what the civil-rights complaints were throughout Colorado.

When the JBC said it was going to cut my budget by 10 percent, I threatened to cut state bank examiners because I knew banks were also inspected by federal examiners. The bank presidents protested loudly and my budget was not cut.

It was during this period that I was able to hire some young, energetic staffers or appoint them to boards. Many of these people would go on to work for me while I was mayor.

Ringel introduced me to a young architect whom I appointed to the passenger-tramway board. Jennifer Moulton went with me after a ski-lift accident to inspect the gondolas. Those mountain people must have done a double take when they saw a black guy in a ski jacket and city leather boots climbing the mountain in a snowstorm to see whether we should shut down the gondolas.

Despite protests, we did shut down the gondolas at the Colorado ski resorts until we were assured of the safety of the skiers.

Moulton served as my planning director when I was mayor and earned a national reputation for her historic preservation and redevelopment of downtown Denver. Sadly, Moulton died of a rare blood disorder shortly after I left the mayor's office.

Moulton had advised me on and we had implemented a number of major projects, even though I sometimes had a different view from hers. We used to kid each other that we were like Mayor Robert Speer and his landscape architect, Saco DeBoer, both of whom worked together on Speer's "City Beautiful" campaign in the early 1900s. Our joke included sticking around long enough to have our busts at the City and County Building, similar to those of Speer and DeBoer.

After Governor Lamm appointed me to his cabinet, I still had my eye on politics and asked the governor to name me to the first reapportionment commission for Colorado. The group was looking at redrawing districts for the legislature. I wanted to serve on the commission to maintain the boundaries for District Seven and District Eight to ensure minority representation.

I made sure at the reapportionment meetings that I sat between two powerful Republicans: Speaker of the House Carl "Bev" Bledsoe and Robert Lee. Lee served as the Denver County Republican chairman, a Denver Election Commission member, and as the right hand of cable-television founder Bill Daniels.

Lee asked me one day why I was sitting next to him.

"Because I know the Republicans are going to screw the Democrats, and I want to learn from you so that twenty years from now I can screw some young Republican who will be sitting next to me," I told him.

I met Theresa Donahue while serving on the reapportionment committee. Ringel later hired Donahue to work in the Office of Consumer Counsel and oversee the Sunrise/Sunset Committee.

(This committee decided which state agencies or laws were outdated.) Donahue would serve on my staff when I was auditor and mayor.

"I always thought that Wellington's style of management was similar to Dick Lamm's," Donahue said. "He would bring on people with a lot of different perspectives and interests and let them run from a broad framework along with what he could support."

Ringel also hired Greg Romberg, who helped run the new Office of Regulatory Reform.

"Wellington saw the value of this office in substance and politically," Romberg, a political consultant, recalled.

I had a great staff that I could rely on. I still carry a letter that Mike Gorham of the Real Estate Division wrote to thank me for a promotion.

"He was the best boss I worked for, and I'm not just saying that because he appointed me to the job," said Gorham, who worked for seven different directors. "He was a coalition builder and recognized the potential in many people."

I saw my staff as a team, and success would only be achieved if we worked together.

"I had directors in the department who would keep their reports to the governor close to the vest and we, as division directors, had to pry the information out of them," Gorham said. "Wellington always told us what we needed to know. The directors appreciated that because it helped us do our jobs."

I also met a man who would be a strong political supporter. I set up a roundtable talk about energy issues and invited Bill Coors, the one Independent member of the Republican Coors family. Coors pushed a project that used steam from the Coors Brewery in Golden to run a power plant.

"While serving together on the roundtable, Bill's daughter committed suicide," Ringel recalled. "Wellington wrote him a note of condolence. Bill wrote back a note that started out, 'Dear Welly.' Bill wanted to be warm and personal. He's the only person I know who ever called Wellington 'Welly.'"

Coors and his wife, Rita Bass, have remained my good friends and political supporters.

At the Department of Regulatory Agencies, I was enjoying the challenge of the new job and making contacts with people such as cable-television mogul and Republican Daniels. Daniels and I got to know each other when he was setting up the Children's Bank, and I helped him get through the licensing process.

The seeds of my wanting to run for mayor were planted when I met Detroit mayor Coleman Young in the 1980 Carter reelection campaign. In 1983, I thought Denver may finally be ready for a minority mayor.

Denver was unique because it was a city that gave minorities opportunities based on their ability to get the job done.

People in Denver are also deathly afraid of being considered racists, not being fair-minded, and not being objective. I believe some of that philosophy is because many people moved to Denver through the military and from other parts of the country. Unlike in the South and East, the people of Denver did not have generations to build upon racial stereotypes or economic issues of family titles and social pedigree.

The western pioneer spirit is also prevalent in that people only care if you can really cut it and get the job done. If you show genuine potential, they will take a chance on you.

As Mayor McNichols sought a fourth term in 1983, I thought the time was ripe for the voters to give a minority the chance to lead the city. But I jumped into the mayoral race too late and learned some valuable lessons.

Chapter Fourteen

1983 Mayoral Campaign, James Thompson

I saw the 1983 mayoral race as a way for me to get into local politics. I thought voters were tired of seeing Mayor Bill McNichols and District Attorney Dale Tooley, who had faced each other in two previous elections, fight it out again.

Months before the mayoral race kicked into high gear, I was worried about a showdown in the legislature between Representatives Miller Hudson and Federico Peña because both men lived within the new legislative district's boundaries. It turned out that Hudson didn't run for reelection, and Peña was already gearing up for the mayoral race.

Unlike my previous campaigns, where I sat down with family and friends and discussed whether I should run, I let my eagerness get in the way. I entered the race late and before putting all of the organizational pieces in place.

I was itching to get into a local campaign and announced my candidacy when others—especially Peña—had their organizations already in place and their campaigns under way.

Another one of Governor Richard Lamm's cabinet members, Monte Pascoe, also ran for mayor that year. When I met Governor Lamm and Roy Romer, who was Lamm's chief of staff at the time, I told them I wanted to pursue the mayoral job.

"You're getting into the race too late," Governor Lamm warned me. "It takes a huge amount of money, and I don't think your chances are too good."

He couldn't change my mind.

"Well, it's something I feel like I have to do, and I want to take a leave of absence," I told him.

Romer said a leave would make it look like I was not a serious campaigner. He recommended to Governor Lamm that I should resign, and they would consider taking me back if I lost the city election. So I resigned, as did Pascoe.

"Wellington Webb did not do his real homework for the 1983 mayor race," recalled legislator Gerald Kopel.

Even my longtime supporter and friend Dan Muse thought I had made a mistake by entering the race.

"I thought it was so silly," Muse said. "I told him it was a waste of his time and a waste of my time."

We had an interesting field, with Mayor McNichols, the incumbent; Tooley, the district attorney; Peña, a legislator; Steve Schweitzberger, a community activist and an amicable guy who ran in every mayoral election; and Harold Sudmeyer, a Socialist who ran just to have fun.

Mayor McNichols could be a crotchety old guy, but I liked his bluntness. He declined to go to the dozens of town meetings and forums set up during the campaign.

"Why should I go to a lynching when all of them there want to lynch me?" he said.

Mayor McNichols believed he would get to the runoff. He just wasn't sure whether he would face his nemesis, Tooley, or one of the newcomers.

Tooley had been politically wounded by me, Wilma, and Rich Castro when we persisted in questioning him about the lack of prosecution on what we believed to be unwarranted police shootings. Wilma, as a state legislator, requested a coroner's inquest into the use of deadly force by a police officer resulting in the death of an eighteen-year-old, as well as an investigation by the Justice Department.

Tooley, who was once seen as a liberal, was now viewed as a conservative. Many people felt that Mayor McNichols should pass the mantle on to a younger mayor. Peña became the liberal and the fresh face.

When it became clear that I wouldn't even make the runoff, my goal was merely to save face. I wanted to finish at least fourth and in front of Pascoe. That competition came from the fact that we were both in Governor Lamm's cabinet and Pascoe was a Seventeenth Street lawyer.

One of the first news articles about the entire field of candidates reported on our campaign contributions. Tooley, as expected, had the most, at $350,000; Mayor McNichols raised $305,000; Pascoe, $210,000; Peña, $169,000; and I had a measly $45,000.

I knew $45,000 was the most I was going to raise, and I did exactly what former governor Steve McNichols warned me not to do. I told Wilma I needed her support to try and have a respectable showing in the election. In order to do that, we placed a second mortgage on our house and borrowed $25,000.

We got one big contribution of $1,000 from Tramwell Crow, and we were so excited, we put out several press releases on that one donation.

I am still struck, humbled, and honored by the smaller donations I received for that election. While I was campaigning at one bus stop, an elderly black woman holding a small coin purse gave me a dollar for my campaign.

I tried to give the dollar back to her and she told me, "I want you to put this in your campaign. I am investing in you."

I attended as many public events as possible to get my name in the press. I called the media when I taped a note on Mayor McNichols's office door at city hall when he refused to answer my questions on pending city issues. "Webb tells McNichols: I want answers" read the headline next to a photograph of me tacking up the note.

On St. Patrick's Day in 1983, four of us candidates attended a celebration hosted by legislator Dennis Gallagher. McNichols, Tooley, and Pascoe agreed to put on silly green hats. McNichols looked like a tipsy leprechaun. I refused to wear the hat because it clashed with my big Afro and goatee.

When I saw the photograph later, I knew Peña was smart to have skipped that event. We all looked like we belonged in a carnival.

Getting sustained press coverage for my campaign became impossible.

"We used to meet each Sunday and lay out the issues for the week," recalled Greg Romberg, who worked in Regulatory Agencies. "This was before faxes and e-mails, so we had to hand deliver any press releases. The releases were supposed to arrive daily. I later found out that the press releases were always late and reporters just stopped coverage. I guess they figured if someone couldn't get their press releases in on time, he also couldn't run the city."

I appreciated the people who supported me and worked on the campaign. City Councilwoman Cathy Donohue was chairwoman of my campaign. Mike Stratton and Tim McKenna ran the campaign.

"Oh, God, I was McNichols's nemesis," Donohue recalled.

She was excited that the longtime mayor would face a strong slate of candidates.

"Every time Wellington ran for office, I was a big supporter," Donohue said. "He handled himself well and was good to work with. He also was someone I just liked, and he liked me."

Arie Taylor was dealing with her own demon, alcoholism, and couldn't help me with this campaign.

"He got into the race too late and with so many other candidates with more visibility," Theresa Donahue said. "He learned from it."

The campaign allowed me to visit different parts of the city and to understand the issues of each neighborhood, an experience that would prove to be invaluable for the 1991 mayoral race.

Pascoe got support from the environmentalists, even though our voter approval records as legislators were both high.

The Hispanic community rallied around Peña, including my friend Rich Castro. Castro didn't spend much time in the legislature that year because he was registering as many people as possible for the city election.

Maria Garcia Berry supported Pascoe, but she also encouraged her lobbying clients to give my campaign some money.

"Nobody saw the Peña phenomenon coming—at least I didn't," Garcia Berry said.

My brother Joe gave me a blunt assessment of my chances. He was a police officer at the time and was able to gauge my support citywide.

"State legislators think that everyone in the state knows them. Well, I just want to tell you that a lot of people who live in the city have never heard of you," Joe said.

If I had entered the race earlier, I may have had a chance to reach more voters.

The black elected officials put off any endorsement, yet the day after the primary, their support of Peña hit the newspapers. What that told me was that the black elected officials had cut a deal with the Peña people long before the primary.

The black community also really didn't think a minority could be elected mayor, whereas the Hispanic community saw the opportunity and grabbed it. Peña and Tooley were the top finishers, with Mayor McNichols coming in third and missing the runoff. Mayor McNichols's long political career ended in 1983.

"Wellington Webb did get in the 1983 mayoral race late, but he finished a strong fourth," recalled Stratton. "Then he supported Peña. His support for Peña was key for the runoff."

Tooley called our house and asked for Wilma and me to endorse him. He thought if he got my endorsement, it would help him overcome Peña. But it was clear that I would endorse Peña. I thought it was important that if Denver, Colorado—a primarily white community— was willing to elect a minority as mayor, then I should wholeheartedly support that candidate. It would remove another ceiling for all politicians of color.

I remember the day after the primary when Mayor McNichols, Pascoe, and I walked from city hall to the Colorado Convention Center to endorse Peña. All these people divided like a great sea as the old man, Mayor McNichols, came over to congratulate the man who would go on to be the city's first Hispanic mayor. Mayor McNichols was never going to endorse his longtime rival, Tooley.

Behind the scenes, Tooley was always suspicious of Peña's victory but was smart enough to never raise the issue publicly; the new voter registration was so heavily Hispanic. Some Tooley folks claimed that there were people with the same Hispanic surnames who had registered more than once. They even said the voters were being bused in from the nearby communities of Brighton and other places outside the city limits.

I felt good about Peña's victory, but I was also overcome with feeling sorry for myself. This was the first time I had lost an election.

I was walking from the convention center to my car when a woman came over and stopped me.

"Don't feel bad. You didn't win this time, but you'll win next time," she told me.

I learned her name was Dolores Dickman and she was a neighborhood political leader who cut her political teeth in the union movement.

At the time, I didn't really take in her comment. I couldn't help but focus on how my lack of political organization doomed my campaign from day one. I tried to bolster myself by remembering I finished fourth out of a field of seven candidates and I didn't make a fool of myself in the debates. In fact, I did quite well.

"He took the loss in 1983 very hard; he takes everything hard," Muse recalled.

With my spirits low, I knew it was time to get out of town and take a much-needed trip. Wilma and I flew to San Francisco and then drove to San José and San Luis Obispo. We spent time with friends and went to San Simeon to see the great wealth of the Hearst Corporation. When we went to catch a train to Los Angeles, we found out a mudslide had taken out the train. We ended up on a bus to Los Angeles instead. All that I could think of on the bus ride was that 1983 was not a good year for me.

Wilma and I enjoyed vacations to California. After my unsuccessful mayoral race in 1983, we visited San Francisco and Los Angeles. There, I shaved off my goatee, following the advice of a Denver voter who told me some people could not get past my height, goatee, and Afro to listen to my message.

I also remembered a conversation with a white voter who told me she was going to vote for me, even though she didn't think I would win. Then she gave me a piece of advice.

"I'd like you to do two things: the next time you run, shave the mustache, shave the goatee, and trim some of your hair to let your real personality show," she said. "And smile some more. For a lot of my neighbors in southeast Denver who don't know you, when you frown and you stand six-foot-four and you have a goatee, they never get past that picture to hear what you have to say."

I went into the bathroom during our trip to California and took a long look in the mirror. Now, Wilma really liked the goatee. When I came out of the bathroom without the goatee, she asked me to grow it back.

"I will someday," I assured her. "I will soon."

The goatee never came back. But I refused to make more drastic physical alterations in 1991, despite the advice of a paid consultant.

I learned several things from the 1983 campaign, including that the politics of appearance is important. If someone feels comfortable with the way you look, they may listen to what you have to say.

I also realized that it didn't help me to attack Mayor McNichols, even though others agreed it was time for him to leave office. He gave me a job when I was struggling with my salary as a legislator. I respected his ability to stand up for his supporters, and they felt he would never sell out his friends.

How peculiarly life turns, because eight years later, Mayor McNichols would endorse me in my 1991 mayoral bid.

I returned to work at the Department of Regulatory Agencies, but I knew I could not stay there long. Romer was running for governor in 1986, and his style of leadership was very different from Governor Lamm's. Lamm would let his cabinet "do their own thing," whereas Romer was a hands-on person.

Romer liked to talk with his hands. When Romer was Governor Lamm's chief of staff, cabinet member Morgan Smith once hid the chalk Romer used at cabinet meetings. We knew if the chalk was missing, Romer couldn't do anything elaborate on the chalkboard. That was the shortest cabinet meeting in our recent memories.

Governor Lamm reinstated me after the 1983 race and nominated me as the top state government official in 1984. The Distinguished Service Award was presented to me at the National Governors Association's convention.

While I continued to think about my political future, Wilma's reputation as an outstanding legislator was growing. I was the first in our family to be elected to a state office, but Wilma had been groomed for the position as an outstanding student at Manual High School. She also credited her experience with Mobil Oil as invaluable.

When Wilma announced she was running to succeed King Trimble after his election to Denver City Council, many people were blown away by her speech. They knew her as Wellington Webb's wife, a mother, and a Democratic activist who was involved in community issues. What they were about to learn was that she fit the Colorado House of Representatives like a hand in glove.

Wilma practiced what she preached on her campaign signs: "She is the right candidate who confronts the right issues."

One of her first actions was to take up my unsuccessful battle during my tenure in the legislature in introducing a Dr. Martin Luther King Jr. holiday bill. She fought that battle for four years, never caving in to the Republicans who each year killed the bill. Every session, she would bring a new bill back with different strategies for success.

Speaker of the House Carl "Bev" Bledsoe had Representative Frank DeFilippo, a former New York City police officer, defeat the bill in the House State Affairs Committee, which he chaired.

DeFilippo had been elected from a strong Republican-dominated district, and he took no political heat for the demise of the Dr. King holiday bill. In fact, he probably received a lot of kudos for his part in killing the legislation.

Bledsoe once showed me material about Dr. King that he had no clue I had already seen. The material claimed that Dr. King was a womanizer and Communist. It included a photograph of Dr. King at a Communist training camp. Bledsoe asked what I thought about Dr. King in light of this information.

"Well, I don't believe this is true," I told him. "You ought to see some of the materials I was sent about you. I didn't believe that either. They said you're a right-wing bigot from Hugo, Colorado, who doesn't care about anything but cattle and white people."

DeFilippo helped defeat the bill for two years. Then, in 1983, he had a change of heart. He was fed up with being the bully, and the bill was sent to another committee. We have since become close friends.

Republican Betty Neale supported the Dr. King legislation the first time I introduced it and when Wilma finally got it approved in 1984.

"I just felt it was an important milestone and should be recognized," Neale said.

Colorado has a Dr. King holiday because of Representative Wilma Webb's leadership. Wilma persevered and ignored numerous racist and unkind comments directed at her in obtaining the passage of the Dr. King holiday law.

For me and Wilma, the Dr. King holiday will always have a special significance. We provided leadership in the ten-year battle to adopt the holiday, then helped coordinate the Dr. Martin Luther King Jr. Colorado Holiday Commission for sixteen years.

Since 1986, Denver has celebrated Dr. King's birthday in a combined parade and march, for which Wilma coined the word *marade*. More than 15,000 people marched in the first celebration. Denver's event now has a reputation as being one of the largest Dr. King celebrations, with an estimated 50,000 people marching each January in his memory.

In 1994, President William Clinton joined hands with other marchers and sang "We Shall Overcome."

"We are a mixed marriage. I am white and my wife is black," said Michael Gorham, who worked for me in Regulatory Agencies. "From the time my children were young, we went to the Martin

Luther King Jr. statue in City Park on his holiday, and the Webbs were always there. We marched as a whole family all the way until my kids got out of high school. It wasn't just another holiday, but a very special day, and made possible because of Wellington and Wilma Webb."

Ebony magazine did a story about the Webbs of Colorado and highlighted Wilma's work in the legislature. She addressed issues ranging from energy to getting more minorities jobs and scholarships. She introduced tax incentives to get more businesses and jobs to Five Points.

She had become a real advocate for the disenfranchised, children, education, business, women, and civil-rights groups in particular.

Wilma was also probably one of the few legislators who took home suitcases full of legislation to review.

"Why are you bringing all of this legislation home?" I asked, knowing that wasn't my habit when I served.

"I actually study the legislation," Wilma said. "I know I'm going to be asked questions, so I need to be prepared."

Wilma was a no-nonsense leader, and she had the ability to work with Republicans. That proved to be a big asset for me farther down the road.

In her first term, she became a major voice in the Colorado General Assembly. She was the first black woman to serve on the Joint Budget Committee (JBC). Bledsoe, as speaker of the House, tried to punish Wilma by removing her from the JBC after the Dr. King holiday bill was adopted. He unjustly said he could remove all committee members, even if those members—such as Wilma—were elected to the position by their own party members.

Bledsoe appointed another Democrat to Wilma's seat, but the Democrats successfully fought the action in court, and Wilma kept her seat on the JBC.

So when the newspapers were talking about a Webb in the mid-1980s, it was Wilma in the headlines and not Wellington.

When I went back to Regulatory Agencies after the 1983 race,

I felt really down. That disappointment wasn't so much about not winning, but about not giving the election my best effort. I didn't do it right. I vacillated on the decision to run and then it was too late. I not only let down myself, but the people who supported me. I was very hard on myself and everyone around me. So to suggest I was a difficult person to live with for a while is not an understatement.

"He talked a little about the race, but you had to bring it up," recalled Joan Ringel. "I think it was jarring to him. He was sad because he gave and gave to this community, and the first time he asked the city for something big, it didn't work out. That hurts."

I was also dealing with a personal tragedy. The Fourth of July is supposed to be a time of celebration with family, but in 1983, I had watched a man die.

James Thompson was my son Allen's father-in-law. Thompson gathered the family at his home for the holiday, after which he planned to take a trip to Florida. Allen was stationed in Korea with the 101st Airborne. Wilma and I went to see our daughter-in-law Carola at that barbecue at her dad's house on the Fourth of July.

As I close my eyes, I can still vividly see the horror unfold.

The four of us were sitting on Thompson's porch. Thompson was so happy to have about twenty of his children and grandchildren running in the yard with sparklers and laughing. Then we suddenly heard a thud. Thompson stopped talking and kind of slumped forward. We grabbed him. I saw his eyes roll back into his head. As he lay there, Carola put her hand behind her father's head, and it was covered with blood.

Then all bedlam broke loose. We started hollering, "Call 911! Call 911!" Kids from ages three to seventeen were running through the house screaming and crying.

The fire trucks started showing up, and police officer Dave Michaud, who would later serve as my police chief, arrived and started asking questions.

In the confusion, someone called my son Tony and said, "Get over to Carola's father's house right now. Your dad has been shot!"

My son and his wife, Rosemary, raced to the house thinking I was injured.

Thompson was dead on arrival at Denver General Hospital.

The mystery of what happened suddenly became clear: someone celebrating the Fourth of July had carelessly and thoughtlessly shot a gun into the air. Well, the bullets come down. One bullet broke through an awning and went directly into Thompson's neck, lodged in his heart, and killed him instantly.

Thompson's son, Harry, had just gotten out of the navy. He was so angry when he arrived at Denver General and heard his father had died that Harry drove his fist into a wall and broke his arm.

The next day, we went back to Thompson's house because we had to deal with the press. It was hard because it was the family's time to grieve and not deal with reporters.

I believe the person responsible for Thompson's death did not do it intentionally. But in one senseless act, a family lost a husband, a father, and a grandfather. I hope the person who was responsible for his death paid for it in conscience, because no one was ever arrested and brought to justice.

The three vivid memories of that awful day still burn in my mind. First, everything seemed to be in slow motion. Second, this was the first time I had seen someone die. I thought Thompson had suffered a heart attack or stroke until we saw the blood. Seeing his eyes roll into the back of his head is something I will never forget. And finally, I can still hear his family's pain through their screaming: "Father! Daddy! Grandpa!"

Chapter Fifteen

Auditor

After my initial disappointment with the 1983 mayoral race, I regrouped at the Department of Regulatory Agencies and enjoyed the next few years on the job.

I also was involved with the American Israel Friendship League and went to Washington, D.C., with Denver's Jewish community to support Soviet Jews.

"He didn't seem despondent or depressed after the 1983 race," recalled Michael Gorhan, who worked at Regulatory Agencies. "It was more a fact of life, and he was moving on."

I was on the Denver Public Library Commission and agreed to help Mayor Federico Peña with his 1987 reelection bid. Dale Tooley had died suddenly in 1985 from cancer and would not be part of this race.

I also was working with Sue O'Brien, who was the campaign manager for Roy Romer's bid for governor in 1986. O'Brien was Governor Richard Lamm's press secretary, so this was a new role for her.

Cathy Donohue urged me to run for an at-large city council seat in the 1987 election. Before I attended the council meeting, Maria Garcia Berry and I met for lunch.

"I remember that day like it was yesterday," she recalled. "Wellington told me he was going to run for a city council at-large seat and I said, 'Are you nuts? Why on God's earth don't you run for auditor?' Auditor Mike Licht was going to challenge Mayor Peña, and the auditor's race was wide open."

I went to a council meeting where the thirteen members were having a huge debate over trash collection and alleys. I thought to myself, "I don't want to do this. I've been dealing with presidents of banks and savings-and-loans and insurance companies. I don't want to debate with twelve other people over trash collection."

Wilma agreed that the auditor's office would be a natural fit after my experience at Regulatory Agencies. We got some people together—Joe Webb, Tyrone Holt, Lucious Ashby, Deborah Tucker, Theresa Donahue, and Garcia Berry—and had a retreat in the mountains to talk about our organizational plan. Garcia Berry, who was a successful lobbyist, said we would need to raise about $100,000 for the race and I should be the first to announce my candidacy.

I began reading everything I could about former auditors. The most effective auditor, in my opinion, was longtime auditor William McNichols Sr., the father of Mayor Bill McNichols and Governor Steve McNichols.

I'm sure my choice of McNichols Sr. as the city's best auditor would not be shared by former mayor Quigg Newton. On more than one occasion, McNichols Sr. refused to sign contracts when the council tried to spend bond money approved for specific projects to cover such costs as paving streets. McNichols Sr. ran the office the way the people who created the position visualized: as a watchdog.

I asked several people I knew from Governor Richard Lamm's administration for support in the auditor's race.

"I told him if you run like a liberal Democrat, I will not help you," recalled Joan Ringel. "If you run pro-business, I will gladly help."

On November 18, 1986, I announced my candidacy for auditor for the May 1987 election. Unlike the 1983 mayoral race, I was going to announce early and maybe scare off some other candidates. I had a record in Regulatory Agencies of protecting taxpayers and consumers. I had been on the library board and had a lot more city exposure than I did in 1983.

Auditor Licht had been at constant odds with Mayor Peña. One example was that Licht had reported to the press that the city was

186

running a $10 million deficit, whereas Mayor Peña had insisted the city was $16 million in the black.

I promised voters that I would be a truly independent auditor and an aggressive watchdog for the taxpayers. Because I was a member of Mayor Peña's reelection committee, some critics said I would give the mayor a free pass. But I made it clear that I would objectively keep an eye on the mayor and city council. I would criticize or support the mayor and council when appropriate.

I was pleased that several council members showed up for my announcement of my candidacy for the auditor's seat, including Bill Roberts, Cathy Donohue, and Hiawatha Davis. Also present were State Senator Regis Groff, Lieutenant Governor Mark Hogan, and Congresswoman Pat Schroeder, who was chair of my steering committee.

Some of the people who worked for me at Regulatory Agencies ran my campaign. Diana Rich was my campaign manager, and her husband, Hugh Humphries, also helped me with the campaign. Deborah Tucker, my press spokeswoman at Regulatory Agencies, took a leave of absence to work with the media for my campaign.

More than 300 people cosponsored our first fund-raising event, and Governor Lamm introduced me.

One thing happened that I did not anticipate: Licht was so despised that the council was seriously considering asking voters to abolish the auditor's position. At one time, Cathy Donohue even thought about running for auditor so she could eliminate the office.

"I still believe that there should be an accountant for the city, and [we should] give the audit function to the council," Donohue said.

I went before city council and testified as to why the city should keep the elected auditor position. Councilman Sal Carpio initially voted to abolish the office and then changed his mind after we spoke. Sam Sandos was absent from the meeting, and the issue died on a 6–6 vote.

Cathy Donohue and Councilman Ted Hackworth were still unhappy, so I challenged them to debate the merits of maintaining the auditor's office. They both came to support my candidacy.

What I would later learn as auditor—and, to a greater extent, as mayor—is that council members want to be sitting in the mayor's chair and want more control. That's why they often play to the television camera at the council's Monday night meetings: they want the spotlight on themselves.

I got through that battle, and the campaign was running smoothly until a few months before the election. Four new candidates entered the race: Joe Ciancio, a north Denver Democrat who served on the council and was a member of McNichols's cabinet as the Parks and Recreation director; David Lewis, who worked in the auditor's office; Richard Grimes, a barber who thought the office should be abolished; and Bill Schroeder, a Republican and former Denver Public Schools Board of Education member (who is not related to Pat Schroeder). Both Joe and Bill had name recognition and longtime political support in the community. Ciancio worried me the most. I went to one of the popular Italian restaurants in northwest Denver and spoke to members of the Italian community. They said I had a lot of cojones for campaigning on Ciancio's territory, and if Ciancio didn't make a runoff, I would get their support.

I liked campaigning in northwest Denver because of the variety of cultures. I learned about the neighborhoods by visiting the Catholic churches. Within a twenty-block radius, there's Our Lady of Mount Carmel, which is historically Italian; Our Lady of Guadalupe, established for the Latino community; and St. Dominic's, whose foundation was established by Irish immigrants. All three congregations also had strong union ties.

There was another territorial war between me and Ciancio during the campaign. My favorite spot to wave at motorists was at Federal Boulevard and Alameda Avenue. People can see you while they are driving in all directions. Ciancio got to my corner earlier one day than I did. I was forty-six years old at the time, Ciancio was sixty-four, and we were acting like prostitutes trying to stake out the best spot.

I asked political consultant Eric Sondermann, who had come up with Mayor Peña's slogan, "Imagine a Great City," to help with my advertising. He suggested we raise about $40,000 for radio ads because they would get more play than one television commercial. He coined my campaign slogan, "Thoroughly Qualified, Totally Fair."

Developer Larry Mizel, along with Ruben Valdez, Garcia Berry, and black elected officials, helped raise the big money. As with all of my campaigns, Wilma and Joe worked very hard to make sure I was successful.

My campaign was building momentum, and I got endorsements from the Board of Realtors, Denver Area Labor Federation, members of the black postal workers union in Denver, the black newspapers, council members, and *The Denver Post* and *Rocky Mountain News.*

Another strong endorsement came from the gay and lesbian community. Members remembered me introducing the first antidiscrimination bill to protect the rights of people of all sexual orientations. I also was the first public-sector official to serve on the board for the Colorado AIDS Project.

We were able to garner support from my record in Governor Lamm's cabinet.

"Wellington had a reputation in the Lamm administration of being a very good manager with the budget and personnel," said Mike Stratton. "With the auditor being the budget watchdog, this was a good position for him, and it put him in a good position to eventually run for mayor."

By early May, we had raised $68,000, compared to Ciancio's $17,000 and Schroeder's $10,000.

The newspapers kept saying that if elected, I would be Denver's first black auditor. I didn't want to be labeled a black candidate. I wanted people to look at me as the right person for the job.

Mayor Peña was having a rough time with his reelection. Republican attorney Don Bain came out with some very comical commercials that showed Mayor Peña surrounded by bodyguards.

I had hoped to get 51 percent of the vote in the primary and avoid a runoff. Mayor Peña's people were praying I got 49 percent, because he needed me in a runoff to get out the minority vote.

The night of the primary, my campaign workers wanted to open the champagne when the results started rolling in, but I knew the vote was too close to celebrate yet.

I ended up with 57,000 votes, or 49 percent, and faced Schroeder, a nice and decent man, in the runoff. Mayor Peña and Bain tied with 47 percent. We both were ready for round two.

"I think this was the first time that two minorities were running for a top public office, with Wellington for auditor and Peña for reelection," said John McBride, a northeast Denver activist. "I had my doubts that they both could get elected, but people of Denver vote for the person, not the color of their skin."

On the night of the runoff, it was finally time to pop the corks on the chilled champagne. I won the auditor's race with 91,000 votes, or 63 percent, to Schroeder's 52,000 votes, or 36 percent. To his credit, Schroeder came to our campaign headquarters like a gentleman and congratulated me.

"At times, we got a little testy with each other, but we were men enough to shake hands early, and we can shake hands now as well," I told Schroeder during my victory party.

"I will do absolutely nothing to interfere with your office," Schroeder responded that night. He kept his word.

Mayor Peña won the election by only 3,026 votes over Bain, in large part due to the high turnout of black voters in northeast Denver. It would be a rough four years for him.

"Peña was just shredded by the media on a daily basis," recalled Paula Herzmark.

I was the only candidate running for office that year who supported a ballot item that would have used a percentage of the city's budget for the homeless. The issue failed by 62 percent of the vote. During my terms as mayor, I worked to get the homeless money and leased a city building to the Colorado Coalition for the Homeless for $1 for thirty years to convert to about a hundred apartments. But because I didn't do even more, there were homeless advocates who said some very unkind things about me at the end of my tenure. It reminded me that you can support a group on nine out of ten issues, but if you weren't there for them 100 percent, you became the enemy. I faced similar treatment from some of the unions.

As with all of my jobs, I wanted to leave a mark on the auditor's office. I began assembling my staff with the help of my transition team: Garcia Barry; attorney Jim Bull; CPA Ed Meyer, who had worked with me at Goodrich Grocery as a butcher when I was in high school; and Hugh Catherwood. Hugh, a former city-budget director, also was staff director for Mayor Newton. He negotiated most of the fights between the auditor and mayor's office and the city council and the mayor's office.

Even before I was sworn in as auditor, the media began asking if I planned to run for mayor in 1991. I honestly can say that I was so thrilled to be back in an elected position that the future didn't enter my mind. My goal was for voters to remember me doing a great job as auditor, and it was going to take a lot of work to turn the office around.

I asked all of the auditor's staff, including supervisors, to write down their job descriptions, including what they did and who they reported to. This helped me understand who was really doing the work in the office, whether they had titles or not.

I also met with Joe Shoemaker, a former legislator and lawyer who understood city politics. I asked Director of the Department of Public Works Bill Smith, a longtime city employee, to advise me when city issues came up because, unlike most politicians, I knew that the wisdom of longtime employees can be invaluable.

My first acts as auditor were to resolve outstanding conflicts between former auditor Licht and Mayor Peña, including a lawsuit over Denver General Hospital and unsigned contracts for architectural work at Stapleton International Airport.

I liked Licht, but he threatened to sue me when I reversed his financial statement to show that the city actually had a $9.2 million surplus. Licht had been playing with the figures to make Mayor Peña look bad before Licht entered the mayoral race.

I also wanted to professionalize the office, and I used my handful of political appointees to hire people. I brought in CPA Patti

Beer, made her my deputy auditor, and put her over the audit section. I appointed CPA Tom Migaki, who was working in the finances section at Stapleton, as director of general accounting. Humphries was my director of budget and management. When he resigned, I hired CPA Charles Rutland to run that division. Jim Martinez and Elbra Wedgeworth later joined my staff.

"Wellington Webb wanted to bring some respectability and accountability to the auditor's office," said Migaki, a Denver native and second-generation Japanese American.

Rutland, from Macon, Georgia, had met me in 1984 when he started the first Great American Cookies company franchise in Denver and was looking for investors. Rutland had watched the auditor's race from the sidelines.

"I was always a political agnostic," Rutland said. "I didn't believe in the political god. But Wellington appeared to be committed to change. Before he hired me, he didn't ask if I was a Democrat or Republican. It wasn't important to him. He wanted a CPA and someone who was technically qualified. He didn't know I was a Republican."

I also pushed for modernizing the city's technology and finally getting the city's payroll computerized. The workload was large for me and my staff.

"I was twenty-six when he hired me," Rutland said. "He wasn't afraid of a bunch of young people. Of course, we were all unmarried and could work until midnight and get up early the next day. He was the kind of leader who made you want to do well."

In 1989, I brought Theresa Donahue over from her state job at Regulatory Agencies to the auditor's office.

We started making some commonsense changes. Businesses had complained to me during the campaign that it took months for the city to pay its bills to the private sector. I made sure the bills were paid in a timely manner. I also strongly enforced the city's prevailing-wage ordinance. The law requires that contractors working on city projects pay a wage calculated by what is the going rate for federal projects in the same city. The auditor's office wasn't keeping an eye on these projects, and contractors were getting away with paying lower salaries and keeping the savings as their profits. My policy created a strong working relationship with the Colorado Building and Construction Trades Council.

I also wanted to find a new way to work with the mayor and council. I planned to attend the mayor's weekly meeting with council members, which took place in the mayor's office. The mayor reviews contracts and projects with department heads and the council.

The initial comment out of the mayor's office was they didn't know where I would sit. If I sat with the council, I would appear to be aligned with them. If I sat near the mayor, it would appear I favored him.

So I did the next best thing. Ted Glickman was my first liaison to the city council and mayor. He attended the meetings and then reported back to me. Wedgeworth, who would later be elected to the city council, eventually took over that job. I was the first auditor to have a staff member hear firsthand what was going on in those meetings.

I also set a new policy that if the auditor's office found problems in a city agency, we would work with the agency to correct the issues instead of feeding the information to the media. Previous auditors would do the work of reporters and run reports for them instead of making the journalists do their own digging. Therefore, the stories were rife with quotes from the auditor attempting to score points with voters. I instructed Tucker as my spokeswoman to change that policy. Reporters had to file Freedom of Information requests and sort through the hundreds of vouchers and bills themselves. I'm sure I made no friends with the press, but I wanted to be fair to the departments and not embarrass them in the media. There were times the departments or council ignored our concerns, and then we went public with the information.

One example is when we publicized the discovery that the NBA Denver Nuggets owed the city more than $206,000 in unpaid taxes. The city hadn't previously audited the team, which was struggling financially.

Even though I had a much better relationship with Mayor Peña than the previous auditor, we had some clashes that Mayor Peña's supporters never forgot. Among our disagreements, I supported two Park Hill housewives who opposed a plan to place park department offices in City Park. One woman said the city's charter did not allow city offices in designated parks. The issue went to court. A judge agreed that the city charter prohibited parks from being used for city operations such as office space.

We also disagreed with a budget issue over Denver General Hospital, which was deeply in debt.

Although it may have appeared that Mayor Peña and I were at odds in the newspaper headlines, overall I supported his administration. When a recall effort against Mayor Peña began in 1988, I spoke out strongly in support of the mayor. I thought the recall effort was blatantly unfair and, to some degree, racist. I thought Peña took on more animosity, not because of his policies, but because he was the first to change the old guard from Mayor McNichols's era to his new guard. The questions and scrutiny were tough because he was the city's first minority leader.

I also opposed the recall because it would have hurt the city's credit rating.

New people were in charge, and the old guard resented the city government's openness to new ideas, new policies, new people, and a plan for a new airport.

I would soon be faced with my own political crisis because of an issue called "The Webb Fund." I would also face personal crisis due to my involvement in a near-fatal car accident.

Chapter Sixteen

The Webb Fund, Car Accident,
Mayor Federico Peña's Announcement

Becoming auditor increased my expenses. This is one part of public office that many people never get a grip on. Serving in an elected office is more suited to wealthy people.

There were things I wanted to do as a public official. I thought it was important to send out sympathy cards, fiftieth-anniversary cards, and birthday cards to longtime residents. The same was true of flowers for special occasions and funerals. Some people say these are nice things to do and also politically smart.

The question becomes, who pays for such items? You can't use public funds, so unless you are personally wealthy, you have to find another way to pay for the items. Legally, you can set up a fund that is made up of private donations.

Mayor Federico Peña had such a fund simply called The Mayor's Fund. Former mayors Bill McNichols and Tom Currigan had funds called, respectively, Billy's Boosters' Club and the Tom Tom Club.

Most of the funds raised between $15,000 and $20,000 annually.

With the help of my friend Lucius Ashby, we set up The Webb Fund.

The first fund-raiser was hosted by cable-television magnate Bill Daniels at his home, called Cableland. We had it in February and called the event Leap Forward with Webb.

This was not a secret fund-raiser. More than 300 people showed up, and we raised about $20,000.

As a family, we faced a dilemma of whom we should invite to our daughter, Stephanie's, wedding. I thought it was important to expand the guest list to include other elected officials and VIPs. That required more expense, which we took out of the fund. If I were wealthy, I would have been able to pay for it out of my pocket.

Questions arose as to whether that was the appropriate way to use the fund. The issue came up again during the 1991 mayoral race. The fund was legal, but this was an easy headline for my opponents to try to make me look bad.

After the 1991 election, I sent checks to the Internal Revenue Service (IRS) for $2,056 for federal income tax and $367 for Colorado income tax to cover the money we spent on Stephanie's wedding from The Webb Fund.

In 1994, my CPA sent me a letter stating that the statute of limitations had expired and the federal government could not accept the $2,056. I responded to the IRS telling them to accept the money as a voluntary tax payment.

The State of Colorado accepted the $367 even though the statute of limitations had expired.

I never made it public, as I was not required to, that I made the payments, but I kept the records in case anyone ever asked.

That political headache was minor compared to a real near tragedy.

Sometimes your life starts to move out of control when you try to juggle too much. I was at a fund-raiser for Gail Schoettler, who was running for state treasurer. I needed to leave that event in southeast Denver and pick up Wilma for a reception in honor of Reverend Paul Martin, the new pastor of Macedonia Baptist Church.

I wanted to keep my political base strong, but at this time, I had no intention of running against Mayor Peña if he were to seek a third term. I thought the incumbent mayor, who had weathered some tough issues, deserved my support. My goal was to get another four years in the auditor's office.

These things were on my mind when I was driving along Colorado

Boulevard and decided to change lanes. All of a sudden, to my horror, I saw a woman's face in front of my windshield. It was clear I had hit a pedestrian. My instincts caused me to slam on the brakes and pray this woman was alive and not badly injured. She had hit the windshield and fallen onto Colorado Boulevard.

When I got to her, she wasn't moving. I was worried oncoming traffic might not see her, so I moved my car and shone the headlights onto the oncoming traffic to warn motorists.

I called Wilma and told her to call 911 and please come to the accident site. A witness who saw the accident also called 911. Later I learned that the woman, who had on dark clothing, had run out in front of my car. Her name was Teresa Carroll. She lived near Colorado Boulevard and was on her way home when the accident happened.

The whole thing was just a flash in my mind; it happened so quickly. Wilma and I headed to the hospital and continued to pray for the woman. I thought she was dead.

I spoke to a hospital psychologist who had been sent to see us because of the trauma of the accident. This nightmare was even more frightening than watching James Thompson die. How was I going to deal with a fatal accident?

The headline the next day was "Webb Injures Pedestrian." Deborah Tucker put out a press release relaying my sincere hope that the woman would recover and that the accident was under investigation by the police. The car was impounded, and police checked the skid marks to see if I was speeding.

"All that Wellington could think about was if the woman was going to be okay," said Charlotte Stephens, who worked in the auditor's office. "That's all he cared about."

I did not get a ticket as a result the accident, and we settled the insurance claims. Carroll later supported me in the 1991 mayoral race with a contribution and her vote.

Most of all, I was thankful Teresa Carroll recovered.

Once that trauma settled, I began focusing on my reelection for auditor in 1991. I was really proud of the fact that some people who later became my critics while I was mayor, namely Councilman Ted Hackworth, recognized that I brought professionalism to the auditor's office. We expanded the staff and brought in qualified people who understood finances and audits. We were less political than previous auditors.

I would have been content to spend another four years making even more improvements as auditor. Then a single phone call changed my future.

I was attending a fund-raiser in Detroit hosted by Mayor Coleman Young for my reelection campaign. I picked up the phone, and one of Mayor Peña's aides, Penfield Tate III, told me that in about an hour Mayor Peña was going to announce that he was not going to run for reelection. The news was a bombshell. Mayor Peña had silenced most of his critics and survived a recall effort. Why was he leaving office now? But as I would later realize, it is always good to go out on top.

I knew I had to make a quick decision whether to continue my reelection for auditor, a much safer route, or throw myself into an open mayor's race.

Wilma was still serving in the Colorado House of Representatives, and she was attending a convention in Saint Thomas with other black elected officials. I called her about Mayor Peña's decision and asked her to share this with only one other person: Arie Taylor. In hindsight, telling Taylor was like broadcasting the news on CNN.

I asked Wilma to meet me at home as soon as possible and left the fund-raiser in Detroit. After learning the news about Mayor Peña, people in Detroit joked with me whether the checks should be made out for my race for auditor or mayor.

Most people were stunned by Mayor Peña's announcement. But those who worked at city hall saw the toll the job had taken on Mayor Peña, including his battle scars with the council over the new airport.

"I was not surprised when Peña made his announcement," said Cathy Donohue, a council member at the time. "He saw that there had to be an outsider to get that airport opened."

What I didn't learn until 2006 is that my good friend Paul Sandoval also didn't think Mayor Peña would seek a third term, and

Sandoval was preparing a campaign for someone else.

"Peña was married by then, and his wife didn't like politics," Sandoval recalled. "It was a grind on him. My gut was telling me he wouldn't run, and we quietly got a campaign going for Pat Grant."

Grant, a former legislator, was serving as president of the National Western Stock Show. Sandoval got Grant's campaign under way at the urging of our friend Bill Daniels, who promised to help Grant raise $1 million for the race.

A couple of weeks before Mayor Peña made his announcement, Grant told Sandoval the National Western Stock Show board wasn't thrilled with the idea of Grant running for mayor. He pulled out, and Sandoval later campaigned for me.

Shortly after Mayor Peña's announcement, I quickly polled my auditor's staff, and six of seven urged me to run for mayor.

"I asked him if he was really ready to deal with the press that would cover everything from how many times he went to the bathroom every day," recalled Theresa Donahue.

Charles Rutland was in New York at a bond conference when Deborah Tucker sent him an urgent message to call her.

"I was worried something physical had happened to Wellington," Rutland recalled. "When she told me Peña was not going to run for reelection, I didn't believe her. I thought it was a joke."

Rutland caught the next flight from LaGuardia back to Denver.

"I wanted to get to him before others told him not to run or that he couldn't win," Rutland said. "I told him, 'Not only should you run, but you can win.'"

Jim Martinez also pushed hard for me to run for mayor.

The most important discussion was with my family. Wilma and I invited family members to our home and explained to them the difficulty of a mayoral campaign. We had a house full of about thirty people. We told them they would all be suspect, and anything they did could wind up in the newspapers and hurt the campaign. We had all of our children, their spouses, and their children; brothers and sisters; and nieces and nephews at the meeting.

We then went to our pastor, Reverend W. T. Liggins, and prayed together. On Sunday, he brought us before the congregation and announced that the next mayor of Denver would be a member of Zion Baptist Church.

I knew I had my nuclear and extended family, my political family, my church family, my high-school family, and my true friends behind me. They believed I could win, despite the doubters.

I also knew my biggest competition could be one of the original members of my political group, Denver District Attorney Norm Early.

"It looked like Norm Early was going to get into the race, and he was the 800-pound gorilla," said Maria Garcia Berry. "I told Wellington and Wilma if they could look at themselves in the mirror every morning and be willing to work harder than anyone else in the race, they should do this. But they had to want it more than anyone else. I thought this was his time and he should go for it."

Denver Post columnist Chuck Green was enamored with Early. He described him as a cross between John F. Kennedy and Reverend Jesse Jackson. He saw me negatively, as a professional politician with a forced personality and as little competition for Early.

Peter Blake of the *Rocky Mountain News* also tagged Early to be the likely winner.

Meanwhile, Freeman Cosmo Harris, publisher of the African American *Denver Weekly* newspaper, wrote editorials calling for my candidacy.

There also was some talk that Councilman Bill Roberts might enter the race. I had always thought that Roberts might be the city's first black mayor. Before Mayor Peña ran, I thought Councilman Sal Carpio would be the first Latino mayor.

Everyone thought it was a sign that Mayor Peña would run for reelection when Roberts resigned his council seat and agreed to be Mayor Peña's deputy mayor and director of the Department of Public Works. Roberts, whose family owned Empire Construction Services, was as stunned as anyone by Mayor Peña's announcement.

"I thought about running for mayor, but my family agreed it

was time to grow our company," recalled Roberts in 2004, about two years before his death. "It was a very tough decision. I always wondered how it would have been to be mayor. Politics is fun, and a challenge, and Denver's mayor is very strong."

Before Roberts announced he wouldn't run for mayor, a conservative white friend of mine, banker Walt Emery, came into my office.

"Two colored fellows running for mayor is enough," Emery said. "Three is out of the question. All that you guys are going to do is cut each other up."

His comments reminded me of another comical moment from when I was auditor. I came in late one night to my office and found one of the security guards, who was about seventy, sleeping in my chair. He jumped up with his flashlight—thank goodness he didn't have a gun—and yelled at me, "You better get the hell out of here before the auditor comes in."

I told him the auditor said I could use his office. It was quite ironic that a city worker didn't know he was sleeping in my chair.

I spent a couple of days talking to people about the mayoral race and thinking of the consequences. There's always the fear of failure. I was more afraid this time because if I lost, I would be seen as a two-time loser.

Eventually, I overcame that fear and decided to pursue the job.

Once I decided to run for mayor, I needed to get a good organization in place. We had to make sure that the campaign didn't come out like the one in 1983 did, which was half-assed, backward, and slow getting started.

I asked Paula Herzmark to be my campaign chair and Ruben Valdez to be my treasurer. People never understood why I wanted them both so badly. They're smart, qualified people and my friends, but also, I am superstitious. When we were all in Governor Richard Lamm's cabinet, every time that Valdez, Herzmark, and I were on the same page, we were always successful.

Herzmark was very hesitant. I knew she was being lobbied by people to keep me out of the race. She told me the easiest decision would be to run and the more difficult decision would be not to run. But if I decided to run, she would be my campaign chair.

"I really thought that if he went through with the campaign and he didn't just lose but got annihilated, it would hurt any efforts for his political career," Herzmark said. "I cared too much for him personally to see that happen."

Valdez's support would help me in the Hispanic community because his name appeared on all of our advertising.

"I thought once Peña decided not to run, Wellington would," recalled Valdez, who immediately agreed to be treasurer of the campaign.

I asked Steve Welchert, who worked for Governor Lamm and was a debate coach for Mayor Peña, if he would run my campaign. We had worked together on the city's largest bond project in 1989, which poured millions into roads and parks, the National Western Complex, and several street viaducts.

"While I was flattered, I decided to run myself," Welchert said. "The domino started when Wellington ran for mayor. There was an open auditor's seat, and in a moment of insanity, I decided to run for auditor."

Early was already coming in as a favorite and was snatching up the established political people for his campaign. Mike Stratton, who ran my 1983 campaign, suggested I talk to a young man named Mike Dino.

Dino was a Denver native who was the deputy campaign director for Governor Roy Romer's reelection campaign, which Stratton managed. He also ran unsuccessfully for a University of Colorado regent position, so he had seen both sides of a campaign.

"Dino was the perfect match for Wellington," Stratton said.

Dino, who was twenty-six at the time, heard through Cole Finegan that I might run for mayor. Finegan, who was new to Denver but had run other successful congressional campaigns in Oklahoma and other states, would eventually run Early's campaign.

"I didn't know Wellington," Dino recalled. "I saw him as aloof and distant but thought he would be a formidable candidate. He knew the city and would be a substantive candidate."

Dino had a degree in banking and was working with his father, Sandy, who was part of the Resolution Trust, whose mission was to clean up savings-and-loan scandals.

"I went with him to New York to close down some savings and loans," Dino said. "I thought I would be getting out of politics. I didn't think campaigns were that much fun."

Dino spent time after Governor Romer's campaign traveling to watch the Colorado State University Rams in the Holiday Bowl and the University of Colorado Buffaloes win the national championship in Miami. Meanwhile, I was leaving messages for him to call me.

"I knew why he was calling. I thought to myself, 'I do not want to do this,'" Dino said.

When we finally met, Dino played up his campaign experience, whereas I said I would raise a mythical $1 million.

"Oh, man, when he said $1 million, I knew that was unrealistic," Dino said. "Romer didn't raise that kind of money, and he was the incumbent governor."

I didn't know that Dino almost didn't take the job.

"Mike Stratton told me the campaign would be like getting my master's degree in politics," Dino said. "Mike told me Wellington was not going to win and would be a good third place. I would be done in six months and then I could move on. I thought, *Okay, I can do this.*"

I agreed to pay Dino $2,500 a month to run the campaign. He asked for a $10,000 bonus if we won the election, which is a common practice in large campaigns.

"That's when I really got to know Wellington's frugalness," Dino said. "He said, 'Your bonus will be if we win.' I just said, 'Okay.' I think the key is that we really hit it off right away. We're both tall and we both played basketball, although he was a better player than me. There's an unspoken ability for athletes of the same sport to relate to each other."

I knew our finances could be a little shaky. I took what money I had left from my auditor's campaign, and I paid the rent on our new campaign office at Seventeenth Avenue and Ogden Street and the phones through the entire election period. We may not have had a dollar or dime left, but we would have an office and phones throughout the campaign.

At our campaign headquarters' opening, legislator Dennis Gallagher introduced me to the crowd.

"The auditor knows where all of the bodies are buried," Gallagher said, calling me Denver's next mayor.

In December 1990, we asked Mike Donilon, a national pollster, and campaign veteran Mandy Grunwald to do a poll.

I asked everyone to gather at my home to hear the results. Dino and I were the last to arrive. When we walked in, the faces in the room looked like someone had died. And from the poll's results, the nearly dearly departed appeared to be me.

The poll showed that only 7 percent of Denver voters would vote for me if the election had been the day the person was called. Early came out with 67 percent.

"If you ask me whether I think you should run or not, I would have to say no," Donilon frankly told me.

Grunwald, who went on to work for national presidential campaigns, agreed my race would be an uphill battle.

We ended the evening with the rest of my political eulogy by projecting that all of the smart money would go to Early.

Bob Ozinga of the Colorado Building and Construction Trades Council gave me a great big bear hug before he left.

"I'll be with you until the end," Ozinga told me. What he meant was, he knew I was going to my political death if I ran, but he would be there with me as I died on the campaign battlefield.

Wilma said she didn't believe the poll was an accurate indicator.

"There is no way in world that you could have been a state representative, HHS director, Regulatory Agencies director, auditor, and only register 7 percent," she told me.

I believed the poll. It was a snapshot of what voters were thinking that day. So it was a long night of trying to decide whether to proceed with the race.

Early the next morning, my brother Joe showed up in his police cruiser. He barreled up our sidewalk with his gun belt over his shoulder while buttoning his shirt.

"There were a lot of 'experts' who told Wellington he had no shot," Joe recalled. "The poll said no one knows him and he had only 7 percent and to forget about it. He looked demoralized. I came back to his house on my way to work the next day and told him, 'Don't you think about giving up. This is a street fight. It doesn't matter what people say. You have to stay and fight.'"

I laughed at Joe and told him, "Wilma and I came to that same conclusion last night. We'll take a shot at it."

But I also told him the race would be like the fight at the OK Corral. It was going to be a reckoning. It would be about the last man standing. We were underfunded and outgunned. We had a smaller campaign staff. All of the party operatives were conveniently unable to assist for fear of what would happen if someone else won and they were punished.

Joe was ready for the election battle. He had just finished night law school and was offered a fellowship. Instead, he gave up that fellowship to work on my campaign.

As Joe drove away from the curb, all that I could think was, *How the hell do we move up from 7 percent with the election just six months away?* I knew that if I could get enough votes to come in second and force a runoff, I had a good chance to win.

We started having a series of meetings at our house with former Manual High School classmates.

"No one really expected Wellington to win," recalled Ruthelene Wesley Johnson. "But we got Manual graduates, called Manualites, and the East High School Angels, where the Webb children went to school, and we worked for him."

At the same time, Dino started building his campaign staff. He hired a young kid from southeastern Colorado, Greg Kolomitz;

another young guy, Ken Smith, who had worked on some national campaigns; and another young campaign worker, Charles Ellis.

The average age of my campaign staff was twenty-six.

The seasoned campaign professionals who didn't join the Early campaign went to work for Republican attorney Don Bain, the former chair of the state Republican Party who had nearly beaten Mayor Peña in the 1987 race. Bain, who had worked with me on the library commission, was seen as the top candidate next to Early.

I remember my campaign crew coming to my meetings wearing blue jeans, sweatshirts, sandals, or tennis shoes. Little did they know that a short time later, they'd need three-piece suits.

"We were not the pick of the litter," Dino recalled. "Norm and Don had bigger budgets, and we were the third fiddle. But we were not slackers. We did what we had to do, although we didn't always do it efficiently."

The staff fed off of the competition of beating Early's people.

"It was an intense, personal campaign," Kolomitz said. "They were the 'haves'; we were the 'have nots.' It was the insiders versus the outsiders."

Herzmark suggested that Arnie Grossman do the media work. He had worked for Pat Schroeder. I also wanted Venita Vinson, whom I had known since the early 1970s, and Charlotte Stephens to work with Dino, especially in the black community, in addition to Wilma and my brother Joe.

The campaign staff was rounded out with community activists Mary Sylvester and John McBride. My auditor's staff also helped on the campaign when they weren't in the office doing their city work.

Tom Migaki helped organize every Asian event, whereas Martinez and Sandoval worked hard in the Hispanic community.

My oldest son, Keith, who owned a gay bar, helped immensely in organizing support in the gay and lesbian community. (When I was fighting for preventing discrimination based on sexual orientation in the 1970s, I never dreamed our oldest son would be gay.) He fought to save my political life.

Keith took Wilma and me on a tour of gay bars, and some of the patrons were surprised when I asked for their vote. Never before had a candidate so aggressively asked for the gay community's support. Keith also rallied gay newspapers to run advertisements in support of my candidacy and for endorsements. He would come through for me again in the 1995 race.

My other children, Tony, Allen, and Stephanie, organized their friends from high school and college to support me. They also provided free labor along with my brothers, nieces, and nephews by handing out campaign literature and campaign signs.

My family never relented. They felt if I lost, they lost, too. If I won, it was a victory for the entire family.

The agonizing task of raising money in 1991 was tackled by Rita Kahn, Fabby Hillyard, and Donna Good.

I knew that we might not raise the most money or get the most headlines or be the favorite candidate. But I also knew that I, Wilma, our family, and my campaign staff would do one thing: work our butts off for the next six months.

Chapter Seventeen

1991 Mayoral Campaign, Doubters, Tennis Shoes

While Mike Dino and I were trying to get the campaign into full gear, others were pleading with me to get out of the race.

"We begged him to death to get out of the race," said Paula Herzmark, my campaign chair. "I was afraid it would hurt his career if we allowed him to get mauled by Norm Early. His own staff was telling him to get the hell out. I don't think he ever seriously considered quitting.

"It still embarrasses me that I was so wrong," Herzmark said. "It says a lot about Wellington that he didn't quit. And Wilma never would let the campaign go down the drain."

In the black community, the issue was, if we're going to back a candidate among two black men, let's back the one who appears to be able to win. Even though many in the black community had known me longer and I had helped many of them, they put their support behind Early.

"My thoughts were that both guys had proven to be good public servants," recalled former city councilman Bill Roberts. "People did agonize about the race. The black community in Denver is not that large, and not that many are active in politics."

In some cases, black families were split on who they were supporting. As I drove through black neighborhoods, I often saw campaign signs for both me and Early in the same yard. Even spouses were split on who they were endorsing.

Individuals in the black community knew this mayoral race was like a Muhammad Ali versus Joe Frazier boxing match. People outside the black community just saw it as two black politicians possibly knocking themselves out.

The black community knew this was a real contest between two African American political groups and the competition that started with Arie Taylor and Regis Groff was finally going to come to an end with Early and me.

What most people also didn't understand was that the black community is not monolithic. We're individuals who make individual choices.

So it was no surprise that once Early and I announced our candidacies, the lines were drawn in the sand. The same people who supported Taylor in the black community ended up supporting me. The same people who backed Regis and Gloria Tanner ended up in Early's corner.

Some people tried to make me feel bad that having two black men in the race endangered both of our chances, thus I should bow out.

But I knew the real difference between me and Early was that my roots in the community were deep. When push came to shove, the people who knew me best would work harder than ever to make sure I didn't fail.

"While Paula was telling him to drop out gracefully, I told him that was bullshit," said John McBride, a black activist who joined my campaign. "Norm looks like what white folks think a black mayor should be, and that's why a lot of people supported him in the beginning. Yeah, Norm's a *GQ* magazine kind of a guy. Wellington was homegrown with grassroots support, not only from blacks, but from Chicanos. Norm had no connection to the black community."

My neighbors and classmates at Manual High School expanded my grassroots campaign.

"I was one of the people who wrote him a recommendation telling people he would make a good mayor," said my grandmother's longtime neighbor Ira Slack. "There was another black fellow running, Norm Early. I liked him, but not enough for him to be mayor."

Members of my auditor staff also encouraged me to stay in the race.

"By this point, I had become a political evangelist," said Charles Rutland. "I was filled with the Holy Spirit, and the polls didn't matter. Wellington wasn't the glamorous candidate, but he reflected Denver. Denver voters are sophisticated, and they vote for the candidate of substance."

But it became clear that organizations were lining up early to support Early.

"The chamber could not relate to Wellington," said Joan Ringel. "Peña was more preppy. Wellington was a black man happy to be a black man. He was not going to be an Oreo to make them happy."

I dismissed the so-called political experts and got ready to officially announce my candidacy.

When I made the announcement on February 4, 1991, I was surrounded by the oddest assortment of supporters—and that was on purpose. They included three bankers I had worked with previously: Berne Hart, chairman and CEO of the United Banks of Colorado; John Coates, chairman of Century Bank of Cherry Creek; and Walt Emery, president of the Bank of Denver.

Reverend Acen Phillips of the Black Ministerial Alliance, who never wavered during my entire political career, was there next to Emery, a conservative banker. Emery, on occasion, still used the terms *colored* and *Negro*, not because he was a racist, but because those were the terms of his generation.

"Norm and I were friends," Phillips said. "Norm couldn't understand why Wellington would not back down when Norm had all of the money and the political strength. Norm wanted him out of the race. But Wellington had a vision, and I believe that vision comes from God."

At the announcement, I was surrounded by my family and longtime supporters from the legislature, city council, and northeast Denver.

"Everyone on the podium was pretty black, as expected,"

Herzmark recalled. "Edna Mosley, a black Aurora city council-woman, grabbed my arm and said, 'We need to get some white folks in that front row.' I appreciated her comment because of the many campaigns I had been involved with when I said, 'We have to get some black folks in the front row.' I loved it. There was a certain symmetry to it."

February was a good month for the campaign because the *Rocky Mountain News* did an unscientific poll that said I looked like a front-runner. That was followed by a successful Democratic Party event at East High School.

"Ken Smith was a great advance guy," Dino recalled. "He had Webb signs everywhere at East. Early's people blew off the event. Webb got the press. The poll came out first and then the Saturday event. We felt like we were rocking. For the first ten days, it looked like we had life and there was enthusiasm."

Smith, a Denver native, had worked on state and national campaigns, including the unsuccessful presidential runs for Pat Schroeder and Gary Hart. He didn't know me well, but Jamie Byrd, a mutual friend of Taylor's, gave him some advice.

"She told me that Taylor would kick my ass if I didn't work for Wellington," Smith said. "I knew Wellington would be a long shot, but I needed a job. People in my circle said I would identify more with Wellington than Norm."

Smith found out quickly that the campaign had little money. For instance, we had no cash to buy more paper for the copy machine or for postage to mail campaign literature.

In contrast, the Early campaign was able to equip its field workers with cell phones, which were new technology in 1991.

"Cell phones were as big as bricks back then," Greg Kolomitz said. "Someone in our campaign found a shoe box, and we made a fake cell phone."

Some of my campaign staff also pitched in to pay for a toy cell phone they bought at a local department store. They'd pretend the phone was real when they were around Early's people.

We never lost our sense of humor or our sense of humbleness.

My fund-raising was also greatly lagging behind Early's and became one topic at our weekly morning campaign meetings.

"I hated going to those meetings so much that I couldn't eat," Dino said. "They were critical of what was not happening, what we were not doing, and that the writing was on the wall."

Dino also was feeling the pressure of Venita Vinson, who wanted to take over the campaign; Charlotte Stephens, who scheduled all of the events in northeast Denver; and Herzmark, who was critical of our every move.

"I accepted Mike for who he was," Stephens said. "Some people thought he was arrogant and a member of the 'White Boys Club.' He was ambitious. He had tunnel vision and was adventurous. Arrogance doesn't have to be thrown out as a dirty word. As my grandmother told me, arrogant people know who they are and are confident."

Deborah Tucker, my spokeswoman for the auditor's office, gave the campaign a strongly worded memo titled "Lack of Discipline on Schedule" on February 21, 1991.

"I am concerned about Wellington's health, his inability to capitalize on speeches, personal appearances, and press responses, therefore threatening our fund-raising capacity and eroding our support base," she wrote. "Wellington is literally functioning on 'automatic control' like a robot."

Tucker wanted to take away the burden of me telling people I couldn't be at every event. She demanded I have a structured schedule.

"If we don't protect Wellington's time and quality of appearances, nothing else we do will matter," she wrote. "He'll look terrible all of the time, he will appear to be drained and unresponsive at crucial debates and speeches—trust me—there will be no sympathy from opposing camps nor the press."

As Tucker was pushing for structure in the campaign, I continued to get pressure from the black community to drop out of the race. I heard the Black Ministerial Alliance was going to endorse Early, so I asked for a meeting with the pastors. Stephens asked me if I was going to take some supporters with me, but I wanted to go alone. I agreed to have her drive me to New Hope Baptist Church.

Reverend Phillips stood up for me along with about a handful of pastors from smaller churches. But the rest of the ministers said they would endorse Early, even though they had known me longer. Then they asked me to sign a pact that said if Early made it to the runoff, I would support him, and Early would support me if I made it to the runoff.

"I'm not signing a pact," I said to the shocked ministers. "I'm not sure Norm is going to make it to the runoff. It could be me and Don Bain."

Then I asked what the ministers thought was inconceivable: "What happens if Norm and I run against each other in the run-off?"

They thought I was so arrogant, so silly and backward to think that I really had a chance.

Stephens waited for me in the car during the meeting.

"He came out and I could tell he was hurt and angry," she said. "He felt the ministers' endorsement was key. We just drove around for about forty-five minutes, and he was still pissed. Then he came up with a strategy to focus on the elders in each of the congregations. He also worked with the Jewish, Muslims, Buddist, and the Catholics. We went to enough churches to secure a spot in heaven."

I always had a comfort level with church people because I was raised in the Baptist church. Although most of the black pastors endorsed Early, I knew their members didn't always agree with them. So I made sure that I was escorted into each of the churches by some of the oldest long-standing members who had credibility.

When I went to Shorter Community AME Church where Reverend J. Langston Boyd supported Early, I walked in with Ira Slack, Omar and Jeweldine Blair, and Bill and Winnie Coker. Each of them had been a member of the church for forty years or more. That signaled to the rest of the congregation that the old-timers were in my corner.

At one point during the campaign, I met up with Denver Archbishop James Francis Stafford during a celebration at Our Lady of Guadalupe Church. Archbishop Stafford and I walked side by side in a procession outside to honor the Virgin Mary. Archbishop Stafford was handing out prayer cards that had a picture of Jesus. I told him I needed Jesus too, and asked him if I could hand out my campaign literature. I said if people have a prayer card of Jesus with my Webb card, I know that I would win. He laughed and I walked behind him, handing out my campaign literature.

We would collaborate two years later when Pope John Paul II brought World Youth Day to the Mile High City. The pope later promoted Archbishop Stafford to be a cardinal in Rome.

Some members of my church, Zion Baptist, also didn't think I would get elected. But our pastor, Reverend W. T. Liggins, kept the faith. Every Sunday, Reverend Liggins would say, "Well, let me introduce the next mayor of Denver," before he brought me in front of the congregation.

I promised him that when I was elected, he would do the invocation at my inauguration. He had a huge smile on his face when I came through with a victory. He died less than two weeks after I was elected.

With all the negativity around the campaign, Dino tried to do something positive and convinced me to see an image consultant. Jo Farrell had worked with other politicians, including Governor Roy Romer.

"At the end of the day, I want you to end up talking like Jesse Jackson," she told me during our first session.

Well, I know Jackson and we are friends, but I didn't need to talk like him.

She also told me to shave off my mustache and get my teeth bonded. I've had a gap between my front teeth since I was a kid. She said all celebrities in Hollywood get their teeth bonded.

"You know, I've had this gap in my teeth for my entire life and it's been good luck for me, so I'll keep the gap," I told her. "And I'm going to keep my mustache. It's part of who I am and what I am. If people are only into cosmetics, I'm not going to win."

I had shaved my goatee after the 1983 mayoral race, and there would be no more cosmetic changes.

I also didn't think that visiting a dentist would help cure my fund-raising troubles. Chris Romer, the governor's son, was raising money for Early's campaign, whereas Bain's campaign was soaking up the rest of the cash. Our fund-raising efforts were demoralizing. No one would return our calls.

"We got no money from the big people," said Fabby Hillyard, whose previous experience was raising money for the arts. "But there were little old ladies baking pies and giving us the money from the sales. Every dime we got was from a voter or people who would volunteer. Norm got thousands of dollars from people who didn't even live in the city and couldn't vote."

Rita Kahn, an investment banker, combined a fund-raiser with my fiftieth-birthday celebration in mid-February.

"Ten people showed up," Dino said. "There was no energy for fund-raising."

It also didn't help that even though we didn't have money, we got ourselves into a donation controversy. Mayor Federico Peña made some bold moves during his last days in office. One of those was to limit individual campaign contributions to $3,000 per candidate. Previously, the city had no limit on individual contributions.

Our campaign was poor, so I publicly said I would go one step further and limit each individual contribution to our campaign to $2,000, although I had taken a $10,000 donation from investment bankers when I was auditor.

"I wasn't happy when I learned of the $10,000 donation and having to justify it," Dino recalled.

The controversy over The Webb Fund also resurfaced. *Rocky Mountain News* reporter Kevin Flynn wanted to review all of the donations in the fund, and Early brought up the issue at every opportunity.

"There were only two times I saw Wellington angry during the campaign," Dino recalled. "When The Webb Fund came up during the runoff and when there were deals being made to get him out of the race. That pissed him off. Otherwise, he was on an even keel."

When the Early campaign attacked me with negatives ads, several supporters came to my defense, including Richard Lamm, Berne Hart, and Emery.

"We needed the prominent Anglos to counter the goal of the ads that projected Wellington as some black guy who ran things on the sly, that this guy from the ghetto was cutting deals to take care of his kin," Dino said.

But before we could even get to the runoff, things looked bleak. In March, Dino slashed the staff's salaries, including his own. I was advised to shut down the campaign until we could raise some money.

"If you shut it down, you'll never get the momentum back," Wilma warned me.

Instead of shutting it down, we decided to be the first campaign with ads on television. We only had about $27,000 in the bank, and Herzmark convinced me to give $25,000 to Arnie Grossman for the ads.

Grossman came up with three ads that attacked lawyers. Early and Bain were both attorneys, so we knew the lawyers would back them. The ads basically asked voters, "Who would you want to protect your tax dollars: an auditor with experience or a lawyer?" We did it tongue in cheek, but the joke turned out to be on us. We had climbed slightly in the polls before the ads and then dropped after they aired. The only benefit was we had more name recognition.

Dino didn't like the ads and was worried about the future of the campaign. We often would meet at my house, where Wilma would help with campaign suggestions. She also often cooked for the campaign staff after her long day at the state legislature.

"The staff didn't work for me; they didn't answer to me," Dino said. "They did respect Wellington and answered to him and sometimes listened to me, but that was hit or miss. Wellington was the glue that held us together."

Dino was eating dinner at his parents' home when his mother,

Former governor Richard Lamm really came through for me in the 1991 mayoral election when he not only endorsed my candidacy, but he also defended me against negative attacks by my opponent.

Shirley, urged him not to be discouraged about the campaign.

"My mother is a woman of great faith and said I couldn't quit," Dino said. "My dad told me to cut my losses because what I was basically doing was rearranging the chairs on the deck of the *Titanic*. Fortunately, I listened to my mother."

Although the television ads fizzled, a more successful idea was telling voters our position on a number of issues, a blueprint we dubbed "The Webb Plan." It gave voters an idea of what I would do as mayor.

"The Webb Plan took a lot of work, but it showed Wellington did know the city; he knew the issues, and he had a plan," said Theresa Donahue, who wrote most of the plan, with the help of community activist Mary Sylvester.

Hillyard was the only one who had a computer, so she typed up the plan. She did her own editing to make sure it would fit on one sheet of paper.

Initially, the staff and press were not impressed by the document.

"The Webb Plan did not energize the staff, but in the end, it worked," Dino said. "It showed that Wellington wasn't a pretty boy who was just shaking hands. Every week, we could show how smart we were, and we liked that."

Then a couple of things happened that helped our campaign. The first gulf war broke out, and that allowed us to regroup while the spotlight was off the race and on the war. Then I took a strong position on two issues: the controversial construction of Denver International Airport (DIA) and a call to end court-mandated busing within the Denver Public Schools.

"I knew that once Bain came out against the airport, we could come back quickly and distinguish Wellington from Bain," said Donahue.

Less than twenty-four hours after Bain said the airport should be mothballed, Donahue and Sylvester had me prepare for a press conference where I told voters we must proceed with construction. Early was nowhere to be found.

Bain made his announcement before his own campaign got results of a poll they were doing about the airport. The poll showed 67 percent of Denver voters agreed DIA should be built. This definitely hurt his campaign.

Early also made errors in judgment when he fired Chips Spryer and Mary Alice Mandarich, longtime Denver political workers, as his first campaign managers. They were replaced by Cole Finegan. It looked to me like Early was getting rid of his longtime supporters for a newcomer.

"It became clear that Cole was a professional, but Norm was not a good campaigner," Dino said.

Cole came back to politics in 2003 when Mayor John Hickenlooper appointed him as the city attorney, and later he also served as Mayor Hickenlooper's chief of staff.

I surprised a lot of people—including Wilma—when I proposed ending court-mandated busing in the Denver Public Schools. Like other cities nationwide, Denver was ordered to integrate its schools. Some students were bused to schools miles from their homes.

The concept was initially embraced by some members of the black community because many neighborhood schools in low-income areas were allowed to fall into disrepair, whereas other schools siphoned the funds for the students from middle- and upper-class households.

But the Hispanic community, as well as most whites, did not support busing, and the black community was split on the issue.

What wasn't foreseen was that busing caused many students to not be able to participate in after-school activities, such as music or athletics. The integration also created some racial tension, which caused George Washington High School to temporarily close.

"Wellington asked me what I thought about him coming out against school busing," Dino recalled. "He said the court order served its purpose, and he supported going back to neighborhood schools. I thought it was great: a black candidate for mayor calling for an end to busing. It was front-page headlines."

219

I did not accept the premise that the only way black students could learn was to be in a classroom with white students.

Other members of the black community agreed.

"Busing was a sad chapter that became a political football," said Roberts. "It was a very disappointing time for me. It was not the Denver I loved and bragged about to my friends in Georgia, where I came from."

I did not consult with Wilma, who was a member of the Joint Budget Committee and fighting to maintain transportation funds from the legislature for busing. The cuts would have negatively impacted the Denver Public Schools.

Although my announcement put Wilma in a difficult position, I guessed right with voters. My position against busing gave us an immediate boost in southwest Denver, where Councilman Ted Hackworth, a former school-board member who opposed busing, was popular with Republican constituents.

The next boost for us came when *The Denver Post* quizzed all of the candidates on city issues. I came out on top by correctly answering most of the questions. Bain and Early looked silly. The rules were the same for all of us. *The Denver Post* reporter allowed all of the candidates to answer the questions over the phone.

"It was hilarious," Dino said. "He'd get the questions, and most he would answer correctly right away. But the ones he wasn't sure about, he would repeat out loud. There were six of us running around the office looking for the answers. ... The next day, we got a big headline. We were so proud of ourselves."

Despite those good fortunes, I considered dropping out of the race in early April.

The deadline to keep my name off the ballot was approaching. The Denver Area American Federation of Labor and Congress of Industrial Organizations endorsed Early. Bob Ozinga fought to get the Colorado Building and Construction Trades Council to endorse me, but losing the big unions was discouraging.

I didn't know that Dino was also leaning toward me dropping

out before a remark by Early reignited his competitive spark.

"Norm and Cole were talking after a forum and saw that I couldn't find my way out of the building," Dino said. "Norm said, 'Hey, you're going the wrong way.' It was snippy and snotty and felt like he was rubbing salt in the wound."

Dino drove me and Wilma home from the forum, and we spoke briefly in the car outside our home.

"Wellington thought it might be time to get out because he didn't get the labor endorsement and the money was still not coming in," Dino said. "He could keep his name off the ballot with no embarrassment. If what happened with Norm after the forum [hadn't], I may have agreed."

We decided to wait to make a decision until I returned from a fund-raiser in Los Angeles hosted by Reverend Paul Martin and Johnnie Cochran. Reverend Martin, a fellow member of Kappa Alpha Psi, moved to Denver in July 1990. He wasn't interested in the mayoral race until he read a newspaper report urging me to quit the campaign.

"I wondered why a newspaper was blatantly endorsing Norm Early and declaring him the winner when the race was really just starting," Reverend Martin recalled.

Then Reverend Martin got a call from Los Angeles mayor Tom Bradley, also a fraternity brother, who heard my campaign was in trouble and wanted to help. Reverend Martin had worked with Mayor Bradley on several issues when he lived in Los Angeles.

I knew Mayor Bradley, but we were not close. Reverend Martin tracked me down, and we discussed that I needed help raising money. Reverend Martin relayed the message to Mayor Bradley, and his people set up the fund-raiser with Cochran, also a fraternity brother.

The cost was $1,000 a person, and the event took place at a Kappa member's home in Marina del Rey.

"Most of the people who were going to the fund-raiser were life-long friends and they asked me, 'Who is Wellington Webb? We understand he can't win the election,'" Martin said. "I told them, 'Don't ask questions; just give him your money.' Wellington reminded me a lot of Mayor Bradley, and I told them he did have a chance to win."

Before going to Los Angeles, I told Wilma and Dino that if I raised at least $10,000, I'd stay in the race. If I came home with less money, we would bow out gracefully.

"Wilma and I both went to the airport to meet him, and he came back with $10,000," Dino said. "We got a little adrenaline rush and decided to send Finegan a fax. The fax said, 'We're still here, Norm.' Wellington had such a big grin on his face. I was happy for him. I was amused at how giddy he was. We were delighted with ourselves."

I couldn't let my past friendship with Early hurt my campaign.

"Wellington was aggressive with Norm," Dino said. "He showed him pretty quickly that he wasn't going to let whatever friendship they had stand in the way. Wellington was ready to take him on."

Our joy over the $10,000 didn't last long. Our weekly campaign meetings began to focus on an exit strategy. There was talk by some campaign workers that if I quit, Early would give me a cabinet position, such as director of public works. I wasn't part of those conversations, nor would I have accepted a job from Early. I also doubt he would have wanted me in his cabinet any more than I would have wanted him in my cabinet.

Rocky Mountain News reporter Brian Weber convinced Roberts and Tyrone Holt to go on the record that the Early camp wanted to deal me out of the race.

"It unnerved the Early folks that Roberts talked," Dino said. "I was freaked out a little because the story could have gone either way. Wellington could have looked like he was trying to cut a deal, but it rolled over on Early. It also led to one of the best commercials, where Wellington looks into the camera and says, 'Norm, we don't do it like that in Denver.'"

Once we made it clear I wasn't dropping out, I continued to concentrate on the forums. I was doing well against the other candidates, but we weren't moving up in the polls. We were also getting poorer by the day and knew we had to think of something quick or the race would be over.

Dino was driving home from Easter dinner with his parents when he stopped to get gas at a 7-Eleven near Sloan's Lake.

"I noticed all these people at the park having picnics," Dino said. "I remember former senator Hank Brown used to have 'Hot Dogs with Hank.' With all of the parks in northwest Denver alone, I thought it would be a good idea if Wellington walked from park to park. It wouldn't cost a lot."

Dino bounced the idea off Jim Martinez and Ken Smith.

"Ken wanted to go a step further," Dino said. "Ken said Wellington should stay in a different person's house every night. I thought, *Jesus Christ, Ken! Can't you just say it's a good idea?* But he was right. Ken was really insistent. I finally said, 'Okay, if we can get a mobile home to rest in.' Ken, as much as anyone, should get the credit for the walk."

Our oldest son, Keith, also had urged me to get out and meet people in different neighborhoods, so he was in support of the walk.

Dino, Martinez, and Smith wrote up a proposal for the walking campaign, and I thought it was a good idea. The concept of the walk was to generate free publicity. We'd get my name in the media without having to buy ads. It was our last-ditch effort.

We knew Wilma had to be with me at the homes so there was never any question of impropriety. But that also meant that Wilma would have to get back home in the morning to shower, change clothes, and get to her full-time job at the legislature.

"I could see that Wilma hated the idea, but we had so few options," Smith recalled. "Wilma was serving in the legislature, and she had a lot of questions, good questions of how it would work. She was very dignified and would be sleeping in people's homes she didn't know and invading their privacy. She would have to get up at the crack of dawn to get back home and then to the capitol."

Once Wilma signed off, we brought the idea to our weekly campaign meeting.

"Arnie [Grossman] thought it sounded like a high-school prank," Dino said. "Venita didn't think much of the idea. Tyrone and

Lucius weren't thrilled. Bob Ozinga offered to get labor people to walk with us."

The only constant labor support during the campaign came from the Colorado Building and Construction Trades Council. Their members walked with me, and their retired members made many of our campaign signs.

I knew we had no choice but to walk the city. I gave my staff ten days to put together a plan before I laced up my tennis shoes and took off on the hardest challenge of my political career.

Chapter Eighteen

The Walk, Upset Victory

My campaign walk through the city was to be carried out like a military operation. This would be unique because for twenty-one days, I would not get into a vehicle or sleep in my own bed, not until the election was over.

That had not been the case for other notable campaign walks, including Lawton Chiles's in Florida, Dan Walker's in Illinois, or Richard Lamm's in Colorado. Those politicians walked during the day and got into a vehicle at night to go home or to a hotel. I would walk during the day, right to a stranger's house, where I would spend the night.

We had to revise the plan in the runoff to allow me to travel by a hired trolley because the planned candidate forums were located miles apart from each other. But for the most part, my modes of transportation were my feet in my size-twelve tennis shoes.

We held a press conference to kick off the walk in southwest Denver. This was the most Republican part of the city. I was walking as the underdog to the theme song to the movie *Rocky*.

"Wellington showed up in his tennis shoes and a light-blue jacket," Mike Dino recalled. "That became a key element and was his idea. He was not the politician in a suit and tie just glad-handing. He was in his street clothes, fighting the elements, and showing people his great smile."

Denver voters wanted something out of the ordinary, and I was doing my damnedest to give it to them.

My feet took me to every neighborhood in Denver during our famous walking campaign in 1991. People started recognizing my light-blue jacket and waving or honking car horns in support because they saw how much I wanted to be the city's leader. We walked through rain, sleet, and snow.

My days started out early, waving from street corners and then walking to the closest business district to campaign. In the evenings, we had a free hot-dog roast at a nearby park and often ended the night with a campaign forum or debate before going to a voter's home to sleep. Everything had to be coordinated to maintain a good flow and allow me to hit all parts of the city.

"We had to make the logistics work," Ken Smith said. "Sometimes I would call twenty homes before finding a place where he could stay. I'm not sure any campaign could do this again."

Smith and other staffers blanketed the neighborhoods with campaign leaflets and information about the free hot-dog roast. The campaign literature said, "Wellington Webb, Denver's Mayor, Walk with him ... Win with him. He knows the way." We also put pollster Floyd Ciruli's quote in the *Rocky Mountain News* from April 8, 1991, on the literature: "Webb is without a doubt the most knowledgeable candidate on how the city runs."

The campaign attracted some great volunteers.

"This guy had a red Corvette and about seven kids, and he volunteered to do the hot-dog roast at each stop," Dino said. "He'd load up his car with the grill and kids and drive all over town."

When I went to a voter's house, my line with everyone was the same: "Hello, my name is Wellington Webb. I'm running for mayor of Denver. I know you probably have not personally met anyone else running for mayor, and I would love to have your support."

Nine times out of ten, the resident had never met a politician in person; they had just seen them on television or heard them on the radio.

I knocked on the front door of one home in southwest Denver. The gentleman who opened the door was dressed in a white T-shirt and bib overalls. I started my script, and he recognized me.

"You're the guy!" he said. "You're the guy!"

Then he hollered, "Ma! Hey, Ma, that colored fella I'm voting for is on the front porch. Come see him. That's the one I told you to vote for too."

Greg Kolomitz was walking with me that day, and he looked at me, stunned.

"He called you colored!" Kolomitz said, and then he asked me if we should correct him.

I said no, just leave the guy alone. He was voting for me, and we weren't going to change his vocabulary. Then Kolomitz got excited and thought the guy might want a campaign sign of large Webb tennis shoes to proudly display in his yard.

I told Kolomitz the guy could never go that far, to endorse me in his front yard, but he would likely tell his friends how he was voting. That was enough for me.

The first night, I stayed with an upper-middle-class white family. Over the next three weeks, I would meet the rainbow of Denver residents, from a Hispanic family that served me green chile and eggs for breakfast, a Jewish family that gave us lox and bagels, and a black family that cooked up pork chops and grits. I rested my head one night in the guest room of a wealthy family near the Denver Country Club, and another night on a cot from army surplus we brought with us to a homeless shelter.

Few homes had beds made for a six-foot-four body, so there were many restless nights of sleep. But I met people I never would have come into contact with during a traditional campaign.

"He was just as comfortable eating in a home where roaches were crawling on the floors to being in a mansion where hired help served his meals," Charlotte Stephens said. "People knew he was real."

The walking route also brought us to the neighborhoods of friends, where we spent some nights. One of our closest friends, Jill Crow, had a home with five bedrooms, and she gave Wilma and me the one with twin beds—we slept in one of the twin beds together. She also had a cat named Wilma, which we thought was comical.

We stayed with Representative Wayne Knox, who had the second-longest tenure in the state legislature. He was an expert on education issues and lived in a modest home in northwest Denver.

Sometimes we would come in late to our host's home after attending an event. That happened when we arrived in Cathy Donohue's central Denver neighborhood. Wilma and I had been invited to the Owl Club Debutante Ball that night. Wilma drove to the ball wearing her formal. I walked to the event and met her there in my tuxedo and tennis shoes.

Donohue knew we would get to her home late. She had a Doberman pinscher and a hunting dog that she said wouldn't bark as long as we called out their names before we came in the house.

"I told Wilma and Wellington that one dog is named Jaycee and the other Penny," Donohue said. "So, just remember J. C. Penney, like the store, and you'll have the names. They came in about midnight, and I heard Wilma yell out, 'Montgomery Ward!'"

We were so exhausted that we both forgot the dogs' name and called out another popular department store name instead.

The next morning, I also forgot something—left on the floor of Donohue's bathroom.

"He left his underwear on the bathroom floor, like most men do," Donohue said. "Well, I knew I had to get his underwear out of my house. I put them in a brown paper bag and brought them to his office."

Later that day, Elbra Wedgeworth showed up on the campaign trail with the brown bag.

"This doesn't have money in it?" I asked her.

She giggled before handing me my shorts.

I wished there had been some cash in that brown paper bag. We were broke but still had to find money to pay for the mobile-home rental, gas, and the literature we were passing out along the way.

Jim Martinez was worried about the poor fund-raising. I told him that if necessary, I would write my name on cardboard boxes and hand them out as brochures. Or I would get scraps of paper and just sign them. I refused to quit.

"He was concerned about the lack of money, yet he made up for it with sweat equity," recalled my friend Ben Jeffers, who made a valiant but unsuccessful run for secretary of state of Louisiana in 1979.

My campaign walk allowed us to get some free press. We called the media daily from our new locations. We knew some reporters would show up just to make sure we weren't cheating and riding in private vehicles.

One day, I saw some kids in a station wagon pointing at me. I had on these old, raggedy Asics tennis shoes I bought one summer when I attended a government senior-executives program at Harvard. The kids noticed me by my bright-blue jacket. I never changed my outfit, except for my underclothes, for the entire walking campaign.

The only place where I didn't let Wilma stay with me was the homeless shelter downtown. We bought an army cot to avoid being accused of taking a bed from the homeless. This shelter had a history. It was established by an independent Catholic priest, Father Woody Woodwich. Father Woody clashed with Mayor Federico Peña over the location of the facility because it was close to the center of downtown.

Father Woody also established a program that gave the homeless cash gifts at Christmas.

I stood in line with the people waiting to get shelter that night. Women and children went in first. Then the men had to pick from a deck of cards. A red card meant admission; a black card meant you slept on the street or went to the Salvation Army, which allowed the homeless to sleep in its chapel.

I pulled a red card and watched television with a group of homeless men. One man told me he wouldn't tell anyone he saw me—he thought I was a Denver Broncos player down on his luck.

I never slept that night. I had one eye open and one eye closed. I took a shower the next morning with the rest of the homeless men and then had kitchen duty. My job was to dispense the food as the people came down the chow line.

We scheduled this stop to be the night before Norm Early launched his $400,000 television advertising campaign. As I stood outside the homeless shelter, I spoke about how campaign spending had gotten out of hand. The contradiction was not lost on the media or voters.

I was amazed by the people who would show up and walk with us. One woman with a baby in a stroller walked several miles. An older lady we nicknamed "The Bell Woman" would show up in tattered clothes, walk with us, and ring a bell.

The wear and tear on my fifty-year-old body was starting to mount up when, fortunately, I was scheduled to stay at a physician's home. I wore athletic tube socks that were normally bloody by the end of the day because of the blisters on my feet. The doctor took one look at my feet and offered to lance the blisters to give me some relief.

My knee was swollen, and I just prayed that my body would hold up through the election. The walk was starting to gain more attention.

"The *Rocky* [*Mountain News*] made Webb's walking campaign real," said political consultant Steve Welchert, who was running for auditor. "The rest of the press had to cover it too."

My campaign staff started to get some hope that their hard work just might pay off.

"Prior to the walking campaign, we tried everything but got little or no press," said Kolomitz. "Then the television crews started showing up, and the newspapers. I remember saying to my wingman, Charles, who I called Chaz, 'You know, this shit might actually work.'"

The publicity was also a double-edged sword. Now when we went to someone's home, there was a crowd to greet us. After twelve hours of campaigning, I was exhausted but ended up chatting with a living room full of people instead of going to bed. I wasn't about to complain, because this gave us real life as we headed into the primary.

I also knew that although I could win votes by staying in strangers' homes, I also could lose votes. I suspected that after we left, their neighbors would call and ask, "What is Webb really like?" I hoped the response would be positive.

I got good feedback along the way.

Parents who, in the beginning of the walk, had scolded their kids when they pointed at me were now pointing at me themselves.

"The nice thing is that people were honking their car horns in support," Dino said. "He got immediate positive feedback and didn't have to wait for polls. It helped that Wellington felt that energy."

We stopped at schools along our campaign route and gave the students campaign flyers to give their parents about the free hot-dog roasts. The children bugged their parents to show up, and it gave me an opportunity to win over additional voters.

But there were glitches. One night after a fund-raiser with the gay and lesbian community, I didn't have anywhere set up to sleep. The person who had signed up fell through. So the campaign staff went to every nearby home whose yard had a "Webb for Mayor" sign and knocked on the door. A couple finally said yes.

When I arrived, I saw the wife cleaning up the house. It was one of those circumstances where strangers were intrigued with my campaign. I met a couple and garnered two votes because of a schedule glitch.

Another time, Dino and I finished a late-night forum and instead of the host home being nearby, we ended up walking more than five miles. We kept walking and walking, and we finally sat on a curb to rest.

A guy drove by and called out to ask if we wanted a ride. I was ready to say, "To hell with the rules, I'm taking him up on his offer." But before I could react, he said, "Oh, that's right, you can't get in the car," and he drove away.

Dino and I cut through alleys and people's backyards. Needless to say, that next morning, I did not get up early to campaign on the street corners. I needed to rest from the night's extra-long journey.

My former colleagues in the legislature watched the race with interest and little hope that I could win.

"Frankly, I thought Wellington's chances were pretty hopeless," said Morgan Smith. "My wife and I went to a hardware store one weekend and when we came out, we saw Webb in his tennis shoes. Wellington looked pretty beat. But he was determined."

Dino and I kept plugging away at the walk and hit a few dicey moments. Once, we walked by two "good old boys" and their hound dog at a run-down garage.

"I was ready to just walk by, but to Wellington's credit, he stopped to chat with the men," Dino said. "The dog wouldn't stop barking, to which one of the men said, 'That dog doesn't see many people like you.' He wasn't rude. He just said it matter-of-factly. The guys weren't even registered to vote. It showed Wellington's absolute ability to relate to different people."

Then came the day the Election Commission would decide the order of names on the ballot. Arie Taylor drew the candidates' names out of a hat. She was my good-luck charm, and my name came out first.

Meanwhile, Early's people were trying to get him out more to campaign. He looked pretty wooden walking downtown, shaking hands.

I still worked hard in northeast Denver because I did not take one vote for granted.

"One thing is that some people say the Webbs are aloof, and people call them the King and Queen or Duke and Duchess of northeast Denver," said John McBride. "But Wellington is great one-on-one. When he got to them in person and gave out the free hot dogs, people responded."

We poured our last money into radio ads urging people to get out and vote.

"Wellington needs your support for mayor," Wilma's voice said on the ad. "I urge you to walk with Wellington and win with Wellington. He knows the way."

In another ad, I said, "I grew up in Denver. ... I've been here when you needed me. Now I need your vote on May 21. I need you to stick with the vote for the home team because your vote counts."

The basketball coaches at Montbello and East High Schools also did an ad for me. These schools and coaches were well known for their outstanding basketball teams. "We think it's time to have someone who graduated from the Denver Public Schools as Denver's next mayor," they said.

The mounting attention from the media was starting to get to

Early's campaign workers.

"I remember Dino coming in and telling us that the Early guys were mad because 'Webb is on the radio or television *again*.'" Kolomitz said.

The ongoing criticism from conservative columnist Ken Hamblin also helped my campaign. Hamblin is black, but I think he hates black people. Every time Hamblin went after me, my support in the black community rose just a little bit more.

The arts community endorsed me in their May 1991 issue of *Icon*. Ted Pinkowitz wrote: "Webb knows the arts issues as well, if not better than the other candidates. He views the arts as an industry that provides jobs, taxes and enhances the image of our city. The arts have proved their economic clout to Webb and he plans to use that clout to expand the role of the arts in the future development of this city. I believe we should support him. He is the best chance for the arts in Denver."

My commitment to the arts community was proven when I turned Mayor Peña's public-arts policy into a law requiring 1 percent of funding for all new public building projects go to public art. I also supported a $110 million addition to the Denver Art Museum, which included a $62.5 million bond approved by voters. In addition, Wilma played an important leadership role as chairwoman of the Mayor's Commission on Art, Culture and Film.

We got a huge boost when the *Rocky Mountain News* endorsed me. They gave kudos to Early and Don Bain for being committed to the city, but in the end said I rose to the top.

"Denver is lucky in 1991," the May 5, 1991, *News* editorial read. "Its three leading candidates for mayor are intelligent, honest, capable leaders with impressive careers. To tell the truth, each would make a decent mayor; but of the lot, Wellington Webb would make the best."

The endorsement said that as mayor, I would work to give Denver residents more-efficient basic city services.

"Of the three campaigns, Webb's is the most grounded in substance and attuned to the unglamorous, urgent needs of the city," the editorial said.

The same day, *The Denver Post* endorsed Early.

"If we had to sum up Norm Early in a sentence, we'd call him a man who was hard on criminals because he had to be—and soft on kids because he wants to be. It's an attitude and reflection of values that we find appealing."

A few days before the election, the polls showed that Early might win outright and there would be no runoff. He was at about 48 percent in this poll, and I was at about 17 percent.

"Bain's campaign manager, Doug Goodyear, called me and said they thought the numbers were wrong," Dino said. "If Wellington made the runoff, Bain would endorse him."

I knew going into the primary that everyone associated with the campaign gave it our best shot. Now, it was up to the voters.

Even at the beginning of the campaign, I truly believed that, through will and determination, I would beat either Early or Bain if we met one-on-one in the runoff. My greatest fear was that I would finish third in the primary and never get to compete in the runoff.

We watched the results from a suite at the Oxford Hotel downtown. At the end of the night, I achieved my goal: I got 30 percent (36,674 votes), and Early garnered 41 percent (50,004 votes).

When the votes were announced and we knew that we reached the runoff, I cried. The tears were my sense of relief and joy for getting the opportunity to compete with Early one-on-one.

Bain finished third, with 32,812 votes. The rest of the field included Steve Schweitzberger with 1,580 votes; Errol Stevens, 612 votes; George Knapp, 470 votes; and Larry Walsh, 240 votes.

"Today we showed that substance wins over style," I yelled to supporters that night. "Norm! Here we come!"

I didn't have to wait long to see Early. I think it was an error in judgment for him to come over and congratulate us that night. He was the front-runner. We should have been going to him. It was like he knew that even though he had more votes, he would be chasing me in the runoff.

"Norm seemed stuck in a situation and wasn't sure if he really wanted to be mayor," said Maria Garcia Berry. "He was a good district attorney, but he was appointed by the governor after Dale Tooley died and it came easy to Norm. Then, instead of fighting, Norm had reservations from his gut if he wanted to do this."

Against all odds, two black men were making history and heading to a runoff. Instead of making a big deal out of that, I made the subtle reference that now it was a race between two men with mustaches.

"Wellington Webb really believed in a way most of us didn't," said Dan Muse. "Many of us thought there was no way the city of Denver would send two black candidates to a runoff."

The next day, we got up and waved thank-you signs at busy downtown intersections during the rush hour.

"Some people were honking and maybe thought Wellington was already elected mayor," Dino said.

But round two had just begun, and we needed money. Donna Good, who was well known for her fund-raising skills, had been on vacation with her family in Italy for most of the campaign. Ken Smith urged Donna to come back early and help us raise some money for the runoff.

"The fund-raising was horrible," Good said. "Every Democrat—well, almost every Democrat—had given to Early. Norm had raised about $1 million."

When I made the runoff, Good tactfully explained to the movers and shakers that I wouldn't hold it against them that they had given Early money. But she also would not let them off the hook if they said they had already given their limit of $3,000 under the new city law.

"I'd tell them that now their wife or daughter could write a check," Good said. "Wellington got a lot of checks from wives."

Fabby Hillyard was also burning up the phone lines seeking money.

"All of the big boys had written him off early, but by the runoff, we had momentum," Hillyard said. "The money started coming in from people who wanted to cover their butts. They'd give us a line about how they listened to Wellington's message and liked what they heard. We took their money, but we didn't take their baloney."

In a few short weeks, the campaign raised more than $100,000 to do commercials for the runoff. The money included another fund-raiser in Los Angeles, once again set up by Reverend Paul Martin and Johnnie Cochran.

Dino's dilemma was coming up with a strategy for the runoff, whereas I concentrated on getting ready for my one-on-one debates with Early.

"I kept thinking, *How do we top the walk?*" Dino said. "*Does he now ride a bike?*"

Dino and I agreed we would do another walk, up to the runoff on June 18, 1991, although now I could ride in Bain's trolley car. I let Dino get to work on the details of the second walk, and I focused on lining up endorsements.

Among the other unsuccessful mayoral candidates, Bain endorsed me and gave me a pair of tennis shoes. Stevens, who had worked for the administrations of Mayor Bill McNichols and Mayor Peña, also campaigned hard for me after the primary, as did his wife, Rebette. He felt ignored by the press before the primary and also attacked Early pretty hard, especially on the savings-and-loan scandal.

"I was even more convinced that Early brought nothing to the table," Stevens said. "He didn't seem motivated. He really didn't want it in his gut. Wellington and I wanted to be mayor in our guts, and we were motivated to work. Webb made a personal commitment to win."

I asked former Mayor McNichols for his support, and he endorsed me.

I knew it was important for me to do well in our first televised debate. When we looked back on history, everyone remembered that John Kennedy outshone Richard Nixon in the first presidential debate. Few people know Nixon did well in subsequent debates.

It was gratifying when two of my opponents in the 1991 mayoral race, Errol Stevens (far left) and Don Bain, endorsed me in the runoff with Norm Early. Bain even gave me a pair of tennis shoes for the runoff.

Dino's brother, Perry, traveled with me to the debates and always had a boom box. We'd play the theme to *Rocky* to pump me up. But people also could hear the lyrics to L. L. Cool J's "Mama Said Knock You Out" blaring from an empty office, where I usually spent time alone before the debates.

At the first televised debate at Channel 9, I wore a tie that had small baseball players on it, which was Jim Martinez's idea, as a way for me to show support for Denver's efforts to get a Major League Baseball team.

During the debate, I emphasized that as mayor, I would authorize two police officers for each patrol and go back to providing better basic services for the residents.

"I think the citizens are concerned with trash pickup, concerned with filling potholes, and a lot of those issues aren't really glitzy," I told a panel of reporters at Channel 9.

The issues with the police were suggested by my brother Joe, who quizzed his fellow officers about the needs on the force.

Early looked nervous during the debate, almost like he had shrunk a few inches. He tried to cram before the debates, but that just made him look uptight. I knew the issues, and that relaxed me.

Early also tried to rattle me by talking about The Webb Fund. I countered by saying I had a piece of paper in my pocket with the name of Early's campaign staffer who tried to get me out of the race. I pulled out a piece of paper, but only I knew it was blank.

We used the same tactic at other forums with the help of Taylor.

There was gossip that Early had had some problems in the district attorney's office. Taylor put out the rumor that she had documents that would hurt Early, and she showed up holding a big envelope marked "Top Secret" in clear sight for Early to see.

It is not an exaggeration to say that Taylor and Early really disliked each other.

The reporters helped me in the first televised debate by painting Early into a corner as a Peña clone.

"The real issues aren't if you are pro-Peña or anti-Peña," I responded. "The real issue is, is this mayor going to be pro-Denver and fight for Denver."

I had raised the issue about Mayor Peña earlier in the campaign. I challenged Early, who some called a Peña-clone, to give me three policy issues on which he disagreed with Peña. I also asked Bain, who had nothing good to say about Peña, to give me three policies on which agreed with Peña. Neither could respond, which put me in a good light of being the only truly objective candidate.

Many people thought that because Early was the DA, he would do better than me at the debates. He was a great district attorney, but he was running for mayor, and no amount of natural charisma could cover his lack of knowledge of citywide issues.

I finished up that debate with two statements: "I am not running to be mayor of the black community; I'm running to be mayor of Denver. My twenty-one days of walking also is the way I will govern; I want to stay close to the people of this city."

The tone was set for the runoff. I was still the underdog, but now Early was chasing me.

"Wellington caught Norm Early in a mistake," said John Bailey, a community activist who worked on my campaign. "Norm tried to run a suburban campaign in an urban city. He was hoping his name recognition and identity would make the difference. But as a district attorney, he was also seen as a prosecutor putting black people in jail.

"Then Wellington puts on his sneakers and goes and meets the voters," Bailey said. "He was a man who kept the books as auditor and did what many politicians didn't do—he took the time to go out into the community and shake your hand."

Early tried to take his campaign to voters by filling in for people at a different job each day. I was already doing that as part of the walk, including pumping gas one day.

"People saw Norm's moves for what they were—too little too late," Dino said.

The negative ads were also tardy and backfired when people such as Lamm spoke out against them. I felt that if Early was going to go negative, he should have done it early in the campaign.

"Wellington told his campaign staff this was war and we were going to treat it like a war," Dino said. "We needed that focus to be victorious."

Jim Monaghan's ad that ended with me saying, "Norm, we don't do it like that in Denver" may have sealed Early's fate.

"Norm's campaign was doing stuff because they saw it as kill or be killed, while I suspect that Norm probably just went home and went to sleep," Dino said. "Wellington was the key to the walk. If Wellington isn't who he is, the walk wouldn't have worked."

At the annual Juneteenth parade in northeast Denver, both Early and I sensed the outcome of the election. The organizers of the parade, who were good people, faced a dilemma when they put Early and his campaigners at the head of the parade. My campaign staff was upset and wanted an explanation.

The parade organizers thought that Early, as the district attorney and state official, outranked me as auditor, a city official. The truth is that we were both independently elected officials and no one outranked the other.

But rather than fight, I said that we would take our spot at the rear of the parade and march right behind the horses.

"The Bible says, 'Thou who shall be last shall be first and thou who is first shall be last,'" I told my campaigners. "We will be the last people in the parade, and we'll just have to avoid the horseshit."

When we came into view of the crowd, they broke into spontaneous applause and began following us. When I looked at Early, I sensed he knew his fate.

I also believed I had a chance because of Denver's political history. I read every book on Denver politics, including *The Old Gray Mayors of Denver* and personal essays, and several things were clear: no district attorney had ever been elected mayor and no city council member had ever won. About every third or fourth auditor was successful in making the transition to the mayor's seat, the last one being Tom Currigan.

My mayoral campaign in 1991 was placed at the end of the city's annual Juneteenth parade in northeast Denver, but it was clear we had momentum when people in the crowd cheered and some ran to shake my hand.

The runoff was on June 18, the same date that the Duke of Wellington defeated Napoleon at Waterloo. I constantly told this bit of history to the columnists who had written me off from the start.

I also believed that my long public-service record would bring out constituents whom I had built up since the 1970s. I had planted my political roots by working on Jesse Jackson's People United to Save Humanity operation, by working with the poor in the community, and by teaching the black-studies college class, and my constituents had grown with my election to the state legislature in 1972.

I suspected I would get support from a variety of people whom I served along the way, including the adopted people who appreciated that I fought for them to find their birth parents and the gay and lesbian community who appreciated my antidiscrimination bills. The businesspeople knew me from my time on Regulatory Agencies and my work as auditor.

I was much more involved with the Democratic Party than was Early. I hoped the longtime Democrats remembered that and, in the end, would support me.

Wilma's good working relationship with Democrats and Republicans in the legislature, along with my friendship with Republican Bill Daniels, helped us with that segment of the vote.

Strong supporters who helped me in the Hispanic community included Ruben Valdez, Paul Sandoval, Don Sandoval, Rosemary Rodriguez, Phil Hernandez, and Ken Salazar. I also had a consistent record of supporting issues in the Latino community.

What surprised me and hurt me somewhat was when Rich Castro endorsed Early. Castro felt that when I was auditor, I was too aggressive toward the Peña administration on financial issues. Castro died suddenly from a heart attack during the campaign. His death was a blow to Hispanic activists who were ready to support Castro's run for Congress.

I later pushed to name a city human-services building for Castro in recognition of his years of activism and service to the city and state.

I also expected to get votes from residents who appreciated my work as a Denver Public Library commissioner and as a Colorado AIDS Project board member.

I was exhausted from the second walk but now was able to have a little fun.

Wilma and I were eating dinner in a restaurant after a rainstorm when an awning fell down. We got soaked.

"Is the district attorney on the roof?" I quipped.

The press picked it up, and the comment was all over the media the next day.

Denver's weekly newspaper *Westword* predicted I would win the runoff. "At this point, no matter how much Early spends on television commercials and glad-handing, he can't buy himself the election that once looked like a walk," wrote editor Patricia Calhoun. " ... The men-who-would-be-kingmakers will have lost a big one to the voters."

The Post continued to endorse Early and the *Rocky Mountain News* stuck with me.

For many of us, the last few days of the runoff were a blur. We went back to the Oxford Hotel to wait for the results.

"Webb Wins in a Walk," read the large front-page headline of *The Denver Post* the next day. I got 66,511 votes compared to Early's 48,702 votes. *The Post* did a cost comparison showing that Early's $218,000 raised for the runoff alone cost him $4.48 per vote compared to my $129,000 at $1.94 per vote.

The night of the runoff, my family and campaign staff stood in a circle and we prayed that God would give me the strength and wisdom to lead the city toward a successful future.

"People thought we would get smoked, and that made the victory even sweeter," said Tom Migaki from the auditor's office.

Ken Smith felt a sense of pride when I pulled him onto the stage and embraced him.

"We had won against every incredible odd," Smith said. "We had pulled off something that the press and mainstream did not think possible."

The streets outside the hotel, which the police had blocked off from traffic, were packed with my supporters screaming the impossible: "We won! We won!" Among those celebrating were my classmates from Manual High School.

"Not only was I proud that we elected an African American mayor, but also that he was a schoolmate of mine," said Ruthelene Wesley Johnson.

The media spotlight on Manual was finally positive instead of just focused on the problems.

"At the time, Manual didn't have a great reputation, so it was good to show our classmates did succeed," said alumna Connie Skillern Hall.

Denver Post reporter George Lane wrote about my election, Wilma's successful political career, and about another graduate, Norm Rice, who had been mayor of Seattle since 1989.

"You guys must be proud as hell right now," Rice told Lane, one of the first black journalists in Denver to work on a large daily newspaper.

Both Early and Peña came over and congratulated me the night of the election.

I know the walk made the difference. Someone asked me if I could do the walk again, and I'm not sure that I could. We walked through every neighborhood in Denver. We spoke with every ethnic group, every religious group, and every group, straight or gay. We shook the hands of employees on the early morning, daytime, and night shifts. We slept in the homes of forty-two residents, most of them strangers.

My campaign was like an island. There was no place to go, no ships coming to rescue us. We either saved ourselves or we all would have drowned politically. We created our own lifeboat to victory, and the reason it worked was that people saw I genuinely wanted to be Denver's leader.

Mixed in with the thrill of victory was the relief that I didn't feel the agony of defeat, as I had in 1983.

"I ran into Wellington after the 1991 election, and I said I was so proud of him," recalled Greg Romberg. "His response was, 'Too bad this didn't happen eight years sooner.' I told him that he was wrong, that he wasn't ready eight years earlier to be mayor."

The day after the runoff, we were back out at a busy downtown Denver intersection waving signs and thanking voters.

"Did I finally relax? We had ten days until the inauguration," Dino recalled. "I was freaked out again. There was a lot of work ahead of us."

I made sure that no other new mayor would face that unworkable deadline again. The council changed the rules to allow thirty days between the runoff and the inauguration in order for a new mayor to get a cabinet in place.

While everyone was partying on election night, the reality set in that finishing the construction of Denver International Airport (DIA) was now my job. I think people elected me partially because they knew that I was neither a cheerleader nor a pessimist about the airport. I was a realist in that the size of the airport project was one that national governments take on. If we failed to complete the project, it would be my fault.

Victories and successes have many mothers. Failure has only one father.

The saying "Be careful what you wish for" rang true a few times during my first term. DIA consumed my waking hours. The four delayed openings, the botched baggage system, and the bogus investigations clouded everything we did those first four years.

Chapter Nineteen

First Term: Cabinet, Unheralded Projects,
Unexpected Violence

The ten-day period after winning the election became a whirlwind of press interviews and naming a transition team to help me choose cabinet members.

At the same time, we had to plan my inauguration. We wanted the inauguration to be special given the fact I was the first African American to be elected mayor of Denver. We also wanted it to be classy in the sense that it reflected our values.

Wilma and Ken Smith worked tirelessly to get everything in place. Because of my love of history, primarily the Greek and Roman civilizations, it was clear the event would take place at the Civic Center downtown.

We also wanted to make the inauguration especially memorable for northeast Denver and decided to walk two miles from our home to the Civic Center. It was a hot July day, and our family was followed by a large crowd of friends and campaign supporters.

My mother was recovering from a stroke, but we brought her from her assisted-living home to the ceremony. My Aunt Frances came from Mississippi.

Wilma's mother, Faye Gerdine, was there as well, and Wilma's sister, Luanna Slay, and her husband, Charles Slay, came from Michigan.

The police department insisted that I wear a bulletproof vest. The unexpected weight was a tight fit under my new tailor-made suit. The bulletproof vest and weight also symbolized how my life was changing.

Wilma suggested we invite the Denver Symphony Orchestra, but the musicians were concerned that the hot weather would make it difficult for them to play their instruments. Smith found a large red-and-white tent that served as a backdrop to shield the musicians from the hot sun. I feared the tent might look hokey, but it kept the instruments cool enough to be played and made for a nice backdrop.

My favorite piece, "Fanfare for the Common Man," filled the air at the Civic Center while the crowd fanned themselves with the paper programs.

I didn't make the council members and auditor an afterthought in the ceremony. The elected officials proudly walked up the aisle to applause before stepping onto the stage.

The cheers grew louder when Wilma and I walked down the aisle to the "Battle Hymn of the Republic."

Onstage, I was joined by the people who stuck out their necks for me when I was a mere footnote in the election.

I was pleased by the inclusiveness of the day and that every community was represented at the event. That inclusiveness would later be misunderstood, twisted, and nearly cost me a second term.

The inauguration included recognizing the only three businessmen who supported me throughout the campaign: Berne Hart, chairman and CEO of United Banks of Colorado; Walt Emery from the Bank of Denver; and John Coates, chairman of Century Bank of Cherry Creek, who had advised me on business issues when I was auditor.

Hart, who was a Republican, was the master of ceremonies.

Los Angeles mayor Tom Bradley and Atlanta mayor Maynard Jackson sent their chiefs of staff, and my good friend Ben Jeffers came from Louisiana.

Mayor Federico Peña and his wife, Ellen, were very gracious that day. We welcomed other members of the Hispanic community, led by former state representative Phil Hernandez.

We also made sure that all segments of the religious community were included. Rabbi Steven Foster and his wife, Joyce, who worked with me and Wilma on Martin Luther King Jr. activities before I was elected mayor, were on the stage. She would later become a city councilwoman and my good friend.

Rabbi Foster prayed for me and the other elected officials, as did Protestant and Catholic clergy.

There was never any doubt that my Baptist pastor, Reverend W. T. Liggins, who stuck by me the entire campaign, would do the invocation.

"God moves in mysterious ways," Reverend Liggins said, recalling how I had an impossible dream with limited resources but an overabundance of faith. "He walked liked Joshua, and the walls came tumbling down!"

He ended the invocation by thanking God that the community chose a leader based on his abilities, not the color of his skin.

Wilma held our family Bible, the pages of which had often been turned by my grandmother and were yellow with age, as I took the oath of office. It was the same Bible I put my left hand on when I was sworn in as regional director for Health and Human Services and for city auditor.

We ended the event on a lighthearted note with the symphony playing the theme song to *Rocky*.

The excitement of the day carried over to the inaugural ball that evening at the Colorado Convention Center. The event was open to everyone, and the first floor was so crowded when we arrived that we went upstairs and watched the people dance and talk. Among the crowd were the residents who allowed me and Wilma to sleep in their homes. We gave them each a special plaque, similar to the ones Jimmy Carter had given to people who opened their homes to him and his family members during his presidential campaigns.

"Wellington Webb being elected mayor was more than pride for me and for Denver," said longtime black resident Ruby Kirk Gray. "It was truly a blessing."

As I later looked at a video of the inaugural events, I couldn't help but remember that anyone elected mayor can never fully know or understand what lies ahead. I didn't have a sense of the demands, the

My wife, Wilma, held our family Bible on July 1, 1991, while Colorado chief justice Luis D. Rovira gave me the oath of office as Denver's forty-second mayor. Denver voters choose leaders based on their ability to work hard, their vision, and their leadership.

level of decisions that I would have to make, and that the more decisions that I made, the more likely I'd be to make some mistakes.

One mistake I immediately corrected was the vehicle I would use as mayor. I drove a city-owned Mercury as auditor and knew the police department had ordered a Lincoln for me to use as mayor. When the car arrived, it was cherry red. Of course, no one in the police department admitted who ordered the color. I said the "police ghost" must not have known that red is not my most flattering color, and I told them to reorder one in black or midnight blue, which the department did.

When Kevin Flynn of the *Rocky Mountain News* inquired about the switch in vehicles, we didn't tell him about the color but said I needed more seating space because of my height, which was true. Flynn actually went out and measured both vehicles. Despite his report that both vehicles were the same size, I still believe the second car's backseat not only had more head room, but also was a more appropriate color for a mayor.

My goal with the first cabinet was to hire a third of the people coming out of the campaign who shared my values and were competent for the job. But for the remaining hires, I wanted people—some of whom I didn't know—who had the technical expertise to do an outstanding job.

I also believed that current city employees had often been overlooked even though many were qualified to be managers.

When we went looking for cabinet members with only two weeks to complete the hiring, we accepted applications from the campaign staff, current city employees, and the public at large.

I felt that one of the most important positions was the city attorney, who has to be a great manager and also share my values. I chose Dan Muse, who had been part of my political circle from the 1970s.

I had also known Venita Vinson from my days at the Colorado State University Manpower Laboratory, and she had worked with me on all of my political campaigns. She previously worked as Congresswoman Pat Schroeder's district manager. She had also been my eyes and ears in the community, so I brought her in as my first chief of staff.

Wilma lobbied for Mike Dino to be chief of staff, but instead I appointed him as director of intergovernmental relations. He worked with me and other mayors in the metro area concerning local, federal, and state government.

I promoted Bill Smith, deputy of public works, who was overseeing construction of the new airport, to manager of public works. I reappointed George Doughty as the aviation director, but he would now report to Smith.

I was unsure of Doughty because he had a my-way-or-no-way attitude. But I thought the consistency on the airport project superseded my personal views.

I brought in Bruce Alexander, a retired banker, as manager of parks and recreation and as my deputy mayor. I did this for a couple of reasons. I told Republicans that I would open the top jobs to everyone, and Alexander was a Republican. He was also a member of a long-established Denver family and involved in the Denver Botanic Gardens. He had ties to the business community, which did not support me in the mayoral campaign. He was also older than me, and I believed I could learn from him.

Jennifer Moulton was an ideal choice for planning director. She would become the driving force behind downtown's revitalization and the city's park expansion. I always believed she was the best city planner in America. Moulton had also written position papers for me during the 1983 mayoral race. Philosophically, we were like two guards on a basketball team, each knowing what the other would do before it was done and complementing each other.

One of the most self-satisfying appointments was for my good friend and political ally Arie Taylor. When Taylor first came to Denver, she worked at the City Clerk and Recorder's Office. In 1983, she campaigned for Mayor Federico Peña and had hoped he would appoint her as the city's clerk and recorder. Other jealous members of the community said Taylor didn't have the right polish and verbal skills for the job. She was heartbroken. Shortly after the 1991 election, I called her.

"Arie, you've always cared more about elections than anyone I know. How would you like to be the city's clerk and recorder?" I asked her.

I heard muffled cries, and she said she'd call me back in the morning. I was tremendously happy that I was able to make her dream come true. I knew Taylor would fight for everyone's ability to vote.

The out-of-the-box appointments included naming Steve Newman of the American Federation of State, County, and Municipal Employees as the director of human rights and community relations. Usually this position went to a minority because the job often dealt with unrest within the black, Hispanic, or Asian communities. My thought was, "Why can't a white guy who is sensitive to the needs of ethnic communities do this job?"

Newman's union also sent out several mailings to all city employees during the runoff, which really helped our effort.

I appointed the first and—to date—only female manager of safety when I asked Beth McCann, a former deputy district attorney, to take the job. I picked McCann to oversee the police and fire departments, even though she had campaigned for Norm Early.

The police had a security team for Mayor Peña, and when it came time to decide who would head my detail, I chose a man with fifteen years of service on the police force, including several as a detective and sergeant. He also happened to be my brother Joe, and I frankly underestimated the negative reaction from some people.

I wasn't hiring Joe. I was just giving him a new assignment. Who better to watch my security than my brother? We also saw ourselves somewhat like the Kennedy brothers. Jack Kennedy appointed his brother Bobby to be his attorney general.

We came up politically the hard way. We didn't have a mentor, so to speak, or someone in the party or an elected official to follow. Our mentor in politics was our grandmother, but she operated on the precinct level. Everything I and my political allies did was learned through trial and error, by developing an army of volunteers, by fighting for what we believed in, and through our ability to take risks.

"It's hard on a family who happens to be black," Joe said. "Anything you do cannot be an individual effort, and you never get credit. It always has to be some form of cronyism or nepotism."

Despite the criticism, I would choose Joe for the job again in an instant.

I reappointed Fire Chief Rich Gonzales.

The toughest search was for the police chief. I received many anonymous letters and calls, then finally selected longtime police officer Jim Collier. We both later came to the conclusion that he didn't suit the job. Another top choice, longtime Denver officer Dave Michaud, took the police chief position about a year into my term and stayed with me the longest.

I rounded out the rest of my first cabinet and mayoral staff with qualified people, including several people who had worked on the campaign.

In those four years, the benchmarks were real clear. The first thing we had to do, whether we were able to complete anything else, was to open Denver International Airport.

We had campaigned that we would be a nuts-and-bolts administration, that I would be a blue-collar mayor who would deal with everyday issues.

Everything that first term got overshadowed by the airport, but of particular pride to me was the revitalization of downtown; saving Denver General Hospital, later renamed Denver Health Medical Center; the opening of the addition to the downtown library; and the law that requires 1 percent of all public construction project dollars be allocated for public art.

"Downtown Denver used to have no stores that were open in the evenings and there was nothing to do," recalled Connie Skillern Hall, a high-school classmate. "People lost hope and weren't keeping up their property."

The city council struggled to revitalize downtown, and my goal was to first attract housing and retail and then worry about building a new hotel. In 1990, there were 2,700 residences downtown. That had ballooned to about 8,000 in 2003, the year I left office. Those numbers don't include the Golden Triangle area near the City and County Building, where lofts quickly replaced abandoned buildings once downtown residences became popular.

"Before the 1990s, we couldn't get anyone to live downtown and no one would come downtown after 5:00 P.M.," recalled former councilman Bill Roberts. "Now, cities come to Denver to see how we turned things around. People now want to live downtown because they are close to all of the amenities."

My first action as mayor in 1991 was to call for a Downtown Economic Summit. We invited all of the stakeholders, including property owners, store owners, individuals with leases, and others interested in downtown.

We broke up into subcommittees and discussed a plan on how to keep downtown safe, how to deal with cleanliness, and how to upgrade downtown and the surrounding neighborhoods. When a downtown starts to decay, the next victim is the surrounding neighborhoods. I believe that every city's downtown is a signature for the community's stability and vitality.

The work on downtown, headed by Moulton, helped me build a relationship with the business community.

"His message was that we could bring downtown Denver back and even better," said Dino. "He put city resources in downtown. Government can't determine all the economic factors, but whatever dollars the city had, they went to downtown."

During that time, we thought that Macy's was going to open a downtown store. We had a parade, but the Spider-Man balloon we had rented had a flat left leg, which really reflected how that deal never got off the ground.

Bill Mosher started the Downtown Denver Partnership and united the downtown businesses.

"The business community got on board," Dino said. "Webb had something to focus on with the business community with housing and tourism. This was the first big thing that said what Webb was all about."

We put more money into downtown to improve the business district, which in turn attracted new businesses. We put more police downtown, which in turn made it safer. We kept all of the cultural and sporting venues downtown, which in turn gave people a reason to visit and live downtown. These things brought a desire for people to live downtown and the demand for new condos and lofts. We had generated a twenty-four-hour downtown.

I also was able to settle an outstanding lawsuit against the city concerning downtown. The Peña administration wanted to spur retail development along the Sixteenth Street Mall, and the Denver Urban Renewal Authority condemned some property.

Scott Moore, a property owner whose great-grandfather John Evans was a territorial governor of Colorado, felt the city was offering unfair compensation for the property and he sued.

When I was elected, another developer, John Denton, wanted to build an outside mall along Sixteenth Street, but he could not proceed because of the pending lawsuit.

City attorneys had no luck negotiating with Moore, so I invited him to have drinks with me at the Brown Palace Ship Tavern.

After he had had five scotch and sodas and I had had five rum and Cokes, I thought it was time for me to propose a truce.

"Wouldn't it be something if you, the great-grandson of a Colorado governor, and me, the great-grandson of a slave, sitting together in the Brown Palace—where at one time black people were not allowed—were to settle this lawsuit without attorneys?" I asked Moore.

After another round of drinks, he agreed. A few years later, the Denver Pavilions Mall opened with retail shops, a movie theater, and restaurants.

Moore would later host a fund-raiser for me in the 1995 reelection at his mountain ranch, where I believe I was the first black guest.

I also stepped in and resolved another dispute that could have gotten ugly. During my 1991 campaign, I promised to make the city less cumbersome for businesses. A former colleague in Governor Lamm's administratioin, Jim Monaghan, called me one day with a prime example of a bureaucratic city blunder.

Monaghan's boss, billionaire Phil Anschutz, had been given the proper city permits to rebuild a railroad roundhouse in the Central Platte Valley where trains change direction.

When the project was in its last phase, Public Works inspectors said they found a design flaw and told Anchutz's people they would have to tear down a section and rebuild it.

I called Public Works, and when I was assured the flaw was not a safety issue, I told them we could not hold up a project because of our oversight in the design.

Word got back to me that the Public Works employees were criticizing my intervention and threatened not to sign the certificate-of-occupancy permit for the project. I promptly told them if they didn't sign the final approval, I would.

My point was, I don't care if you are a small business or a billionaire, city staff stupidity, and in some cases arrogance, would no longer be business as usual for Denver.

A vibrant downtown and good business climate were just one part of my plan for a vital, growing city. The second important piece was a healthy community. My goal was to save the city's public hospital.

Denver General Hospital was founded in 1860 when two Denver politicians had shot each other and decided the city needed a hospital. I knew about the financial problems when I served as auditor, and by the time I was mayor, the facility faced a $39 million deficit.

"I put an ad in *The Wall Street Journal* trying to sell the hospital, and nobody wanted it," recalled Patty Gabow, chief executive officer of Denver Health. "It's hard to run public hospitals. Most of the people are uninsured. How can you run a business when most of the patients don't pay?"

I teamed up Gabow with director of hospitals Tom Moe to find a way to save the hospital. The problem was that, as a city agency, the hiring and purchasing rules caused impractical and expensive delays.

For example, the hospital wanted to buy a piece of radiology equipment, but by the time the order was approved, the equipment was outdated and the hospital had to start the process over.

"It took more than four years to buy one piece of equipment," Gabow said.

The city's Career Service rules also weren't flexible enough to deal with crises. During the first gulf war in 1991, several nurses were in the National Guard Reserves and got called up for duty. The pay for nurses went up nationwide. By the time the city's Career Service got around to increasing the pay, the war was over.

The creation of a hospital authority would cut through the red tape, but it also meant the city had to give up one of its largest departments to an independent board. I created a task force to study the issue and put together all the pieces to make it work.

"His plate was full with the new airport, and he could have said, 'Donna, I can't deal with the hospital,'" recalled Donna Good, who was part of the task force. "Instead, as part of a team, he really listens and thinks. He let us go forward."

The hospital was the only safety net for the poor and uninsured, and I couldn't let it close on my watch.

Denver Health is now a spectacular model for the rest of the nation. Other cities have struggled for decades with how to save their public hospitals. Denver transitioned to a hospital authority in four years, and the hospital has thrived and expanded under the authority.

"I think most politicians would not give up their second-largest department under their control," Gabow said. "It took a lot of courage, and at the end of the day, it was Mayor Webb who had that courage."

It was quite humbling in November 2006 when the hospital named a new building in my honor. The Wellington E. Webb Center for Primary Care, a 75,000-square-foot facility, allows patients to have doctor appointments, get X-rays, have lab work done, and visit a pharmacy all at one location. The honor shows me that our hard work to save the hospital was recognized. The Denver Health Foundation also launched a $1.5 million Wellington E. Webb Endowment for Community Health, which will provide money for research in the areas of access to care.

I'm pleased to have my name associated with the best public hospital in the country.

Although I knew we had to do something about downtown and Denver Health, my administration faced unforeseen social problems the first term with gang violence, the Ku Klux Klan disturbances on Dr. Martin Luther King Jr.'s holiday, and a conflict between the Italians and Native Americans over Columbus Day.

I believe that anyone can manage when everything goes well. The great managers and their staffs are the ones who find ways to deal with unforeseen problems and fight their way through for the best of the community.

The media dubbed 1993 "The Summer of Violence." The brazen shootings began on May 2, 1993, when ten-month-old Ignacio Pardo was hit in the forehead with a deflected bullet while visiting the Denver Zoo. He got caught in the cross fire of gang violence but thankfully survived his injuries after brain surgery.

On May 30, sixty-two-year-old Louise Brown was shot and killed in her kitchen in northeast Denver. Her teenage nephew had a history of gang violence, and police said that the ten bullets shot into her home were probably meant for him.

A few weeks later, six-year-old Broderick Bell was shot in the head by a stray bullet fired from a carload of gang members. He also survived.

Other brazen shootings had injured and killed innocent bystanders, and the entire city was on edge. It was clear that many gang members from California had relocated to Denver and in a few short months managed to terrorize residents.

I galvanized the city to address the problem, even though at one point the media reported violence had actually decreased in Denver from 1992. The overall number of homicides was lower in 1993, but the shootings in broad daylight and in public places shocked and frightened the citizenry.

We joined northeast Denver residents in an antiviolence march on June 17, 1993, following the shooting of six-year-old Broderick Bell during Denver's "Summer of Violence." Bell's mother, Ollie Phason, marched in front of me next to Bell's father, Broderick Bell Sr. (left), and Denver police chief Dave Michaud (right). Photograph courtesy of *Rocky Mountain News*

"[The year] 1993 was a reflection of the whole craziness of that first term," recalled John McBride. "The airport was not going well, and we had other projects left to us to complete by the Peña administration. At the same time, there was violence not only in the black community, but the brown community as well. These kids weren't misunderstood. They were gangsters. People in the neighborhoods knew it. That year was a test of what the administration could be. We adjusted and got things under control."

Liberals and conservatives alike were telling me, "We don't care what you have to do to stop it, but stop it."

Parents made their kids play in backyards, and living rooms facing streets became empty because of the fear of stray bullets.

We had already started town-hall meetings when ten minutes before one was about to begin, Bell was shot and injured in front of his home.

"He was very upset when we saw the blood in the street," said Charlotte Stephens, who was with me that evening and eventually ran the city's nonviolence program, called Safe City. "Wellington was angry. He was not going to let those little bastards take over his city. He said he was going to chase these fools out of Denver."

The town-hall meetings made it clear that we had to increase efforts to get these kids and young adults jobs and we needed to segregate the pretenders from the predators. We began curfew programs to get kids off the streets. We approved new penalties on gun cases and created police-impact units, which I referred to as "search and destroy."

Some people feared we were letting the police go too far, but several minority communities welcomed the enforcement because the violence was in their neighborhoods. My view was, if you broke the law, I didn't care what ethnic group you belonged to.

A mother called me to complain that her child was just riding in a car and didn't know the driver had a gun.

"Quiz your kid about who he is hanging out with next time," I told the mother. "I would rather have your child alive and mad than dead and happy."

"He was completely and totally the right person to be mayor at the time," said Dino. "There was a lot of confrontation, and he gave the police department room to be more aggressive. We had a minority mayor to say, 'We are not fooling around with this.'"

The most fundamental principle of any city in America is public safety. If people do not feel safe, they won't call any kind of community meeting—they will move.

"He was always at the funerals," said former manager of safety McCann. "He made personal visits to the families impacted. I think he was truly devastated that young black men were killing each other and shooting children. He didn't want this in his city."

I allowed the police to go after the crack houses and confiscate the cash, drugs, and cars.

"Decent people were trying to live their lives, and they couldn't even let their kids play in their yards because of the drive-by shootings and firebombs," said former police chief Michaud. "Many chiefs told me they couldn't do anything major without permission from their mayors. This guy wasn't that way."

Michaud knew to call me if there was a police shooting. We went together to the hospital to comfort the officer's or gang member's families waiting to know if their loved one had survived the latest round of violence.

"One time, there was a shooting in the middle of the night, and when I called him, he said to come pick him up," Michaud said. "Here was the mayor and police chief surrounded by scared and angry neighbors. That made people notice, including the police officers, that we gave a damn. His presence was reassuring to everyone."

I knew our initiatives were working by late August 1993 when someone drove by and fired fifteen bullets into our car and home while Wilma and I were on vacation. It was no surprise that the gang members knew where we lived because many of them were our neighbors.

Because I grew up in Denver, I knew some of the gang members and their parents, who in some cases also were gang members. Being in a gang is not illegal, and in some cases, the gang members were not bad people. They found something in the gangs they were not getting at home.

When our car was being shot up, Wilma and I were in Maine for a much-needed break.

The violence back home never left my mind, but I also learned an important lesson. The skycap who greeted us in Maine was bewildered that we had left Colorado to visit his state.

"Why the hell are you here?" he asked us. "I've lived in Maine for most of my life and can't wait to get out. If I was from Colorado, I would stay there."

When we got back to Denver, I immediately called a meeting of representatives of the tourism industry, including taxi drivers, hotel clerks, skycaps, and anyone who comes into contact with tourists.

The comment in Maine made me realize how individuals can hurt a city's image with one comment. The people who work in the tourism industry can be the city's greatest promoter or its greatest detriment. I believe Atlanta does the best job promoting its community because I have never heard a negative comment about the city, whether dealing with a guy shining my shoes to waitresses and hotel clerks.

That's the way it should be in Denver.

Another image issue I dealt with after my trip to Maine was making sure to take away any glamour associated with the gangs. The city convinced the local media to stop reporting the gang affiliations.

"I have a scholarship to an Ivy League school, and my cousin, a gang member, has a larger scrapbook than me," one young black man told me.

His comments led to the development of a program that continues to give me great pride. My education coordinator, Carol Boigon, and her assistant, Tish Maes, began the Mile High Scholars in June 1997.

We worked with the Denver Public Schools to have principals and teachers pick students in each grade based on their character as well as scholastics. The students then were invited to a graduation ceremony where their names were called, and each student got a carnation

I focused on education and youth issues during my twelve years in office, including inviting students to my office at city hall and establishing the Mayor's Office for Education and Children. In 1997, we began the Mile High Scholars to recognize youth who are good students and good citizens.

and a certificate signed by city and school-district officials.

The students also received free tickets to city facilities, such as the Denver Art Museum and the Denver Zoo. In later years, the city's professional sports teams—the Broncos, Nuggets, Rockies, and Avalanche—also donated tickets.

Long after I left office, young adults would come up to me and say with pride, "I was a Mile High Scholar." Their parents also placed "My Kid Is a Mile High Scholar" bumper stickers on their cars.

The whole idea was to say to students that it's okay to be smart; it's okay to be a good student. You are going to get recognition, including your name printed in Denver's two major newspapers, for being good citizens, and the kids involved in gang activity will not.

Another role for me was chairing the U.S. Conference of Mayors' Task Force on Violent Crime and making recommendations to President William Clinton. At one meeting, someone asked me why I recommended restrictions on guns and not other weapons.

"Because there are no drive-by knifings," I replied.

I was sitting among dignitaries on the White House lawn the day President Clinton signed his anticrime bill. The mayors and police chiefs nationwide were a big part of why that bill was approved. The nation's mayors rallied around President Clinton when the bill faced opposition from Congress.

The bill gave Denver and other cities money for youth programs. I matched the federal grant that Denver received with $1 million from the city's budget, which funded the Safe City program.

The U.S. Conference of Mayors, under my presidency, sponsored the Wall of Death. The structure showed that every day, nearly eighty-nine people nationwide are killed by guns. The wall had the names of 4,001 victims when it was unveiled. I told television journalist Katie Couric, then host of the *Today* show, that the shooting of fathers, mothers, sons, and daughters should not go unnoticed. I felt the deaths were the nation's unnatural disaster.

The violence in Denver didn't end when the temperatures dropped in the fall of 1993. I attended the funeral for an eighteen-year-old aspiring rap singer, Carl Banks Jr. He was killed by a drunken fourteen-year-old while taking his siblings trick-or-treating.

"This is not what our heritage is about or what we survived slavery for," I said at Banks Jr.'s funeral.

A month later, we were burying another teenager: Geronimo Maestas, sixteen, was shot and killed while walking home for refusing to give up his Denver Broncos jacket.

We pushed forward with the initiatives, including a grant program that allowed community groups to decide how the money would be used. Such things as boxing programs and after-school activities helped keep the kids involved and off the streets.

There is no doubt that the summer of 1993 tested this city's soul. Thirteen years later, it was with great joy that I received a high-school graduation invitation from Broderick Bell—the six-year-old in 1993 who became the face of the "Summer of Violence."

I still fear that the gang violence is cyclical and may plague the city again. The older gang members are getting out of prison, and most of the money for the community programs aimed at the youth is no longer available.

We faced another social crisis just six months after being in office when the Ku Klux Klan (KKK) was granted a state permit to assemble at the capitol the same day more than 15,000 people marched on Dr. Martin Luther King Jr.'s holiday.

Several members of the black community wanted me and Wilma, as the Dr. Martin Luther King Jr. Commission chair, to fight, along with Governor Roy Romer, the Klan's legal permit to be on the state capitol grounds. Although I abhor everything the Klan stands for, I also had to support their rights to freedom of speech.

We encouraged everyone to ignore the protesters, but the emotions ran high. When the fence between the two groups began to tumble, the KKK members ran for cover with the Colorado State Patrol's protection into the capitol and into Denver Sheriff buses, which were normally used to transport inmates to court.

The KKK got the permit to speak on the Dr. King holiday

because the state issued permits on a first-come, first-served basis. The next year, community activists LeRoy Lemos, John McBride, Alvertis Simmons, and Julia Gayles stood in line for thirty days, twenty-four hours a day to make sure the Klan could not get the permit. They slept in a trailer outside the permit office, and members of the King Commission brought them food. They are the heroes in that saga, and Denver's Dr. King holiday has not been marred by outside agitators since.

The King Commission under Wilma's leadership made the celebration a weeklong event. Because she fought for so many years, she was overwhelmed with joy when many Republicans in the legislature finally truly accepted Dr. King as an American hero and participated in the events.

The Columbus Day parade controversy also caught me by surprise. I asked, "Why me? Why Colorado?" I was trying to build an airport, and all of my energy was getting sucked up by social issues.

I later discovered that Colorado was the first state to make Columbus Day a state holiday, in addition to its being a federal holiday. I ended up walking with the Italian group's leader that first year because I did not want violence between the two groups. I agreed philosophically with the Native Americans, led by Glenn Morris and Russell Means, about Columbus. I thought celebrating the contributions of other Italians who became great Americans would be better. But in my job as mayor, I had to protect the rights of the parade participants as well.

The parade didn't take place for the next five years until a more aggressive group, the Sons of Italy, took out the parade permit. We worked with the Native Americans to allow symbolic protests without anyone being hurt, but we did arrest more than 100 people who protested the parade.

This issue will land in the lap of every Denver mayor until both sides find a common resolution.

Looking back at the first term, I felt my administration was like a race car, dodging the dangerous curves of unforeseen violence and social issues. But the only finish line that counted was the opening of DIA. If we crashed or stalled before that finish line, there would be no second term.

Chapter Twenty

Pope John Paul II, Prayer, Airport Trials and Tribulations

An amazing thing happened during the "Summer of Violence": crime went down citywide one week in August when Denver hosted Pope John Paul II and more than 200,000 visitors for World Youth Day.

My staff spent more than a year planning for the event, which would put the world spotlight on the city. They had to deal with such issues as finding homes for the kids to sleep in because Denver didn't have enough hotel rooms.

We put 7,500 cots for youth at a converted bovine beauty salon at the National Western Complex. We placed the overflow of pilgrims in an empty department store downtown and a covered parking garage. Residents from Denver to Greeley to Pueblo also opened their homes to the visitors.

"Wellington got everybody going at full speed to prepare for the event," said Amy Bourgeron, a former Department of Public Works spokeswoman who was part of the planning team headed up by Doug Franssen, director of street maintenance. "We had to be prepared for the international media. It was mind-boggling, but we put together a good team."

Police Chief Dave Michaud sent officers to Miami to learn how the force there had protected the pope during his visit. Denver officers also had to provide security for eighty visiting cardinals. President William Clinton and his family greeted the pontiff when he arrived at Stapleton International Airport, and Denver officers were there, along with the president's Secret Service detail.

"We knew the eyes of the world would be on Denver," said former Department of Public Works director Mike Musgrave.

The visitors spoke fifty-seven languages in all, but the common theme of the week was celebration, joy, and prayer.

I had a couple of minutes with the pope when he arrived by helicopter to Mile High Stadium. Wilma and I presented him with a carved wooden key to the city—whose handle was Jesus' face, and the key portion was Denver's skyline—made by city employee Art Rodriguez. We also gave the pope a book of poems by Thomas Hornsby Ferril, who became poet laureate of Colorado in 1979.

"A meeting between the pope and the mayor was not on the original agenda," Bourgeron said. "Wellington doesn't hesitate to ask for a miracle. He said he needed an audience with the pope. We didn't tell him the pope doesn't usually meet with mayors."

In those few moments, I said to the pope: "Your Holiness, this is the key to our city. I hope this key is an instrument to peace and your presence will help stem some of the violence in our city and have guns turned in, not only here, but throughout the world."

The city employees did a marvelous job of coordinating the huge crowds to venues throughout Denver and detouring traffic without shutting down the town. The only glitch came on Saturday when the pilgrims started walking twelve miles to Cherry Creek State Park in ninety-degree temperatures for the pope's Mass, scheduled for Sunday. The pilgrims didn't like the 86,000 gallons of lemon-flavored water that was donated by Coors Brewing Company. Home owners along the way pulled out lawn hoses for the dehydrated walkers, but by the time the pilgrims got to Cherry Creek, many were collapsing. Arapahoe County Sheriff Pat Sullivan threatened to call off the Sunday Mass.

I didn't want to see that happen, and even though the Mass was outside of the city limits, we called in every Denver paramedic and firefighter by 10:00 P.M. Saturday. We literally took over half of the venue in Arapahoe County, with Stephanie Foote, my chief of staff, coordinating the effort. Sullivan still spoke to the press, because it was his jurisdiction and I wanted Denver personnel to be supportive.

Wilma and I were honored to have a few minutes to greet Pope John Paul II in August 1993 when he arrived at Mile High Stadium for World Youth Day. I asked the pope to pray for the end of violence in Denver and elsewhere.

What the Denver paramedics found at the state park looked like a war zone. Dehydrated kids were lying everywhere, and several were taken to the hospital Saturday night. But by midmorning Sunday, the Mass proceeded. The success of the event is still being heralded by the visitors. Subsequent host cities often have relied on Denver's blueprint to plan for World Youth Day.

The peacefulness of the week was welcomed by everyone.

"The Holy Spirit settled over the city that week, and somehow that grace helped with the violence," recalled Foote.

I never wore my religion on my sleeve, but I thought a day of prayer for the city in the face of the gang violence would be a good idea. I was raised as a Baptist, and I stepped forward for baptism when I was twelve.

We put out a press release on city stationary calling for the day of prayer. An agnostic sued me because he said I was promoting religion with city funds. This was the same guy who sued Denver because of its annual Christmas Nativity scene in front of the City and County Building. He lost that suit because the city's Christmas lights are paid for with private money. I did let him put up a nonreligious display, but in the rear of city hall.

I had to go to court over the day-of-prayer lawsuit. I acknowledged to the lawyer for the agnostic that we used city stationary. When he asked why I replied: "Because I needed help. I didn't know who else to turn to. We had kids shooting each other over gangs and colors, and I didn't think it was inappropriate to ask for guidance from God. I thought maybe if we had all of our clergy leaders calling for a day of prayer together, then the kids might begin to listen."

It was clear through the town-hall meetings that many of the pastors were afraid of the kids and, instead of reaching out, were shunning them from their churches.

I didn't like being sued because of my faith.

The judge then asked me if I wanted to say anything. I commented on how this country was founded on religion and how our currency says "In God We Trust." I told him I put my hand on my family Bible when I was sworn into office and the Pledge of Allegiance includes the statement "one nation, under God, ... "

"I was a Christian before I was mayor, and I'll be a Christian after I am mayor," I said.

A few ministers came to the hearing. My comments slowly got out into the community and took on a life of their own. Conservative Republican and Democratic elected officials said they would go to jail with me if necessary. People who objected to my continued support of antidiscrimination laws for gays and lesbians stopped me in the airport and said they didn't always agree with me, but they admired the fact that I stood up for my Christianity.

I also turned to prayer during the agonizing four years it took to open Denver International Airport (DIA), which was the only airport at the time to have a chapel, mosque, and synagogue in the terminal.

After the fourth delay of the opening, several black clergy had a private prayer meeting with me. Once again, I needed all the help I could get.

In addition to the delayed opening, a controversial issue during the first term was the airport concession policy. The seeds of that discussion started when I was auditor. I discovered that less than 10 percent of the concessions at Stapleton—including restaurants, bookstores, and bars—were operated by Colorado, or specifically Denver, business owners. The city had given one large contract to the Host Marriott Corporation based in Rhode Island. At the time, having just one large concessionaire was common at airports nationwide.

"The concessions were locked up like one big Wal-Mart," said Foote, who was a member of the city council before accepting my request to be my chief of staff.

Wayne Cauthen, one of my political advisers whom I recruited from Martin Marietta to be my manager of contract compliance, brought me an idea. The banks wanted the city's pension dollars. In turn, we could get the banks to back loans for downtown housing and minority business loans.

What most people didn't realize was that many minorities in

Denver, especially blacks, worked for local, state, or federal government or school districts. We had no real base in the private sector, and the loans were very limited. These city loans would allow new entrepreneurs to have capital to start a business and succeed or fail on their own.

We created huge enemies for the administration when the council agreed to terminate Host Marriott for the new airport. Our mistake with the public and media was not adequately explaining the goals of the policy. The perception grew that I wanted to give all my friends concessions at the airport.

"I knew what the mayor wanted to do, and I sat in on every single selection process, which was about a thousand meetings," Foote said. "The whole cronyism thing came up, and we lost sight that what he was trying to do is open it up to local entrepreneurs. Even today, people will say, 'How did that business get a contract?' It makes me angry and it hurts because I sat in a thousand interviews and I knew who could do the job and what they were capable of."

Even with the bank loans, most of these new business owners took out second mortgages on their homes to start the ventures at the airport.

But I would later learn that even some of my staff questioned the process.

"The concession process was out of hand," Mike Dino recalled. "It was a good concept, but enough people who knew the mayor were chosen. The council had less and less trust in the mayor and began micromanaging contracts here and there."

The perception in the community was that Venita Vinson, my chief of staff before Foote, was picking and choosing which bids the city council reviewed.

"Having a woman chief of staff made sense," said Maria Garcia Berry, a lobbyist who acknowledged helping Vinson tackle the job. "Having a woman who's an African American probably caused some people to stop and say, 'What is this?'"

Vinson didn't get along with the media, especially after it was reported that she hadn't filed her income taxes in nine years. Some people, including my staff members, say I waited too long before firing her in 1992.

"What always bothered me is that some people didn't think they were accountable for their actions. It made us all look weak," said Charlotte Stephens, who supported Vinson's firing.

On the other hand, Donna Good was shocked when I fired Vinson.

"This was one instance where he was not loyal and threw her in front of a railroad car," Good said. "And I was leery of him for about a year. Then I realized that because she was so close to him, he was even more let down. He was actually really hurt."

I regret the hastiness of my decision.

I brought in Foote as my new chief of staff. She did an excellent job. Foote later became my Department of Public Works director and deputy mayor, and I promoted Cauthen to chief of staff.

While we were crafting our new concession policy, the city's rules that set percentage goals and other requirements to make sure minority-owned and women-owned businesses got a fair shake to bid on public construction projects was challenged in court.

Concrete Works of Colorado, Inc., sued the city in 1992. A district court judge ruled that the city's affirmative-action program was unconstitutional. That decision was overturned in 2003 by the Colorado Court of Appeals, which ruled that the program was constitutional because it was justified by historical and ongoing official discrimination. The U.S. Supreme Court refused to hear the case, thereby accepting that the city's affirmative-action program was constitutional.

Most people would think the black community was throwing kudos my way for opening up the process to everyone. But what a lot of people didn't know was that the expectations from the black community were unrealistic.

One black man charged into my office upset because he had bought a pickup truck to haul dirt for the new airport and was turned away by the company whose equipment was large enough to haul the guy's truck away.

We got calls from professional athletes—some as far away as New York City—and their business partners who wanted concessions at the airport. Legally, we could not deny them a chance to apply. But I didn't encourage their interest, because this went against the goal of the program to give new opportunities to local businesspeople.

"At first when he got elected, people would ask me if I knew the mayor and I would say yes, I knew Webb," said longtime friend Chuck Williams. "Then they would ask me to ask him to do something for them."

Reverend Acen Phillips knew the pressure I was under.

"There is a lack of understanding," Phillips said. "He opened a lot of doors, and a lot of people didn't go through them. But just look around the airport ... several black entrepreneurs became millionaires with a stroke of a pen. Some of them have given back to the black community, but others haven't."

I believed so strongly in the concession policy, which now is a model nationwide, that I grandfathered in several leases before I left office in 2003. A reporter asked me if I didn't have faith in future administrations to continue the policy. I frankly said no. The only faith I had was in my ability to make sure that minority and women businesses that were successful at DIA had the chance to continue that success.

The concession controversy was fueled by the opening delays and the baggage fiasco.

"The first delay made it look like officials were on top of the game," Dino recalled. "By the third delay, we looked like fools, but it showed his ability and his staff's ability to keep rolling."

City planners first started talking about Denver's need for a larger airport in 1974. Stapleton had to close often because of the weather and got a reputation as the worst airport in the country next to Newark, New Jersey.

The runways at Stapleton were built too close together, so in bad weather, the airport often had only one runway open. That meant airplanes from New York to Los Angeles would get backed up if there were delays in Denver.

My frustration was evident at the delayed opening of Denver International Airport during a visit to the control tower with Aviation Director Jim DeLong (right) and City Councilwoman Debbie Ortega. The airport opened on February 28, 1995.

There were also no direct flights to Europe, and national travelers avoided Stapleton whenever possible.

Safety was the main issue for City Councilman Bill Roberts, who was the first public official to call for a new airport.

"I wanted the airport moved out of town, and Mayor Bill McNichols wanted it expanded to the Rocky Mountain Arsenal," Roberts recalled. "I represented those neighborhoods that were bombarded by noise and safety issues. Some small planes had landed in people's backyards. The churches complained of the noise on Sundays. The schools had to deal with the noise."

Denver and Adams County reached a preliminary agreement in 1985 on a fifty-three-square-mile plot for the new airport. Adams County voters approved the annexation in 1988. A year later, Mayor Federico Peña, although not required to, put the issues before Denver voters, who approved the new airport.

I don't think that Mayor Peña ever got enough credit for the location of the new airport. Many people said it should be located in southeast Denver, where most of the growth was occurring at the time. But Peña had the vision to put the airport on the northeastern border of Denver and Adams counties, which spurred development in that area but included enough open space for future airport and economic growth. It was a masterful decision.

Ground was broken in September 1989 with Mayor Peña's initial optimistic opening of 1992.

I delayed the first opening, scheduled for October 31, 1993, back to December 19, 1993. Then the December 19 date got pushed back to March 9, 1994.

Some of the airport staff was so confident that the airport would open on March 9, 1994, that we had brochures made whose tops were cut to look similar to the unique white tent roof at DIA.

Those brochures became collectors' items when by February 28, 1994, I knew the baggage system wasn't ready and pushed the date to May 15, 1994. On May 2, I had to announce again that the baggage system wasn't ready, but I refused to give a new opening date.

Going before the press to announce each delay was painful, just painful. Then after the second and third time, there was nothing new to say.

We got national attention because this airport was the largest public-works project in the country. At one time, there were 12,000 construction workers on-site and 125 general contractors. The last major airport had been built in 1971 at Dallas/Fort Worth.

The jokes on the late-night shows of David Letterman and Jay Leno continued to pile it on. One older person from the South, whom I didn't know, wrote me a letter and told me to hang in there. "I know you aren't building the airport by yourself," the letter said.

The animosity was also aimed at Mayor Peña and Governor Roy Romer because they had both campaigned for the airport.

We added to the fodder when the city had a gala in November 1993 for more than 3,000 people in anticipation of the grand opening. That party turned out to be fifteen months before the actual opening.

The baggage system was a major reason for the delay, but so were several factors. Bill Smith, whom I admired greatly, died unexpectedly of a brain tumor in October 1992. George Doughty, who disagreed with our concession policy, resigned in May 1992.

Ginger Evans, chief airport engineer, was now saddled with the duties of the two men while also doing her job. She did the best she could, but Smith had never written down much of the information about the airport construction. He kept it in his head.

"It was a disaster for me personally," said Evans, whose three daughters were ages eight, six, and four at the time. "I went from working six days a week to seven days a week. I had a babysitter in the morning and a babysitter at night."

Evans left the project in the summer of 1994 but returned for the grand opening and was part of a ten-year-anniversary celebration in 2005.

When I announced the airport would open February 28, 1995, I still had doubts we could meet the date because of my historical struggles with the project.

The first hurdle I faced was with United Airlines dragging their feet to sign an agreement as the airport's main carrier. Mayor Peña's administration did not get the contract signed before he left office.

Vicki Braunagel, who became the codirector of aviation with Turner West, recalled one of my first conversations with United CEO Stephen Wolf, whom I liked.

"It was one of the mayor's classic conversations," Braunagel said. "He told Wolf either your people come to town and stay until negotiations are done or the whole $45 million deal is off. I could imagine Wolf thinking, 'Oh my God. This guy is in street-fighting mode.'"

I told Wolf I was too new in office to know better. We later met for dinner in Denver at a restaurant called Strings. We both arrived with our attorneys, and we all had a dinner of soup, salad, and New York strip steaks. After our attorneys left, Wolf, who is about my size, ordered another full meal, so I did the same. We sat in a back room at Strings fighting our machismo with food.

Our staffs worked round-the-clock, and we locked in a thirty-year commitment. The one stipulation from United was that the city had to accept the automatic-baggage system, which they claimed had been successfully tested in Texas. We had no choice but to agree, because United was the largest carrier and we needed to get the airport opened.

We also had to fight the Adams County commissioners from undermining the agreement between Denver and Adams County to locate cargo carriers at the north side of DIA. While this location to the north would benefit Adams County, the commissioners went another step and tried to get the cargo carriers to be located at Front Range Airport in Adams County. When I learned of this development, I decided to relocate the cargo carriers to the south side of DIA because the original agreement had been violated. The cargo carriers were pleased because their preference was to be located at the south side of DIA since it is closer to Interstate 70.

At one point, I had an office at the airport, located twenty-three miles northeast of city hall.

"Mayor Webb and his staff literally lived at the airport," recalled Councilwoman Cathy Donohue. "They looked exhausted. They never saw their families."

In order to spend any time with her sons, my chief of staff, Foote, let the boys Rollerblade in the airport's basement while she dealt with one crisis after another. She was very familiar with the airport, having served on city council for ten years and given her background in finance.

"I was wearing a wine-colored knit dress at one press conference where we announced another opening delay, and of course the newspapers picked the worst photograph, where we looked beat up," Foote said. "I could never wear that dress again."

Mike Musgrave, whom I named manager of the Department of Public Works after Smith died, was my "heavy." He made no friends and forced everyone to push ahead.

"I no longer went to work in suits or attended cabinet meetings," Musgrave said. "I worked six and a half days a week. I faced $100 million in change orders and subcontractors who hadn't been paid."

What many people don't realize is that we had to expand the terminal, at an additional cost of $65 million, just to accommodate the $193 million automated baggage system that United wanted. We built a larger airport than Mayor Peña envisioned, and it was a build-as-you-go project.

"My son Eric asked me what was wrong with the baggage system because kids at school were giving him a hard time," Foote said. "I told him I didn't know, but we were going to fix it. People attacked us personally, yet every day we got up and moved forward."

The most difficult aspect for me with the baggage-system failure was realizing that United didn't care if the new airport opened. As far as they were concerned, the longer they stayed at Stapleton, paying lower rent, the better off they were.

United adjusted schedules and had fewer flights into Denver. They did everything they could to slow down the process. United always threw their weight around because they were the largest carrier.

I felt like one of those cartoon characters on a bucking Brahma bull. I was hanging on for dear life, trying to meet another deadline, while the press and public were waiting for me to fall off.

I had never before been in a situation where we continually missed deadlines. Some people told me to fire the people in charge, but it wasn't their fault. They were thrown into a situation, just like me.

I never told *Rocky Mountain News* reporter Kevin Flynn, but he understood the airport better than almost anyone: he chronicled how United, the city, and the maker of the baggage system were at fault.

The television footage of luggage being mangled on a test run showed very clearly that the $193 million automated system was a bust.

"Then the question became 'What do we do?'" Braunagel recalled. "Do we try and require United to do a tug-and-cart? United threatened to cut back the number of flights to Denver and just provide the minimum. Or do we build a new system? Who was going to blink on the issue?"

United officials, now minus Wolf, who had gone to U.S. Air, came to Denver and wanted to meet over dinner at The Brown Palace. Well, that was the shortest dinner in history for me and city attorney Dan Muse. They told me United made a corporate decision and wanted to delay the opening of the airport until 1996. I bluntly reminded them that I was up for reelection in May 1995.

"If the airport is not open by then, I wouldn't even vote for myself," I said. "Delaying it another year is totally unacceptable."

Then Muse and I got up from the dinner table and left the men to eat their meal alone.

We had $3 billion already invested in the airport, and it couldn't open because of the botched baggage system. We had air shows at the new airport, which attracted good crowds, but no passenger planes could land because we didn't have a workable baggage system.

The business community was getting nervous, and I knew I needed their help to move forward with an alternative baggage system. I had to capture the business community and bring them inside, closer than I had ever done before.

The Denver Metro Chamber of Commerce said they could do a better job at the airport, so I welcomed the members to help. They weren't thrilled that our meetings were in public, with the press present, but then they began to have a deeper appreciation for what we faced.

When I called a press conference to say we would not delay the airport's opening, the chamber board members were there supporting me.

The best thing we did was hire German consultant Mattias Franz of Logplan to first inspect the automated system and then design a new system.

When United balked at the Franz plan, we invited United officials to hear another plan. What the airline didn't know was that our city engineer presented a fictional plan that was so convincing that it scared the airline. Our engineer drew up bogus plans, and his acting performance was as good as Humphrey Bogart in the movie *Casablanca*.

The bluff worked. We needed another $63 million to build the new baggage system, but we were finally headed in the right direction.

"I was very impressed by Wellington's willingness to make the right, not politically expedient, decision," Braunagel said. "It was a very difficult time, but I thought [they were] some of his strongest hours."

A month before the airport opened, United announced a $40 fare increase to help cover its share of the increased baggage-system cost. It wasn't until 2005 that United finally admitted the automated system was a failure and sold much of the machine for scrap.

The ray of sunshine that we were finally getting a baggage system that worked was quickly consumed by dark clouds. My lowest of lows with the airport came when the U.S. Securities and Exchange Commission (SEC) began investigating our bond dealings.

Several things fed into the investigation. First, the SEC under the Clinton administration wanted to target cities awarding contracts in what they called "pay to play." The SEC enforcement went after local and state politicians they perceived were giving contracts to firms that gave them campaign contributions. They did not investigate members of Congress.

"These cowards," I thought. "The policy should apply to every elected official."

It also was interesting that the majority of the cities targeted were led by black mayors.

Because there would be millions of dollars for bond firms with the new airport, I stayed with the bond firm of Pryor McClendon Counts & Co., which was the firm Mayor Peña had chosen. They were qualified and I saw no reason to change firms.

But Pryor McClendon also happened to be an African American–owned company that had given me a large campaign donation when I was auditor. We added several other bond firms, including minority- and women-owned firms, to get the work on a rotating basis.

The one company I personally excluded was located in New York. An individual at that firm was scheduled to have a fund-raiser for me in the 1991 mayoral race. I flew out to New York and he sent an assistant to tell me the fund-raiser had been canceled. The company then backed Norm Early.

That individual called me after the election, apologized to me for making the useless trip to New York for the non–fund-raiser, and asked if he could come to Denver.

I told him everyone was welcome in Denver. Instead of refusing to see him when he arrived, I personally informed him that as long as I was mayor, his company would not get one penny of city work.

Denver's strong mayor position allows an individual, in some cases, to decide which firms get city work and which firms don't. Some would say my actions with this company were petty, but at some point I had to make a statement that people cannot do anything without consequences.

The SEC investigation forced us to hire a Washington, D.C., lawyer, who formerly was the SEC counsel for enforcement, to defend the city and myself. I remember walking into the SEC's Enforcement Division and seeing thirty men in white shirts and skinny ties and fearing that no matter what I said, they wouldn't believe me.

They did not charge us with anything, but they were considering me guilty based on newspaper clippings and not on facts. The headlines about corruption also raised the suspicions of people in Denver, many who thought I was dead meat and couldn't survive this unfair attack.

This was even more damaging than the baggage-system failure because people who didn't like my administration were painting us as dishonest.

I told Wilma it was my worst experience with a government agency, and she empathized with me. I thought it was unbridled power. I had not been indicted. I had not been arrested. Yet the headlines and the drawn-out investigation painted us as guilty without any evidence.

After five years of dragging the city and me through hell, the SEC found nothing except that some of our paperwork could have been better. We suffered through headlines labeling us as crooks, and even when the SEC sent us a letter clearing the city of any wrongdoing, the agency would not publicly acknowledge that the investigation had been dropped. For the first time, I felt like some conservatives when they talk about the excessive power of the federal government.

"It was frustrating for everyone who worked their asses off for the city," former city attorney Muse recalled. "We followed the rules, but when we showed up in a position of power, the rules changed."

Before the opening, which was attended by 1,000 members of the media nationwide, Foote, along with engineers, operations staff, and contractors, put together a checklist of 1,798 items to inspect. They had to replace the lights in Concourse C because they were five years old. They flushed all of the toilets and discovered low water pressure was caused by soil accumulated in the pumping stations.

Those checks were made while birds, trapped inside when the unique white-tented roof was installed, flew around the concourses. Their offspring still make the airport their home and have become a novelty for some visitors.

I was extremely proud of the city workers when they moved 100 aircraft, 13,000 vehicles, and 6,000 rental cars from Stapleton to DIA without any interruption in airline service. There was bumper-to-bumper traffic of rental cars, catering equipment, and other airline operational equipment going about four miles an hour for forty-eight hours between the two facilities.

I felt like General George Patton watching the equipment roll by. I was damned proud of our city workers and airline employees.

"I don't think people realize how us little civil servants opened DIA and put Denver on the international map," Foote said.

I still have a small model airplane that says a lot about my first term in office. The plane was made to commemorate the opening of DIA, and three dates are crossed out. It truly was blood, sweat, and tears that got us to February 28, 1995, when two United and one Continental plane landed simultaneously at the airport.

My good friend Bill Daniels got the bragging rights for the first landing when we allowed him to land his private jet, which now hangs in Concourse C, at DIA the night before the grand opening.

My pride in the airport is for such achievements as the concession policy; the artwork, including work by Denver and Colorado artists; the religious spaces on the sixth floor; and the coming together for the first time in history of the African American and Anglo members of the Masons to create the airport's dedication stone.

In the next ten years of operation, DIA would garner numerous awards, including Best Airport in the United States for Customer Service, J. D. Power; One of the Least-Delayed Airports for Business Travellers, *Business Traveller* magazine; One of the World's Five Best Airports, *Official Airline Guide*; and Best Airport in North America, *Travel Savvy* magazine.

It was no surprise to me when Jim Monaghan warned me that I couldn't even run for a second term if the airport didn't open on February 28, 1995.

The headline in the March 13, 1995, of *The Denver Post* said, "Upbeat Webb launches bid for 2nd term." I officially kicked off

It was a glorious day in 2005 with past and current leaders gathered together for the celebration of the tenth anniversary of the opening of Denver International Airport. Joining me to cut the cake were (from left) City Councilman Michael Hancock, Codirector of Aviation Vicki Braunagel, Denver mayor John Hickenlooper, former Denver mayor Federico Peña (who also served as U.S. secretary of transportation), and Codirector of Aviation Turner West.

my campaign at the new Elitch Gardens amusement park, which was relocated from a northwest Denver neighborhood to the Central Platte Valley.

I survived the airport battle without permanent scars to face the nastiest political race of my life.

Chapter Twenty-One

Media, Brutal 1995 Reelection

As long as I've been in politics, one area where I've struggled is dealing with the media.

At one point during my first term, I stopped reading both Denver newspapers.

"How in the hell are you going to be mayor and defend what's going on when you don't even read what they are writing?" asked my former spokeswoman and mayoral aide Deborah Tucker.

Mike Dino quit watching the nightly news and avoided returning reporters' calls.

"We weren't good at dealing with the press," Dino said. "We had no discipline. We couldn't tell a straight story, or we said too much. There was not a lot of patience, and we just got mad and personal."

"Wellington felt there were racist folks in the press who were unfair and had no sense of objectivity," Dino said. "He felt like they had a hidden agenda and were out to get him. It wasn't like he was paranoid like Nixon or anything, but it was overwhelming."

Briggs Gamblin, the former Colorado director of the government watchdog group Common Cause, was my first press secretary after Federico Peña's spokesman Tom Gleason left in September 1991. I allowed Gleason to stay on a couple of months after I took office so he could have five years vested with the city.

I knew Gamblin was a good public-policy person with Common Cause, and I thought he could do the press job. But Gamblin acknowledges he was overwhelmed by the job.

"We had no idea how challenging it would be," Gamblin said. "There is no more-covered day-to-day politician than the mayor of Denver in Colorado journalism."

Gamblin felt many reporters were still shocked that Norm Early lost the election. He had to deal with the administration reacting to the media instead of actively setting the tone of coverage.

"We did not do a good job of explaining the [airport] concessions, and that needs to be laid on me," Gamblin said. "Internally, we got defensive instead of trumpeting that what we were doing was beneficial for Denver. We needed to be a little more seasoned and a little more aggressive."

I knew that living in one of the few remaining two-newspaper cities meant the competition helped spur the sensational headlines.

"I told him some reporters would do a tough story on their grandmother to get their editor's attention," Gamblin said. "He would get it, but his emotions would take over."

I also have never been one to chitchat with members of the media before or after press conferences. At times, my staff would get on me about acting aloof in public when I really was just preoccupied with my full plate as mayor.

"He can be aloof and standoffish," said Charlotte Stephens. "Both Deborah [Tucker] and I always were pulling his chain. We'd tell him to go back and talk to the person who he walked right by and ignored."

My staff got used to leaving me with my thoughts if I looked preoccupied.

"Next to my father, he is the man I have the most respect for," said John McBride. "He is a really good man. He also can piss me off. He'll walk into a room and not speak to you. You can't take it personally. That's just him."

The media even turned on one of its own when I hired Butch Montoya, the news director at 9News, to be my manager of safety in 1994. Beth McCann left the job to work on the Safe City program.

Some critics charged that I appointed Montoya to appease the

Hispanic community. What many people didn't realize was that Montoya had counseled jail inmates for years and was very familiar with the issues in the police, fire, and sheriff departments.

In some ways, there was no way for me to win with the media, and often I just stopped trying.

My supporters also began questioning the press coverage.

"Everything he did was scrutinized and turned inside out so it became a different issue than what it was," recalled Annie Slaughter. "Blacks have a double magnifying glass on them. If they do something that would seem slight for someone else, it becomes a massive issue for them."

During the 1995 reelection campaign, Jim Monaghan addressed our weaknesses with the press. My best decision was hiring Denver native Andrew Hudson, a Manual High School graduate who had worked as a deputy press secretary for U.S. Senator Tim Wirth and as spokesman for the Regional Transportation District.

Gamblin became my liaison with the city council, which was a great fit for him.

"They felt just totally beat-up after the election and treated unfairly by the press," Hudson said. "Looking at the press clippings, Briggs was in an impossible position. He tried hard but could not manage the hurricane around him. Briggs is just too nice and wanted everyone to love him. Reporters took advantage of that, and there was no plan to fight it at a strategic level."

I had previously met Hudson briefly and felt that even though he was only twenty-eight when I interviewed him, he could turn things around. He proved me right when he confronted radio-station talk-show host Peter Boyles and former *Denver Post* columnist Chuck Green head-on about an inaccurate report of thousands of mangled passenger baggage at Denver International Airport (DIA).

"I went on the air when I was still a little green," Hudson recalled. "I got into a screaming match, and we called each other dopes. I got off the phone and my body was shaking. I thought, 'There goes my great job with the mayor.' Then I felt a hand on my shoulder. It was the mayor with a smile on his face. 'You're going to work out just fine,' he told me."

But that memorable day with Hudson almost didn't happen. The 1995 campaign was the ugliest, nastiest political fight of my life.

As the race approached, I assumed Auditor Bob Crider would challenge me and City Councilwoman Mary DeGroot would run for auditor. One day, she sent me a note saying she wasn't going to run for auditor, but she would be in the 1995 race.

Then my staff joked that DeGroot might run for mayor because she suddenly was wearing makeup and dressing in a red suit jacket.

I told Wilma I wanted to meet with political consultants Eric Sondermann and Floyd Ciruli to give me an analysis on my administration and our vulnerabilities before we started polling. They made it clear that they were going to support another candidate.

They told me I was vulnerable, especially to white females. Sondermann went on to help manage DeGroot's campaign. To this day, if the press wants a negative quote about me, Sondermann does his best to deliver.

Although I hired Sondermann to work on advertising during my 1987 auditor race, this time around, he likened my administration to Chicago's Richard J. Daley machine.

The airport's successful opening didn't stop the venom streaming from DeGroot's mouth.

The press knew DeGroot and I didn't care for each other. She did her best to make inclusion projects seem like something filthy and called me a crook and a criminal, with absolutely no evidence to support her libelous statements. She questioned my integrity and the integrity of members of my family. She threw out the words *cronyism* and *corruption*.

Her husband later wrote me a note apologizing for calling my administration the most corrupt in the country. Corrupt? Based on who and what? His wife was part of the city council that approved every contract that also was reviewed by the auditor.

DeGroot tried to paint my inclusion program as something

dirty, when in fact my administration reflected the city. No one was left out—whether white, black, brown, yellow, straight or gay, Jewish, Catholic, Protestant, Baptist, or Muslim. My administration truly was a rainbow and included individuals from all income classes.

During my first term, people tried to make an issue of whether I would accept the traditional free membership to Denver's Country Club that was given to all mayors. Well, in 1991, there were no black members at the country club. But instead of buying into any controversy, I accepted the membership, which at the time cost $25,000.

"I said I was going to be mayor of the entire city; that includes the rich as well as the poor," I said.

Still, DeGroot tried to form a rift in the community, even though she couldn't get along with her colleagues on the council.

"The Queen of Mean, as I like to call Mary DeGroot, was the absolute worst person on the council," said former councilwoman Cathy Donohue, who left her council seat in 1994 to head my Regulatory Reform Department. "She couldn't get a bill passed. It would have been frightening if she got elected as mayor."

Only three of DeGroot's twelve council colleagues—Ramona Martinez, Ted Hackworth, and Ed Thomas—endorsed her in the runoff.

"People called the office and said they were not voting for me because I was backing Wellington Webb and his cronyism," recalled former councilwoman Joyce Foster, who was reelected. "I had to remind them that Wellington Webb had been very good to southeast Denver with the renovation of University Hills shopping center and improvements at Bible Park. We did it together."

DeGroot's campaign listed my cronies, and among the names of mostly black people was attorney Steve Farber. Farber watched the 1991 campaign mostly from the sidelines because Early's campaign manager, Cole Finegan, worked at Farber's firm.

After the 1991 election, my administration didn't initially use Farber's firm, Brownstein Hyatt & Farber, for any contracts, but that softened into the term.

"In four short years, I went from the number-one enemy of the Webb administration to the only Jewish crony of Mayor Webb," Farber said. "I was supportive of the mayor because he did a good job the first four years and he deserved the opportunity to continue the leadership for four more years."

What was happening in Denver in 1995 also was going on in different parts of the country. I think the best time for black mayors was in the early 1990s, when African Americans were leaders in Seattle, San Francisco, Dallas, Denver, Kansas City, Houston, Cleveland, Detroit, Jackson, Memphis, New York, Rochester, and New Orleans. By the mid-1990s, many of the incumbents were being challenged by white females, often liberals. Less than a third of the black incumbents got reelected.

"He was being attacked day in and day out," recalled Donna Good, who once again headed my fund-raising. "People were willing to believe that he was going to lose."

But as the incumbent mayor, I found that the campaign money was a little easier to raise than during the first election. In 1991, my campaign generated less than $300,000, and that was money from mostly unknown residents. In 1995, I was able to raise $1.1 million, compared to DeGroot's $528,824, from a contribution list that looked like the Denver Chamber of Commerce.

The contributions came from my longtime supporters, including Bill Coors and Rita Bass, Bill Daniels, Sharon Magness, and Merle Chambers.

My other opponents included Crider and, surprisingly, attorney John Frew, who was a friend and a former supporter. Frew figured that he could snag the election when DeGroot and I knocked each other out.

DeGroot's anti-Webb campaign was getting legs when I asked Monaghan, who also served as spokesman for billionaire Phil Anschutz, to run my campaign. He brought in a young guy named David Kenney to help.

I asked some business leaders to be my "secret weapon."

"When you go to these cocktail parties and my name comes up, don't let them know you support me, but find out what their issues are with me, so I can do better," I told them.

I wanted to know what people were saying when I left these gatherings and at the dozens of parties that excluded me from the invitation list.

Denver's upper crust made it very clear that they were concerned about some of the contracts that were awarded. They were relying on the press reports and not looking at the bigger picture of how I was the first mayor to open the process to everyone.

"I don't think Wellington needed then or now to defend what he did or why," Dino said. "He should say he would do it again. This country was brought up on the Good Old Boys Club. Wellington brought new good old boys and women to that club that looked different than folks in Denver were used to."

Former state senator Paul Sandoval, my friend, explained the cronyism charges to voters who were on the fence.

"As far as the cronyism charges, he didn't hide it or run from it," Sandoval said. "He said he hired his friends. To the victor go the spoils. He had every right to bring in people he trusted. He never handed out anything to anyone. You had to go through the city council and channels. It may have been perceived that he did hand his friends things, but that's not how it works in city government."

I was campaigning against a very slick, manipulative, and deceptive candidate who tried to play the race card and divide the city. I kept reminding voters of what we accomplished during our first term: a successful opening of DIA, building a new central library, addressing the "Summer of Violence," and gaining positive press from World Youth Day.

"When I look back at all of the things we had to deal with in the first term, Norm Early would have had a heck of a time," Dino said. "Wellington is as good as it gets in the line of fire. It's his competitive nature as an athlete. He wants the ball when you are down by one and with just seconds left to play. He got disappointed because

295

at times no one near him wanted the ball. They wanted to be on the court when the team was up by fifty points and dunking the ball. When it was close and the heat was on, there were not too many people around him."

Despite my accomplishments from the first term, my opponents ground away at the negatives, but one debate just struck me as funny. Frew kept saying that Denver was like a donut hole: all of the surrounding suburbs were doing well, whereas the city struggled.

I countered: "Denver is not a donut hole but a sweet roll. Denver is the middle, where all of the jelly is. We're much sweeter than our suburban counterparts because we have cultural and sports amenities downtown."

Although I was living this reelection twenty-four hours a day, my supporters and even my cabinet members got complacent. My heart sank when the Sunday before the election, *Denver Post* reporter Christopher Lopez reported I would win outright and not have to face a runoff. I'm convinced that headline kept many of my supporters home on Election Day.

I knew I was in trouble when I checked in with one of my supporters who was waving campaign signs on a street corner.

"Mayor, I don't feel good about the election," Samuel, who was from Nigeria, explained to me. "I keep waving, but they don't wave back."

It stung to lose by ninety-seven votes to DeGroot. She garnered 42.8 percent of the vote to my 42.7 percent. We were headed to a runoff.

"It scared me when he lost in the primary," recalled Ben Jeffers, who flew in from Louisiana, where he served as chief of staff for Governor Edwin Edwards. "I was with him that night, and he was real down, as obviously anyone would be."

I thought Jeffers had gone back to Louisiana when I heard a knock at my door early the next morning.

"I was in a taxi headed to the airport, and I told the driver to turn around," Jeffers said. "I went to Wellington's house and basically woke him up. I figured he needed encouragement. We sat in the living room for several hours and at the end of the conversation, he was pumped up and ready to go."

I had to shake off all my concerns about being a six-foot-four black man going head-to-head with a white female candidate. The gloves came off.

I also shook up my cabinet and reminded them that if I was out of a job, so were they. I looked at the results from their precincts and realized that many of my cabinet members had not worked hard enough—and some not at all—to get us reelected. They had a couple of weeks to redeem themselves.

The loss in the primary was a wake-up call for me and my staff.

"I cried myself to sleep," Good said. "I couldn't eat for a few days. Wellington was walking around with his head practically on the ground. After a few days, I told him, 'You have to stop it and get over it. If you don't get over it, your staff won't either.' Denver was dancing with someone else, but in the end, they would go home with Wellington."

All of my supporters went into high gear for the runoff.

"Peña had a tough reelection too," said political consultant Mike Stratton. "But as he had done a million times, no one can overcome adversity as well as Wellington Webb. The runoff was a good wake-up call for us and the people in the organization. In the long run, it may have been a blessing in disguise, because there may not have been as strong an effort."

Frew supported me in the runoff, but Crider, whom I liked, told me he didn't think I could win and backed DeGroot.

Jeffers urged me to get Dino and Greg Kolomitz back on board for the runoff campaign. He also recruited national political advisers Bill Lynch of New York and Maryann Spraggins of Washington, D.C., to come to Denver and assist us.

"I left the house one morning and I told my wife I was going to do something constructive," Dino said. "I couldn't do it by being an adviser in the mayor's office."

Denver fire chief Rich Gonzales rallied my supporters with a bullhorn during my reelection bid in 1995. The Latino community supported my first mayoral campaign in 1991 and helped me get reelected in 1995 and 1999.

Kolomitz, now working with Maria Garcia Berry, also didn't hesitate to help.

"Up to that point in the 1995 campaign, there wasn't the chemistry of the 1991 race," Kolomitz said. "He wanted to recapture some of that. He had the confidence that we could get the job done."

Foote spent her weekends trying to drum up support for me in grocery-store parking lots.

"The first weekend, no one would talk to me," she said. "The second weekend, they wanted me to answer questions. By the third weekend, people were whispering to me that they were going to vote for him ... Mary DeGroot was vicious with the attacks. Even when the polls showed them neck-and-neck or she was ahead, she was not gracious and had no sense of humor. People who were going to vote for her changed their minds. They told me they didn't like her."

I thought DeGroot's technique of referring to me as *Wellington* and not as *mayor* backfired. I told her on a KOA radio program that only my good friends call me Wellington, and she should call me Mr. Mayor. DeGroot's reaction to tell me to "chill" didn't go over well with voters who thought she should respect the office of mayor, even if she didn't respect me.

She even once accused Wilma of trying to intimidate her by standing behind her at a debate. Wilma was only standing there because we were in a small room at a radio station and there was nowhere else to stand.

My campaign was split on whether we should address DeGroot's charges of corruption and cronyism. Monaghan didn't think it was an issue, but Muse was adamant we could no longer keep quiet.

"Given everything I've read in the newspaper or heard on television, I wouldn't even vote for myself," I told my family members.

I knew I had to offer a mea culpa for my mistakes and also dispel the untruths. In a sixty-four-point letter, I said I didn't do some things well, I was not perfect, but that I was going to do better the second time, and we also listed the many things that we had done well.

We drafted the letter before the runoff, but I wanted to wait to send it. We mailed it during the runoff, primarily to voters south of Colfax Avenue because we knew these were mostly white conservative voters. My base north of Colfax was still strong, but I couldn't just rely on the minority vote. I had to build coalitions.

"I think DeGroot's campaign overreacted in terms of showing a woman could be tough," Gamblin said. "She came off dour and scolding. Then he tells the voters that he has an agenda and he acknowledges mistakes were made and will be corrected. The message was he got it, and most people accepted that because they liked him. Voters were looking for a reason to stick with Mayor Webb. Mary did not give them a reason to leave."

Don Bain, who watched this campaign from the sidelines, said at the time, "People are going to support the devil they know [as] opposed to the devil they don't."

DeGroot also never told voters what she would do as mayor.

"Mary made the same mistake that Don Bain made when he ran against Peña," said political consultant Steve Welchert. "They did not put forward their own platform. You can beat the incumbent to get to the runoff, but then you have to tell voters what you would do as mayor."

This opened it up for us to question her management abilities.

To assure voters I was serious about change, I told my cabinet that everyone—except Police Chief Mike Michaud—would have to resign and reapply if I got reelected.

At the same time, Councilman Thomas was trying to get Michaud to back DeGroot.

"My response was to go public and tell people if she won, I'm out of here," Michaud said.

Our son Keith also wrote a letter to a gay newspaper chronicling my leadership skills compared to DeGroot's.

"I am writing to you today as the proud gay son of Mayor Wellington Webb and First Lady Wilma Webb," Keith wrote. "The choices made June 6 could easily change the amount of direct influence we, our community, will have on City Hall."

In addition to my work for the gay community, Keith outlined how my administration made Denver a better place to live by addressing gangs and violence, and its numerous successful projects, including the opening of the airport.

I also called on the ministers to once again help.

"In the first election, it was one preacher and one politician standing together," recalled Reverend Acen Phillips. "In the second election, it was most of the preachers and one politician standing together. We pulled in white folks from south Denver who had never been involved in politics. Those ministers never dreamed we would be working together, and after the election, some even stayed with the ministerial alliance."

The 1995 mayoral runoff also allowed the black community to finally heal from its political bickering. I opened a campaign office, headed by Arie Taylor and Gloria Tanner, in the heart of northeast Denver. The two women were political opponents but came together to fight DeGroot's accusations against me and DeGroot's opposition to opening city contracts to the entire community.

DeGroot had unintentionally reunited the black community.

I also got support in the 1995 race from Early, Regis Groff, and their supporters, who opposed me in 1991. I couldn't have won a second term without them.

This time, on Election Day, Samuel brought me good news.

"Mayor, I think we did pretty good today because I'm out there waving and people are waving back," he told me with a smile on his face.

Our supporters were not complacent in the runoff. I got 54 percent, or 66,884 votes, compared to Mary's 45.9 percent, or 56,725 votes.

"Ultimately, this is a left-of-center city, and Mary ran as a right-of-center candidate," Sondermann told the *Rocky Mountain News*. "I think it's about as simple as that."

Well, not quite. Mark Obmascik of *The Denver Post* wrote in an election analysis: "In an election age where political races typically are decided by thirty-second television ads, Webb won with a classic

The Webb family celebrated following my reelection in 1995: (from left) my brother Joe, campaign director Mike Dino, and deputy campaign director Greg Kolomitz. Dino and Kolomitz helped me recapture the spirit of the 1991 race for the 1995 runoff.

door-knocking drive. No one could accuse this incumbent of arrogantly sitting back and expecting voters to recoronate him."

I spent the last thirty hours of the campaign awake and shaking hands.

I was physically and emotionally exhausted, happy, and angry simultaneously. I remembered the joy of the 1991 election. I was proud of the resiliency and tenacity of the 1995 victory—without the endorsement of either newspapers—but the sting of the unfounded accusations hurt. It's bad enough to have to deal with my mistakes, but having to answer unfounded, untrue accusations made me angry. It reminded me that politics is not for the weak.

But I was also exhilarated that people stood by me, voted for me, and gave me the opportunity to do some of the programs and projects that I wanted to do. I told reporters this would be my last term, but deep down, I felt this was really my first term.

The four years of my first term were spent basically completing Mayor Peña's agenda, which mainly was DIA. I was a good soldier and never complained about what I found out and what I was left. My only goal then was to build the 85 percent of the airport left to build—and build it, we did.

Now it was my turn to take the next four years and emphasize what I wanted to do as mayor. I had already laid the groundwork of one large project in 1994 when I formed the South Platte Working Group. I wanted to turn ten and a half miles of abandoned railroad tracks, homeless shanties, and garbage dumps along the South Platte River into parks and open space.

I called a press conference on February 2, 1995, to endorse the group's report, called "A Vision for the South Platte River." I announced my plan to bring together city, state, federal, and private landowners to transform the area. A twenty-seven-member commission, cochaired by Joseph Blake, then of Shea Homes, included Casey Davenhill of the Denver Audubon Society, Myrna Poticha of Clean Water Action, and Jim Daniels of the Denver Planning Board.

Joe Shoemaker, a former state senator and father of the Greenway

Trail along the Platte River, was thrilled I was taking on this project.

"I've been through a lot of mayors, but this is the first mayor to come along and say, 'This is Denver's greatest natural resource.' What the mayor is suggesting is like a miracle to me," Shoemaker told *The Denver Post*.

The *Rocky Mountain News* later called me the river's "most important cheerleader."

Mayor Peña laid the groundwork for this project when he cleaned up the abandoned railroad tracks from the Central Platte Valley. Without Peña's work, my administration would never have been able to transform the area.

I named Andrew Wallach, my mayoral assistant, who had also worked for Mayor Peña, as the director for the South Platte Corridor Project. In 1991, the area was an eyesore of abandoned warehouses and railroad yards. By 2003, it was home to a new amusement park, the Pepsi Center sporting arena, the new Mile High Stadium for the Denver Broncos, the city's newest thirty-acre park, and pricey lofts.

But when I announced the project, many people thought I'd never produce results.

"At the time of the first press conference, it was four months before the election, and some people thought it was just the idea of the day," Wallach recalled.

Wallach had tried to get Mayor Peña more involved in the parks system, but Peña balked.

"I think Mayor Peña thought the parks were too much of a Yuppie issue, and he was somewhat cautious of the Yuppie image anyway, so he played against the stereotype," Wallach said. "I think Mayor Webb did the same thing. Some people thought he would have gone to all of the parks and just put up new basketball hoops, which, in some cases, he did. But he recognized that no one had adopted the Platte River, and this became his legacy."

I hired water lawyer Ken Salazar, the former chief legal counsel to Governor Roy Romer and former director of the Colorado Department of Natural Resources, as a consultant on the project. Salazar would go on to be elected state attorney general and a U.S. senator.

"Some people really felt in the beginning that he couldn't do it," Salazar said. "Key people felt Wellington would put out the vision but not follow through. Two or three years later, they said how incredibly wrong they were. It had been successful because he was devoted and led the charge."

I got the support of neighboring communities by extending the improvements to land outside of the city limits in Adams County to the north and the city of Englewood to the south.

In 1996, Great Outdoors Colorado, the state's lottery program dedicated to parks and open space, gave the city $7 million to help leverage more than $20 million in additional state, federal, city, and private funds for the project. The goals included managing river corridors, designing parks to make sure natural habitat is maintained, removing noxious weeds, and restoring native vegetation and wildlife refuge.

The costs included $10 million to help reduce flood dangers and connect the Greenway Trail to communities to the north and $3 million to redevelop an abandoned wastewater treatment plant. Funding for six new parks, which was more than $10 million, came from GoCo, Colorado Division of Wildlife, Gates Family Foundation, Winter Park Trust, and Trillium Corporation.

The South Platte Project became a national model.

"The mayor really became a one-man parks department," Wallach said. "If left to their own devices, the Parks Department would have just wanted more money for maintenance, but the mayor wanted new parks."

I made a land trade with Trillium on a handshake with company president David Syreen before the 1995 election. They got property closer to downtown to develop into lofts, and the city got the land near the Platte. Of course, having new parks made their property more valuable to potential home owners, and the parks created a real community in the heart of downtown.

That was always my goal with downtown: attract new residents and the businesses will follow. It's a blueprint I preach to other cities, which still make the mistake of going after retail first.

"Other mayors look to Denver as an example of how to bring people back into the city and eliminate urban blight," Salazar said.

My planning director, Jennifer Moulton, played a major role in the success of the project, including hiring a real-estate agent who quietly negotiated the land deals with private owners without controversy. She also helped enlist the support of the League of Women Voters, whose members had influence.

The project had youth-education programs whose participants included the Colorado Department of Natural Resources, Colorado River Outfitters Association, Denver Audubon Society, and Volunteers for Outdoor Colorado. Volunteers planted more than 300 trees, 7,800 shrubs, and nearly 7,000 wetland plants. Those who worked on the trails included GoCo, the Downtown Denver Partnership, University of Colorado College of Design, Public Service Company of Colorado, and numerous city agencies.

I gave my State of the City annual speech at Commons Park in 2000.

"People say they don't like the traditional politician, but Mayor Webb came in with the political skills and confidence and knowledge of state, federal, and city politics to make this project successful," Wallach said.

My last State of the City speech was on the Millennium Bridge. I always have to pause when I walk across that bridge because the city's share to make it a reality was $3 million.

This was a signature piece for a developer in Lower Downtown, but he had run into financial problems completing the $6 million bridge.

I first heard of the bridge when Moulton and my chief of staff Wayne Cauthen double-teamed me. Moulton said the bridge would be an architecture landmark for Lower Downtown, much like the tent roof design of DIA.

I looked at the design and said, "This looks like a damn ship."

The bridge was designed to look like a masthead for a ship. The question became how could the city legitimately help pay for a private developer's bridge. The answer was that the bridge would allow pedestrians to get from the South Platte River to downtown, which made it a public-works project.

For Moulton, who was from Boston, the bridge reminded her of home and her passion for harbors and boats. For me, the bridge is a reminder of $3 million in city money.

Another important key to the redevelopment of the Platte Valley was a new arena for the Denver Nuggets and the Colorado Avalanche. Ascent Entertainment, which owned both teams, agreed to build the $160 million facility and sold the naming rights to PepsiCo, Inc. In turn, the city would let the teams out of its lease with the city-owned McNichols Arena and give the owner property tax exemptions and sales tax rebates for the new Pepsi Center.

The teams collect a seat tax for the city, so we still get revenue from the facility. I also insisted the agreement include a clause that both teams stay in Denver for at least twenty-five years. Liz Orr deserves a lot of credit for negotiating this agreement.

When negotiations stalled, I showed up at a press conference with a can of Coca-Cola, Pepsi's top competition.

"You don't pull a gun on me ... because I'll be drinking Coke at every function I go to from now on," I said.

The symbolism didn't go unnoticed.

The Pepsi Center opened in 1999 as a premier venue for sporting events and concerts.

Liberty Media Corp. later bought Ascent Entertainment. The city briefly considered taking over the Pepsi Center before billionaire Stan Kroenke, who also owns a stake in the NFL St. Louis Rams, bought the Colorado teams and arena from Liberty Media. We thought Kroenke would make a long-term commitment to rebuilding the Nuggets, which has proven to be true.

Projects were moving forward when I faced another unforeseen event. I should have gotten used to the unexpected, because it seemed something always happened during my tenure. Denver was chosen to be the site of the Oklahoma City bombing trial.

Suspects Timothy McVeigh and Terry Nichols had been accused of putting a massive bomb inside a rental truck in front of the Alfred P. Murrah Federal Building in Oklahoma City. About 9:00 A.M. on April 19, 1995, the bomb exploded, blowing away half of the nine-story building. The worst terrorist attack on U.S. soil before 9/11 left 168 children, men, and women dead. Most heart-wrenching were the photographs of rescuers pulling the broken and bloody bodies of the children from the building's day-care center.

The trials were moved from Oklahoma City to Denver because of the question of the men having an impartial jury in Oklahoma. Denver residents opened their hearts and, in many cases, their homes to the victims' families, who sat through months of gut-wrenching testimony before both men were convicted.

I had no intentions of allowing another O. J. Simpson–like media circus to happen in the heart of downtown Denver.

"The mayor called me in and told me my job was to make the media behave," recalled Amy Bourgeron.

Through the leadership of the Denver bureau of the Associated Press, Bourgeron successfully got the media to set up ground rules. The coordination included everything from where the television satellite trucks parked to the number of reporters allowed in the courtroom.

The media plan was later used for the Kobe Bryant alleged-rape trial in Eagle, Colorado, in 2003.

I felt good ending 1996 with several city projects under way, but then life's reality hit. December 1996 was difficult because I was reflecting on the deaths of four of my friends. Two basketball buddies of mine, Jerry Trice, who put Weber State on the map in Utah, and Walt Hamlet, who set records at Hastings, Nebraska, both died of lung cancer. Their years of smoking one cigarette after another snuffed out their lives while they were in their fifties.

My former spokeswoman, Deborah Tucker, a heavy smoker since she was a young teenager, also died of lung cancer shortly after she published a short book on the 1991 mayoral campaign.

Harold Parker, the only person who felt like a big brother to me, and was a colleague at Fort Logan, died of a liver ailment.

I was thinking of my own mortality when a routine physical showed my prostate-specific antigen level was high, which is a sign of prostate cancer. Dr. Richard Wright, my personal physician, advised me to see a urologist, who took snips of my body for a biopsy. The urologist wanted to come by the house to talk about the results, and I knew that was a bad sign.

Unfortunately, I was a prime candidate for prostate cancer. I live in Colorado, which has a high rate of the disease—strike one. I'm a black male and was over fifty at the time—strike two. And my father had prostate cancer—strike three. The odds definitely were against me avoiding this health challenge.

Although most people are allowed to fight cancer privately, elected officials suddenly become spokespeople for the disease, whether they want to be or not. The public thought I had a routine surgery, rested up for a while at home, returned to my mayoral duties, and later urged all men to get screened for the disease.

What they didn't know was that for a few days, the doctors held their breath at Denver Health Medical Center because my bowel and stomach had shut down following the operation.

Chapter Twenty-Two

Prostate Cancer, Whirlwind Second Term

When Dr. Richard Wright suggested I have surgery on my prostate right away, I hesitated because, frankly, I was sick of dealing with illness and death. I might have put off the surgery for months if Dr. Wright hadn't insisted. I'm convinced his advice saved my life, because, unbeknownst to me, City Councilman Hiawatha Davis had also been diagnosed with prostate cancer, with a different result. I had my surgery on February 10, 1997. Davis tried to treat his cancer with holistic medicine. He didn't trust doctors and believed, to some degree, that prostate cancer and AIDS were government conspiracies to destroy the African American community.

About this same time, Davis resigned his council seat and went to work for me as a Department of Public Works employee. I campaigned for my former aide Elbra Wedgeworth, who was elected to Davis's council seat and went on to serve as council president.

Months after my surgery, Davis finally agreed to have the operation, but it was too late. Wilma and I visited Davis in his home as he lay in his son's arms shortly before he died.

I often cite our two stories. I listened to doctors and received treatment, and I'm still here. Davis delayed treatment and is no longer with us.

Shortly before I entered Denver Health Medical Center for the surgery, I got a call from Henry Cisneros, who was serving as U.S. secretary of housing and urban development. He told me that he was resigning his position. He said if I applied, my name would be at the top of the list as his successor.

Cisneros told me that Norm Rice, the mayor of Seattle and a former Manual High School classmate, was also on the list, along with Andrew Cuomo, the Housing and Urban Development (HUD) assistant secretary and son of former New York governor Mario Cuomo.

The timing of this news was obviously horrible. I told Cisneros that although I was honored to be considered, I had to focus on my surgery and recovery.

But his call made me realize why President William Clinton had contacted me during the Christmas holiday.

Wilma and I were home one night when the phone rang. It was an operator. She told us the president of the United States was trying to contact me, but our phone number was unlisted. The phone company has a policy of not giving out unlisted numbers—even to the president.

"Hell, I thought the CIA had our home phone number," I told the operator.

We had to give our permission to put the call through.

President Clinton wished us a happy holiday, and we made some other small talk. But I suspect the president was already thinking about who he would appoint to succeed Cisneros. Cuomo ended up getting the promotion.

I'm not disappointed I couldn't consider the HUD job because of my health. I liked being mayor and had promised people I would serve out my term. Still, it would have been fun to be among the national mix as a nominee.

The doctors suggested that while I was having the prostate surgery, I also get an abdominal hernia repaired. They said that that ailment was somewhat urgent because I traveled to third-world countries and needed to avoid any possibility of emergency surgery.

After coming out of surgery, I was reminded of how men deal so poorly with health care. As boys, we are told to suck up the pain, ignore the bruises, and carry on. We often live by the phrase "No pain, no gain."

So, as a brave mayor, I ignored the option of having intravenous pain medication until a very wise nurse gave me some advice. She told me my body was working too hard to deal with the pain instead of healing. She encouraged me to push a handheld button, which released a dose of pain medicine into my bloodstream, any time I felt the pain.

The next day, the same nurse told me to "stay off the button." Those little twitches of my thumb on the button sent me on a trip to a place where everything was light blue. It was like traveling through space. I even thought I saw Captain Kirk from the television show *Star Trek*. I thought to myself, *No wonder we have a drug problem in America.*

But my short adventure with pain medicine wore off quickly when I noticed too many doctors coming in to check me. They put tubes down my nose to drain my stomach, which had become distended. Instead of going home shortly after the surgery, I was kept in the hospital an extra two days.

The doctors' extra attention had some comical outcomes. On my way for an MRI, my hospital bed was too long to fit into the elevator. We were stuck between the elevator and the floor, and the doctors couldn't figure out how to adjust the bed. They called a nurse, who immediately knew what to do.

Then, when they got me to the MRI room, they put me on a really narrow table that slid into the MRI machine.

"If my fat ass falls off this table, just leave me down here," I joked with the technician, "because half of my body is already hanging off this table."

On the second extra day in the hospital, a nurse acted like she won the lottery when I finally passed gas—my bowel and stomach problems were on the road to recovery. Later, I thought of Martin Luther King Jr. and the time he was stabbed by a deranged woman in 1958 while autographing his book, *Stride toward Freedom*, in Harlem.

The woman had driven a letter opener into Dr. King's chest, and it took hours to remove it because the razor tip was touching his aorta. Dr. King later wrote that doctors told him his life was saved because he didn't sneeze before his chest could be opened and the letter opener removed.

I thought about how I would have to write that I survived my brush with death because I farted.

It was heartwarming to receive bundles of get-well cards, from the crayon-drawn pictures from young constituents to letters from political colleagues. The correspondence included notes from Federico Peña, who was then U.S. secretary of transportation; and from Cleveland, Ohio, mayor Michael R. White; Abilene, Texas, mayor Gary D. McCaleb; Columbus, Ohio, mayor Gregory S. Lashutka; Chicago mayor Richard M. Daley; Dallas mayor Ronald Kirk; and DeKalb, Illinois, mayor Greg Sparrow.

North Little Rock, Arkansas, mayor Patrick H. Hays wrote, "I'm sure your tennis shoes will be waiting for you when you get back in high gear."

My health crisis made me realize that women do a much better job of addressing health prevention and then talking about illnesses, such as breast cancer. Men still avoid yearly physicals, and prostate cancer survivors talk to each other in hushed voices.

Men wear blue ribbons during Prostate Cancer Awareness Month in September, but women openly give each other much more support during Breast Cancer Awareness Month in October.

So I now have two birthdays: the date of my birth, on February 17, 1941, and the date of my prostate cancer surgery, February 10, 1997.

That brush with my mortality made my second term that much more of a whirlwind.

One of Denver's prouder moments was the successful hosting of world leaders during the Summit of the Eight event four months after my surgery. President Clinton called me and Governor Roy Romer about hosting the event, which included the leaders from the United States, Canada, United Kingdom, France, Germany, Japan, Italy, and Russia.

I assigned some of my staff to work with the federal people sent to

I greeted President William Clinton when he arrived in Denver for the Summit of the Eight meetings of world leaders in June 1997. President Clinton worked well with the nation's mayors, and we, in turn, supported many of his initiatives, including the Crime Bill.

Denver to coordinate the event. I did not want the city to get kicked to the curb. I was also concerned about cost. I raised the issue with Harold Ickes, a former Clinton adviser, who was the federal coordinator of the event. He told me there was no federal money; it was a freebie. I told him that by working with our senators, we should be able to get some money for security. Denver was hosting the leaders of eight nations in addition to the Okalahoma City bombing trial.

We spent four months of political haggling to get a $1.95 million appropriation from the federal government. The money was used to pay police salaries, overtime, benefits, and equipment costs for the weeklong summit events.

Donna Good had taken a leave of absence to help an ill relative in Boston shortly after the 1995 election. When she returned, I tagged her to work with Ickes on the event and help us raise money for such things as receptions.

I would not settle for anything but first-class events, not only to be a good host for the leaders of these nations, but also to show that Denver could once again shine in the worldwide spotlight.

We reached out to our supporters, including Bill Coors, Bill Daniels, and Daniel Yohannes, who was then president of U.S. Bank Colorado, formerly Colorado National Bank. Johannes and Lieutenant Governor Gail Schoettler, who was geared up to run for governor in 1998, served as the cohosts.

Wilma organized events for all of the first ladies of the countries with Colorado first lady Bea Romer and U.S. first lady Hillary Clinton.

I put Amy Bourgeron in charge of dealing with public relations, and she shortly discovered her budget had disappeared. She initially thought she would get $600,000 for setting up a media center and press kits for more than 1,000 worldwide journalists, but that money was needed for other events.

"The mayor wanted the best, and that included a magazine and a logo, and I had no money," Bourgeron recalled.

The business community recognized the significance of the

event, and through my staff's determination, we raised the money necessary to cover costs. Bourgeron found a graphic artist who created a professional logo for free, which was used on posters, banners, and media kits. *The Denver Business Journal* published a magazine about the event in exchange for advertising revenue. U.S. West, Inc., now Qwest Communications International, Inc., set up the media center at no cost to the city.

"It was amazing PR for the city," Bourgeron said.

I was proud that the main meetings were held at the Denver Central Library in its new wing. The world leaders discussed topics around a new $25,000 birch, aspen, and cherrywood table made specifically for this world-leaders' meeting. The 500-pound table was donated to the city and remained at the library after the summit.

We suspended our no-smoking rule at the library because many world leaders smoked while they negotiated, and we didn't want to offend anyone.

Other highlights were taking the leaders to The Fort restaurant in the mountains west of Denver for real western food, including jalapeño peppers stuffed with peanut butter, and a tour of Red Rocks Amphitheatre.

The initial welcoming reception was at the governor's mansion. I spoke first and welcomed the leaders to Denver and then introduced Governor Romer. He gave a short welcome and sat down. "How did I do?" he asked me. "I thought you did wonderful, but you forgot to introduce President Clinton," I replied.

By this time, President Clinton was at the podium, and he had such a way with the public that the gaffe wasn't noticed.

I enjoyed spending time with all of the leaders, including Prime Minister Jean Chrétien of Canada, President Jacques Chirac of the French Republic, and President Boris Yeltsin of the Russian Federation. All three men had previously been mayors of their capital cities.

It was quite the sight to see large motorcades with heavy security driving through Denver's streets. Many residents stood on sidewalks for hours to catch a glimpse of the leaders.

I was thrilled when federal officials chose the Denver Central Library as the main meeting place for world leaders during the Summit of the Eight in 1997. The city received as a donation a $25,000 birch, aspen, and cherrywood table where the world leaders gathered. Photograph courtesy of *The Denver Post*

A year after the Summit of the Eight, France gave me the highest and most prestigious honor bestowed upon a civilian, called Chevalier de la Legion d'Honneur. The award was given by President Chirac in recognition for my leadership in organizing the Denver Summit of the Eight.

The Legion of Honor was established as a military award by Napoleon Bonaparte in 1802 and is now given to civilians who have made contributions to France.

I was very honored, but I told President Chirac that the award was a tribute to the citizens of Denver who opened their arms to the world during the summit.

The rest of 1997 was spent laying the groundwork for some very ambitious projects for 1998. Like other Denver Broncos fans, I suffered through the four Super Bowl losses and was hopeful when the team faced the Green Bay Packers on January 25, 1998, in San Diego. The Packers were favored to win Super Bowl XXXII.

Wilma and I traveled to the game with Jimmy Rivas and his wife, Janet. We had reserved optimism that quarterback John Elway and running back Terrell Davis would be the right combination to pull off an upset.

Oh, what a glorious feeling when the last second ticked off and the scoreboard read Broncos: 31; Packers: 24. Wilma and I attended the Broncos victory party afterward and heard the stories of Denver residents back home running out of their homes and celebrating in their yards with each other. Some knuckleheads also caused problems by starting fires in Lower Downtown, but those are usually the people who find any reason to be disruptive.

We opened up Mile High Stadium to thousands of people who flocked there to greet the Broncos the night they returned from San Diego. Then the city hosted the largest victory parade in our history. More than 300,000 people packed downtown and watched Elway lift the Vince Lombardi trophy on the steps of the City and County Building.

I felt the time was right to announce my support for the team's long desire for a new football stadium. The city owned and operated Mile High Stadium. The proposal set to go before the state legislature would be similar to the one that built the $215 million Coors Field for the Colorado Rockies baseball team.

Instead of the city owning the football stadium and being responsible for its $5 million yearly operating costs, the six surrounding counties—Adams, Arapahoe, Broomfield, Douglas, Denver, and Jefferson—would charge a penny-per-$10 sales tax.

The $364.2 million facility would include 25 percent funding from the Broncos. In turn, the Broncos would get all of the revenue from parking and tickets. The Broncos also would reimburse the city for police officers working traffic, and the city got the team to pay for improvements to roads in the area.

Broncos owner Pat Bowlen used to always complain he had the worst football stadium lease in the NFL.

"Now that I'm going to support the new stadium, you have to stop saying that," I told him, "because every time you say it's the worst contract in the league, I come right behind you and say the city has the best contract in the league."

The Metropolitan Football Stadium District was created with a representative from each surrounding county. To the surprise of many, I chose Norm Early as Denver's representative. I approached him about the position just as I had, at some point, gotten most of the 1991 mayoral candidates involved in the city. Don Bain's law firm did work for the city, and Errol Stevens worked on the Stapleton redevelopment.

I made the appointments to show that my administration was not petty or bitter. We had the ability to reach beyond the election and make sure talented people were involved in city government.

I knew Early would be independent and fight for the voters. I chose many of my appointees to boards and commissions based on their abilities and not their support of my administration. I did this knowing that if the situation were reversed, I doubt that I would have been welcomed back to city politics.

I knew what it was like to lose the mayoral race in 1983 and that people in power were usually the only ones to reopen the door.

While the legislature worked to put the stadium vote on the November 1998 ballot, I was crafting my own bond issue. I proclaimed 1998 "The Year of the Neighborhood" and then put the decision making in the hands of community activists.

We set a bond issue amount at $98 million, but instead of the city leaders saying which projects would be done, we set up a neighborhood task force to set priorities. I had the most fun watching the process, because everyday citizens had to tell one another *yes* or *no* on each project. I stayed completely out of the process.

"I have to do this every year with the budget," I told neighborhood activists. "Now this is your chance to do this on a very small basis."

We had twenty town-hall meetings in every part of the city to find out residents' concerns and wants. The projects ranged from repairing sidewalk paths in parks to building new police stations and recreation centers.

The school district also had a $305 million bond issue on the ballot that fall to build new schools and improve existing ones, which I endorsed.

Getting one bond issue approved by voters is never easy. There were three on the ballot—the Broncos stadium, Denver neighborhoods, and the school district—and voters approved all three.

Not only were those decisions good for Denver and the region, but they also cemented my decision to run for a third term. There was some talk that City Councilwomen Susan Barnes-Gelt and Susan Casey would challenge me, but that fell by the wayside after the successful bond elections.

That same year, both women tried to turn down a very generous donation to the city.

Bill Daniels had torn down two or three houses in 1986 to build a $7 million mansion, which he called "Cableland" after his pioneer work in cable television, near the upscale Cherry Creek neighborhood. The 24,000-combined-square-foot home and grounds includes four kitchens, two dining rooms, thirteen bathrooms, and a 1,102-square-foot swimming pool. In 1998, he called mayoral aide Jim Martinez and said he and Bob Lee, his longtime Republican friend, wanted to meet with me.

Daniels was getting up there in age and had a variety of careers outside of cable television, including as a sports-team owner and philanthropist. He owned part of the Los Angeles Lakers and the Utah Stars of the ABA. When the Stars declared bankruptcy, Daniels lost a bunch of money but personally paid outstanding bills for the team even though it wasn't required by law.

Daniels was that kind of person.

We met for lunch. Daniels, who didn't hear in one ear, was at one end of the table, and Lee, a chain-smoker, was at the other end. I was in the middle, trying to dodge the cigarette smoke and relay Daniels's message to Lee to speak louder.

Daniels told me he wanted to donate "Cableland" to the city to serve as the mayor's mansion.

"I've given it a lot of thought, and I didn't want to give it to someone I didn't like or respect," Daniels told me. "I love Denver, and I would like for you to take it."

He included a $3 million endowment to cover maintenance costs because Daniels knew the city previously turned down another home without an endowment. He also stipulated that he would continue to live in the home until his death.

While our city attorneys were working with Daniels's estate planners to finish the donation, Casey and Barnes-Gelt were lobbying other council members to turn down the gift. They didn't want me to live there. There was a part of me that wanted to bring this issue to the public for the racist view it was—or maybe that's too strong. It was a personal attack, likely because both women thought I had too much power.

I told Dan Muse that I'd agree not to live in it full-time for the rest of my second term. That did not preclude me from hosting city events there or even spending a weekend at the home.

What Casey and Barnes-Gelt didn't realize is that I had come to a similar conclusion—that I didn't want to live full-time at "Cableland," but for a different reason.

I knew I was going to run for reelection in 1999. It would be hard making the case that the guy who ran for mayor in 1991, lived in a modest home, and stayed overnight in mostly working-class voters' homes was now living in a gated mansion.

And I dreaded the thought of having to pack up our belongings to move to "Cableland" only to have to pack everything again and move back to Gaylord Street when my final term ended in 2003.

The city accepted the gift; two years later, Daniels passed away.

Once the city took ownership of "Cableland," Wilma began working on the home to make it more suitable for hosting official city meetings, charitable events, and diplomatic occasions. She placed a bronze welcome sign with the city seal on it. It renamed the mansion, "Cableland, The Official Residence of the Mayor of Denver."

She raised money, including $10,000 from my campaign fund, and selected official City of Denver china dinnerware, crystal glassware, and silverware engraved with the Denver city seal. A large circular carpet with the Denver city seal was placed in the home, along with the flags of the city, state, and nation.

She also had a large photographic portrait of Daniels placed in a room often used for receptions. In honor of Daniels's mother, Wilma also created the "Reflections and Contemplations Garden of the Denver First Lady" in the yard.

I was able to use "Cableland" for receptions when the city hosted the U.S. Conference of Mayors and National Conference of Black Mayors. Many nonprofits also use the home for fund-raisers, and it has been an asset to the community.

I had one offer before I left office to purchase the home. I rejected the offer because I felt I could not violate the friendship and trust I had with Daniels.

In many ways, I see 1998 as my most successful year as mayor. We finalized the contract with Forest City to redevelop Stapleton's 4,700 acres of airfield into a multiuse residential community. When

The redevelopment of Stapleton International Airport into a residential and commercial neighborhood was awarded to developer Forest City Enterprises, based in Cleveland. City Councilwoman Happy Haynes (right) helped me greet the first new residents in 2002. Stapleton garnered the prestigious Stockholm Partnerships for Sustainable Cities award from the king of Sweden.

completed in fifteen to twenty years, the former airport will have about 12,000 homes and 30,000 residents.

When I left office in 2003, the neighborhoods were already being established, and by 2006, 2 million square feet of retail and new restaurants were attracting visitors from throughout the metropolitan area. Another 1 million square feet of retail will be built. A visitor today would never know that the area once was an airport.

Stapleton has become the poster child for Forest City Enterprises, based in Cleveland. Several national publications have mentioned Stapleton as the model for mixed-use developments.

My personal goal with Stapleton's redevelopment was to make sure there was ample open space. I pushed hard to first set aside parkland because I knew waiting would mean commercial space would be a priority for the developer. That negotiation gave me the designation of being the mayor who accumulated the most park and open space. I was able to get 1,100 acres of park space at Stapleton, which brought the grand total of park space during my tenure to 2,100 acres.

Mayor Robert Speer built up 1,075 acres during his tenure.

"I know how significant a role Mayor Webb played in the Stapleton redevelopment," said Reverend Paul Martin, who served on the redevelopment committee. "There was no precedent for turning a decommissioned airport into a community development. Stapleton is a miracle story."

During the 1999 mayoral reelection, some people complained that I never got a grocery store to reopen at the Dahlia Shopping Center in northeast Denver. I can point to Stapleton, about a mile east of Dahlia, where there's a 1 million-square-foot shopping center, including a grocery store.

The Stapleton redevelopment plan even got worldwide attention and garnered the prestigious Stockholm Partnerships for Sustainable Cities award for Denver, given by the king of Sweden.

Another development goal of the city was to encourage all developers to provide homes for all income levels. Historically, cities nationwide have learned that the concentration of the poor into large high-rise public housing or into one section of a city is bad public policy.

We wanted Denver neighborhoods, including Stapleton, to offer homes that first-time buyers, including teachers and police officers, could afford, along with homes for those with middle-class and upper-class incomes.

Denver's housing market in the mid- to late 1990s was going through the roof. Older neighborhoods were seeing more families moving in and renovating the houses that historically had low mortgages and affordable rents.

Several middle-class neighborhoods saw affordable bungalows being demolished and replaced with higher-end housing. At the same time, many developers were "popping the tops" of older homes by adding second and third stories.

Although we encouraged the revitalization of the neighborhoods, we also saw lower-income residents being forced out by increased rents and mortgages. If we left it to the market alone, many groups of people could no longer afford to live in the city.

City officials in 2000 began working on Denver's Inclusionary Housing Ordinance. We finally got a law passed in 2002 that mandates that for-sale housing developments of thirty or more units that get any government money provide 10 percent of the units as affordable housing.

The law required that new lofts downtown and housing developments in other sections of the city not only house millionaires, but provide units that a recently graduated college student with his first job or a middle-class family could afford.

It is true diversity when a neighborhood not only is home to people with different ethnic backgrounds, but also of different economic statuses.

I also believe that this new law helped boost the number of people who live downtown. Residents, many of them first-time home owners, have neighbors who are athletes with Denver's professional sporting teams. The athletes lived in the penthouses, but the rest of the units are affordable for people of many different income levels.

As planning for the Stapleton redevelopment got under way, Denver also played a key role in the redevelopment of the former Lowry Air Force Base, located south of the former airport.

Our planning department, headed by Jennifer Moulton and board chairman Bill Hornby, spent hundreds of hours working with the Lowry Redevelopment Authority to make sure the area—which straddles Denver and Aurora—was redeveloped properly.

"It was remarkable the degree [to which] Mayor Webb made sure the public was involved in how Stapleton and Lowry took shape," Hornby said. "We had endless meetings. Wellington gave the citizen-advisory boards tremendous support."

The McKinney Act, which stated that homeless organizations have the first right of refusal for closed military bases, caused the neighborhoods near Lowry to fear the worst. I remember attending one meeting at George Washington High School where 2,000 angry neighbors had gathered. Mike Dino warned me that I may want to come in the back entrance to avoid the crowd. My view was that no matter how hostile the crowd, always walk in through the front door and right through the audience.

The debate was ugly, with some people saying the homeless would bring AIDS and crime to the area. A compromise allowed the Colorado Coalition for the Homeless to buy some units but then resell the property and buy units throughout the region. This way, Denver did not take on the brunt of the homeless population but would help distribute homeless families to new Coalition housing throughout the six-county region.

Voters usually reelect you because they like the bricks-and-mortar things they can see you accomplish during your term. But for me, the real joy of being mayor was the ability to help people who were often at the end of their ropes.

Chapter Twenty-Three

"First Tuesday," International Flights, Africa

An important neighborhood issue came to me through my monthly meetings with residents, which I called "First Tuesday." The meetings were set up for ordinary citizens to come in from 5:00 P.M. to 7:00 P.M. and visit with me for ten minutes.

I had some interesting visitors, including one man who signed in as "Jesus Christ" and went on to tell me we had met each other before in different lives. I started keeping my office door open after that meeting so that my police bodyguards could listen to the conversations.

One evening, a group of women from the Overland Neighborhood Association came to see me about their battle to get the defunct Shattuck Chemical Company to remove radium from south Denver. The women included two retirees, a nurse, secretary, massage therapist, and hairdresser. In addition to Shattuck, which produced radium compounds from 1923 to 1984, the women were fighting the Environmental Protection Agency (EPA). The EPA agreed to allow the company to entomb the material at the site, which is just a few miles south of downtown and near the Platte River.

I supported the women's environmental concerns for their neighborhood. If the EPA, which is supposed to protect residents, sided with the chemical company, then the city had to take up the residents' battle.

It took several years, but in 2002, the EPA finally reversed its decision and began working on a plan to clean up the area. Four years later, the chemical waste had been removed and the area was covered with grass.

But the most satisfying "First Tuesday" meeting nearly didn't happen. A woman and her three daughters arrived five minutes before I was ready to leave my office. The family was homeless and living in an abandoned store building. The mother used candles for light and a two-by-four to block the door from other homeless people seeking shelter.

I knew by experience that I needed to check out her plight, and I sent city staffer Alvertis Simmons to the building. He told me her story was true.

I then called Sal Carpio of the Denver Housing Authority and he found the family shelter. I called Head Start and they found the mother a job.

A year later, I saw the mother and children, and I initially didn't recognize them because they looked like a middle-class family.

This family was down on their luck and just needed a little help. It made all of those hours of "First Tuesdays" worthwhile.

Rich people always have access to government. The insiders get taken care of first because they hire lawyers and lobbyists. The people who are most vulnerable and sometimes need the ear of a mayor are residents such as the homeless family and the neighborhood association. "First Tuesday" was their vehicle to get inside the mayor's office, and in these two instances their short visits produced results.

Shortly before I left office, an Aurora mother sent her college-age son to see me. The young man with dreadlocks told me he was studying theater at Howard University, but he was in need of tuition money. One of my staffers called the school and discovered the young man was close to flunking out. My staffer suggested I send a check to another student who was more likely to succeed.

I had a flashback to the moment that my grandmother sent me to see Denver mayor Tom Currigan when I couldn't find a teaching job. There are times you have to take risks on people, knowing full well that they may not succeed.

I wrote a personal check for the young man's tuition. Wilma met with the student and then wrote him a check from the Dr. Martin

Luther King Jr. Colorado Holiday Commission scholarship fund, which she had raised.

We received a note from the young man in 2005: "To my adopted Dad. I just wanted to let you know that I am graduating from college."

He's now pursuing an acting career in California.

To have had the chance to help that young man and the homeless woman who visited me with her three daughters on "First Tuesday" is as important as any major deal I negotiated for the city. These people came to me because they had nowhere else to go. I chose to help them instead of steering them into the bureaucratic shuffle, which often leads to nowhere.

Although those visits were personally gratifying to me, one big payoff for the city as a whole during my second and third terms was getting direct international flights from Denver's airport. Once Denver International Airport (DIA) was open, we had to feed the beast, and that meant creating more reasons for people to fly out of Denver.

Because of Denver's geographical location in the West, the airport is our port to the rest of the world, not unlike the Atlantic Ocean is for the East Coast and the Pacific Ocean is for the West Coast. The airport opens us to the rest of the world, similar to the way in which the Pony Express, stagecoaches, and railroads brought travelers and trade in during the pioneering days of the city.

Our local airlines, which have been primarily dominated by United Airlines and our homegrown Frontier Airlines, offered domestic flights and flights to Mexico and Canada. But in terms of foreign travel, Denver residents and businesspeople had to first fly to Los Angeles or San Francisco to get to Asia, or New York and Washington, D.C., to get to Europe. It was my goal to get nonstop flights from Denver to both Asia and Europe.

We faced a battle with the Federal Transportation Department to get a nonstop flight to London. Mayor Federico Peña had been courting British Airlines for years, and I took up the cause in 1991. The proposal faced major opposition from United Airlines, which didn't want the competition. United passengers had to get connecting flights to Europe in Chicago, New York, or Washington, D.C.

I led a delegation to London to meet with British Airways officials and their board chairman Sir Colin Marshall, but United Airlines continued to block our efforts.

Republican senator Ben Nighthorse Campbell was very instrumental in our four-month dogfight with the Transportation Department. The popularity of the new direct flight to England immediately proved there was a market here for both British Airlines and United Airlines. That would help me later on to lure the German airline Lufthansa—once again emphasizing the "international" in DIA.

Lufthansa officials were very concerned about offending their share partner, which was United, because they relied on United for booking services and joint flights. I flew to Germany and met with the president of Lufthansa, who informed me he was getting information from United that Denver's air was too thin to handle the German airplanes and our runway was too short.

I countered that if the air was too thin for Lufthansa flights, how come the United planes, which were the same size, had no problems? Then I told him we would extend the runway and the lights.

When the work was completed on the runway extension, I mailed the Lufthansa president a chunk of concrete. It was a symbol that the ball was now in his court.

He sent a crew to Denver, and I promptly took them to dinner at The Fort restaurant. I enjoyed taking people who came to negotiate to the mountain eatery, which is at about 7,000 feet, especially if they were from locations at sea level.

Once we had a deal with Lufthansa, United announced daily direct flights to Germany. But as I predicted, those flights didn't last long. Travelers were curious about the German airline, and to this day, the Lufthansa flights are booked.

We were also successful in getting a direct flight to Asia. This was important not only to transport passengers, but also to transport cargo in the belly of the passenger planes. It's much faster for businesses to transport cargo by air than have it sent by truck or railroad to Los Angeles or San Francisco, where the direct flights originated.

Korean Air agreed to extend their leg from Los Angeles to Denver. This allowed travelers in Denver to get direct flights to Seoul, Korea, instead of having to travel to Los Angeles or San Francisco.

This happened almost by accident. While meeting with Japanese and Chinese executives about flights to Asia, we discovered that the president of Korean Air had been to Denver several times before. When we suggested the flight to Denver, he agreed because he had a good impression of the city.

It just goes to show that you should always treat people well because you never know when that person could become your client.

I made one of my most memorable international trips in November 1995 during a trade mission to Ethiopia.

I had been interested in Africa from the time I was a young child and saw glimpses of the country through movies. I always rooted for the underdog in movies, whether it was the Africans over the hunters, the Indians over the cavalry, or the Spartans over the Romans.

I didn't really understand the history of Africa until as a young adult I began teaching black-studies classes. Then I became a sponge, soaking up everything I could learn about Africa. I became quite interested in the African freedom movements and in a lawyer named Nelson Mandela who was imprisoned for opposing apartheid. I participated in protests in the United States in front of the South African Embassy in Washington, D.C., against apartheid and wrote guest editorials in Denver's newspapers.

As a state legislator and the city's auditor and mayor, I opposed any state or city money invested in South Africa so long as apartheid existed.

In 1993, Denver's long relationship with the Sister Cities program adopted Axum, Ethiopia. Dating back to the early 1970s, Denver has also adopted cities in Mexico, Japan, China, France, Kenya, India, Israel, and Italy.

Representatives from Axum came to Denver for the dedication

U.S. Bank Colorado president Daniel Yohannes (left) helped the city and state put together a trade mission to Ethiopia, his homeland, in 1995. This was my first trip to Africa. Among our stops was Denver's Sister City Axum.

of Axum Park. Daniel Yohannes, one of Denver's success stories, came to the United States from his homeland of Ethiopia on a one-way plane ticket and with $150 in his pocket. By 1995, Yohannes was the president of U.S. Bank Colorado in Denver, and he urged me to bring city officials on a visit to Ethiopia.

I initially said the city couldn't embark on such a trip, but then I changed my mind. Colorado lieutenant governor Gail Schoettler cochaired the trip with me and Lottie Shackelford of Little Rock, Arkansas. Lottie had been appointed by President William Clinton to the board of directors of the Overseas Private Investment Corporation in 1993.

This was my first trip to Africa, so I was very excited. I also was proud once we got to Africa and our plane was made up entirely of a black crew, from the pilot to the stewardess. That was the first time I had seen that in my life.

It was also amazing and humbling when we arrived in Axum and were greeted by 10,000 people at the airport. The Ethiopians appreciated the fact that we were willing not only to visit their country, but hopefully to provide more economic opportunities. They named a roadway Denver Street in the city's honor.

During our visit to a village, an older woman approached Wilma and asked who I was. When Wilma told the woman I was the mayor of Denver, the woman turned to me.

"You are not from America! You are from here!"

Then she gave me an Ethiopian nickname, *Abera*, which Yohannes said translates to "Enlightened One."

Dr. Morris Clark, my friend and an oral surgeon, saw firsthand the poverty in Ethiopia when he visited a hospital and was horrified by the primitive equipment.

"I had never seen anything like it," Clark recalled. "I couldn't sleep that night because it was just amazing that people were living in such hard conditions."

Clark and a group of doctors returned to Ethiopia with medical supplies and two generators.

"It was a very moving and life-changing experience," Clark said.

I was fortunate to return to the continent four more times as Denver's mayor.

In March 1998, I was honored when President Clinton invited me on a two-week trip that marked the first time in more than twenty years that an American president had visited sub-Saharan Africa. The group included several other mayors, ambassadors, presidential cabinet members, and dignitaries.

I was so proud to watch the air force crews work on the plane when we refueled in the Verde Islands. But when we got back in the air, most of the passengers were asleep when I learned there was a problem with one of the engines. Alma Brown, the widow of former U.S. Secretary of Commerce Ron Brown, who died in a plane crash in Yugoslavia, was on the plane. There was lots of discussion regarding whether anyone should tell her or others of the mechanical problem, and then the plane made an emergency landing in Ghana.

We were a little late, but they got the plane repaired, and the trip to South Africa was marvelous.

Out of all of the people in my life, Mandela, former president of South Africa, was the one whom I feel has the most bright aura around him. It's almost religious. People speak softer around him out of respect. It was amazing to be in the same room with the man who suffered in prison for so many years under apartheid and came out with no bitterness. Mandela's struggle was one reason that as a young man I wrote letters and carried pickets to protest the South African government.

President Clinton also invited me to join him on a trip to Nigeria in August 2000 to help boost democracy in that part of Africa.

The trade missions were important, but perhaps a larger impact of the trips was opening the eyes of the world to what Africa was really like. I knew that when President Clinton made the trips, the press would follow. The media reports would show that Africa is a beautiful country and that Cape Town is similar to San Francisco. The media would show that most Africans are not living in huts, that many Africans are intelligent and college graduates of some of the most prestigious universities in the world, from Harvard to Oxford.

At the same time, places such as Soweto and parts of Johannesburg show the extreme poverty of the nation, where children cannot afford books for school and beg on street corners to feed their families.

I'm richer for having seen both sides of Africa firsthand.

Some people may not understand why black Americans feel such a strong connection to Africa. Every human being wants to be attached to something. Blacks came to the United States as slaves and lost their identities. Unlike other immigrants who know where their ancestry lies, black Americans had no idea.

That's why the terminology *African American* is so important. Slaves initially just had one name, like you would call a dog or cat. Then blacks, as a group, were labeled *colored*, then *Negro*. There is no "Negroland." Just like Irish Americans or Italian Americans, we are proud of being Americans, but the term *African American* shows that our roots are in Africa.

So, for me, being able to visit Africa was also a sense of seeing the starting point. It was amazing to know that my ancestors were forced to leave their homeland as slaves, and less than 200 years later, I returned as a mayor of a city that is predominantly white. That is quite an accomplishment with all of the bumps and bruises along the way.

I took another memorable trip to Africa with the U.S. Conference of Mayors and National Conference of Black Mayors, which was organized for me by Tom Cochran, the executive director of the U.S. Conference of Mayors. We visited Goree Island, Senegal, and Ghana in May 1999.

Ghana's president, Jerry Rawlings, had visited Denver the month before, when the city hosted the National Conference of Black Mayors. When we were in Ghana, President Rawlings assigned his security detail to me.

The highlight for me was sitting on the dais along with African presidents, vice presidents, U.S. Secretary of Labor Alexis Herman, and Jesse Jackson.

Our visit to Goree Island in Senegal was powerful and emotional. In Dakar, I told the delegation: "In 1619, we left here as slaves. Today, we have come back as mayors of American cities."

My last trip to Africa as Denver's mayor took place in February 2002. The trip was for a delegation of Denver businesspeople and officials to help promote trade between Colorado and South Africa. Members of the National Conference of Black Mayors also came to promote trade among other states with South Africa.

Some city council members questioned the timing of the trip when the city was beginning to face stagnant sales-tax collections. But I also felt that some council members opposed the humanitarian part of the trip, where Wilma and I planned to address the growing AIDS crisis in Africa.

I reached out to Denver's professional sports-team owners—the Denver Broncos, Colorado Rockies, and joint owners of the Denver Nuggets and Colorado Avalanche—and they gave us $45,000 for the trip. Most of the money went to AIDS clinics in the country of Botswana and the South African communities of Soweto and Cape Town.

Wilma and I visited with the doctors in these clinics, who desperately needed medicine and supplies. We gave one clinic $5,000 to buy infant formula to help prevent the spread of HIV from HIV-positive mothers to their babies.

Members of our delegation broke down in tears after visiting a Salvation Army orphanage in Soweto where children whose parents had died of AIDS were orphans. We dropped off a box of medical supplies, but the director of the center asked for another simple item: new underwear for the children.

A mother visiting another AIDS clinic in Soweto smiled broadly when Wilma and I held her tiny baby who had HIV. I learned in the late 1980s about the stigma of AIDS when I served on the board of the Colorado AIDS Project and realized that showing human compassion can go a long way in dispelling the myths of AIDS.

The trip was inspiring, but my enthusiasm was dampened by intestinal problems. I was treated in Namibia, which helped until I could get home. Denver Health Medical doctors discovered I had an attack of diverticulitis.

Traveling to Africa was my dream come true, and I'm appreciative that President Clinton included me and other mayors in his trips.

President Clinton worked extremely well with the country's mayors on a variety of issues. His staff was told to work with the mayors and not just tolerate us, as was done by previous administrations.

He also invited so many mayors to the White House that it was no longer fashionable to pocket souvenirs with the White House emblem on them, which included items from bathroom towels to M&M candies.

President Clinton allowed me to sleep in President Abraham Lincoln's bedroom twice. On one visit, I overslept, and an usher, who was black, came to my room. He told me there was a car waiting for me downstairs. I lay back in Lincoln's bed and asked the usher, "How does it look for a black man to be lying in Lincoln's bed?"

He started to laugh but caught himself.

On another visit with Wilma, I thought what a wonder for me, a black mayor from Denver whose father never graduated from high school and whose great-grandfather was a slave, to have slept in the same room where President Lincoln wrote the Emancipation Proclamation.

It made me realize how far as a nation we had come for me to be a guest of the president of the United States, yet how far we still have to go.

Wilma was smarter than me. She not only took her camera to the White House to record our visit, but she called our friends and family from the White House. We were excited when our loved ones weren't home because then she left the White House phone number on their answering machines. Boy, were some people shocked when they called the number and the White House operator answered.

I was somewhat disappointed when most of the people I called answered right away.

Our relationship with President Clinton and First Lady Hillary Clinton grew over several White House State Dinners.

A short time after an overnight visit to the White House during the Whitewater investigation, I got a call from the Federal Bureau of Investigation. Two agents came to my office and asked me where I had slept in the White House, who I saw, if I toured the White House, and if I saw any file boxes.

After I got done answering their questions, they said that concluded the interview.

"My goodness," I told the agents. "I thought you were going to ask me about the towels, matches, stationary pads, and M&M candies with the White House emblems that I took home for family and friends in Denver."

Tom Cochran, the executive director of the U.S. Conference of Mayors, referred to me as a "triple-crown mayor." I was elected president of the U.S. Conference of Mayors in 1999, president of the National Conference of Black Mayors in 2000, and president of the National Conference of Democratic Mayors in 2002. I was the only mayor to simultaneously serve as president for both the U.S. and the black mayors' organizations.

The U.S. Conference of Mayors embraced my desire to work with mayors internationally. In addition to our trips to Africa, I was the first mayor and only the third American at the time to speak at the German parliament.

"Wellington Webb's declaration that 'the twenty-first century will be the Century of Cities' has resounded across the country and the world; from the statehouse to the White House, from London to Paris, and Beijing to Dakar," read a resolution adopted by the U.S. Conference of Mayors in June 2000.

Although I enjoyed the world travel immensely, I was grounded a few years earlier when I learned a lesson about tempting Mother Nature.

In October 1997, the city put its new snowplow and snow-truck equipment on display near Mile High Stadium for a press conference. I felt like General George Patton looking at the line of public-works employees and their new equipment. I said this crew was ready for anything and announced, "Mother Nature, bring it on."

Well, she took on the challenge. That weekend, the city received thirty-one inches of snow—the worst blizzard to hit Denver since 1969. City streets were impassable, trees were broken from the weight of the snow, and icy highways were littered with accidents.

DIA, which was never supposed to close in a large storm, was shut down, but not because the airport wasn't functional. The flight crews and pilots couldn't get to work, and 4,000 travelers were stranded at the airport.

After Mayor Federico Peña left office, some council members purposely blocked naming the terminal for him. Later, Council-woman Ramona Martinez, with my support, successfully urged the council to name the roadway to the airport for Peña. I was proud Peña got the recognition, because it was his vision and tenacity that made the new airport move forward. I also thought it was petty that the council made it impossible to name the terminal after Peña.

The snowstorm jammed Peña Boulevard with accidents and 120 abandoned vehicles. The wind, at up to sixty miles per hour, reduced visibility to zero. We later installed snow fences to help with future storms.

That snowy weekend, I rode with the snow-removal crews and wore my black cowboy hat. I wanted people to see I wasn't just hanging out at home while the city was paralyzed by the storm.

We even had problems just getting to the snow equipment at the airport. The city administrator with the keys to the fenced yard was unavailable, so one brave public-works employee drove his truck through the fence.

He did it on his own. I gave him a city award for his creativity and ingenuity in a time of battle with the snow. I said everyone else was sitting on their behinds trying to figure out what to do, and he took it on his own to drive the truck through the fence. Of course, he also could have gotten into trouble for damaging city property, but his heart was in the right place.

I also probably should have given my spokesman Andrew Hudson an award for taking time off his lunch hour to shovel the sidewalk in front of my home during another storm. A television station doing a story on the city's law requiring shoveling twenty-four hours after a storm inquired about our snowy sidewalk when Wilma and I were out of town. Hudson put on his winter coat and got some exercise instead of eating lunch so I wouldn't look bad.

As 1998 came to an end, I knew I would run for a third term, despite telling reporters after the 1995 race that eight years would be enough. The Denver Art Museum and Denver Zoo had approached me about a bond issue to improve those facilities, in addition to the need for the expansion of the Colorado Convention Center and the need for a convention center hotel.

The county jail was overcrowded and outdated, and the Denver Auditorium Theater and the Denver Coliseum needed renovation work. Denver was also working hard to attract the 2000 Democratic Convention to the Mile High City, which had last hosted the National Democratic Convention in 1908.

Denver was a finalist in 2000, along with Boston and Los Angeles, where the convention took place. I, along with some of my staffers, spent a lot of time campaigning for Vice President Al Gore's presidential campaign in the Midwest and Florida.

I was still stinging from the 2000 snub and also worried about the high security costs when I stopped Denver's bid for the 2004 Democratic Convention. I attended the Democratic Convention in 2004 in Boston as a vice chairman of the Democratic National Committee.

When I was thinking about running for reelection in 1999, I knew a third term would give me the political collateral to finally address what I call "legacy" projects in northeast Denver. When I ran in 1991, I said I would be mayor for the whole city. That meant that I had to address other projects before focusing on northeast Denver.

The 1999 campaign was really a cakewalk for me, but my main opponent, an African American man, didn't have any credibility as a candidate, so he attacked me for not doing enough for the black community.

Chapter Twenty-Four

1999 Reelection, Columbine, Senate, 9/11, Third Term

Reverend Gil Ford was my only vocal opponent in the 1999 mayoral race. Hiawatha Davis used to call Ford "The Mouth" because he was always critical of everyone.

We already had put in motion some special projects for northeast Denver, but Ford unfairly attacked me for not doing more for the black community.

In 1998, nationally known sculptor Ed Dwight, a former astronaut whose projects included a sculpture of Hank Aaron outside of the Atlanta Braves stadium and a sculpture of Dr. Martin Luther King Jr. at Morehouse College, approached Wilma about a new Dr. King sculpture for City Park.

Well, this was a sensitive subject because Councilman Bill Roberts had taken a second mortgage on his home to help pay for the first Dr. King sculpture, which many people criticized as an abstract resemblance of Dr. King. Dwight had sculptures all over the world, yet in twenty years, he had never landed a commission in Denver.

He brought an impressive proposal to me that included a sculpture of Dr. King above life-size sculptures of civil rights leaders Frederick Douglass, Sojourner Truth, Mahatma Gandhi, and Rosa Parks. The sculpture assemblage is twenty-six feet tall and is made of granite and cast bronze.

Wilma, as chairwoman of the Mayor's Commission on Art, Culture and Film, already had done an outstanding job of bringing international art to Denver, including sculptures *Man* and *Woman* by Fernando Botero and Jonathan Borofsky's sixty-foot-tall *Dancers* at the Denver Performing Arts Center.

Through Wilma's leadership and my support, we raised $1.2 million in private money by 2002 to have the impressive Dwight sculpture installed at City Park.

The city donated the first sculpture, depicting Dr. King and Emmett Till, to the Martin Luther King Jr. Cultural Center in Pueblo, Colorado.

Wilma and I had discussed another vision of a museum or library to highlight African American history and accomplishments. I wanted this facility to be located in northeast Denver, but I didn't want it to compete with the established Justina Ford House, home of Colorado's first African American doctor, and Black American West Museum.

I wanted a permanent, public, secure place to display all of the gifts and historical items given to me during my twelve years as mayor, four years as auditor, and six years as a legislator. I had cabinets full of items, including gifts from leaders in Asia, Africa, and Mexico, on all three floors of city hall, as well as in my home.

The proposal started to take shape after I went to the Schomburg Center for Research in Black Culture in Harlem. This facility has the greatest collection of African American research material and is part of the New York City library system.

I called Denver librarian Rick Ashton and told him, "We're going to build a brand-new library in northeast Denver."

I had no idea how we were going to build the library, but the seed was planted. While I was receiving a National Historic Trust architectural award in Rhode Island, Wilma learned about how cities can use current buildings as collateral to build new structures.

Upon our return to Denver, I was reminded by Jennifer Moulton that the city already utilized this approach. The Denver Capital Leasing Corporation (also known as DCLC), a Colorado nonprofit that was incorporated in 1986, was contracted to finance the building of the African American Research Library.

The Denver City Council endorsed the financial arrangement,

I wanted the $16 million Blair-Caldwell African American Research Library, which opened in 2003, to reflect the contributions of blacks to the city, state, and region. The mural at the entrance, created by California artist Yvonne Muinde, includes local and national black elected officials and other community leaders.

and the $16 million African American research library was built in the heart of the Five Points neighborhood.

The first floor is a regular branch library and replaced an aging branch library. The second floor is for research, and the third floor is a museum that chronicles the influence of the black community in the West. The museum displays include the jazz influence in Five Points and a condensed replica of the mayor's office at city hall.

Denver became home to the only African American research library between Atlanta and Los Angeles.

Wilma declined the suggestion that the library be named in her honor. We decided to name the library for two longtime black community leaders: former city councilman Elvin Caldwell and former Denver Public School board president Omar Blair. Both men were struggling with health issues, and we wanted to give them this honor while they were living. The Blair-Caldwell African American Research Library opened on April 26, 2003, with both men present. By 2005, they both had passed away.

Unlike other cultural facilities or monuments that live hand to mouth because they are based on private contributions, I made sure that the Dr. King sculpture and Blair-Caldwell Library were part of the city. By dedicating the sculpture to the city, I knew future mayors would have to maintain the sculpture as part of the parks system. By making the research library part of the city's library system, I knew the library would outlive me.

After leaving office, I helped form the Friends of the Blair-Caldwell African American Research Library to raise private money to cover needs not in the operations budget. Our board included African Americans and Denver natives Chauncey Billups of the NBA Detroit Pistons; Philip Bailey of the musical group Earth, Wind and Fire; Dianne Reeves, jazz singer and Grammy winner; Pam Grier, movie actress; and my daughter Stephanie O'Malley.

When the 1999 reelection began, the Dr. King sculpture and new research library were just taking shape. Ford painted an inaccurate picture that I ignored northeast Denver, in the hopes he would get votes from the black community.

"Wellington didn't do a good job of telling his story," said activist John Bailey. "But I also thought Gil was cleaning our laundry in public, and it was not good political judgment or action."

Former Atlanta mayor Maynard Jackson once told me that the hardest job in America is to be a mayor and be black. You have so many competing constituencies that you can't make them all happy at the same time. For me, it was compounded by the fact that I was Denver's first black mayor and had grown up here. Once I was elected, people who knew me—and those who didn't—expected me to personally take command of their issues and solve any problems.

Although I knew Ford was being unfair, I had to be careful in the campaign not to act like the big guy in school who picks on the little kid. Ford knew he had no chance of winning, yet it was his right to campaign on any issue he wanted.

A black businesswoman was also in the race but had little name recognition. Some supporters thought I encouraged her to run to make it easier to raise campaign funds. I did not.

Although the candidates posed no real threat, they gave supporters a reason to donate to my campaign fund, which totaled $1.17 million. The candidates also allowed me to continue to inform the public about my accomplishments and agenda.

I won the election with nearly 81 percent of the votes.

In 2003, a new editor at *The Denver Post* resurrected the issue of my contributions to the black community, which I thought was bizarre because he was new to the community and this issue was four years old.

"Most folks in the black community thought he [Mayor Webb] could do their bidding," said John Bailey. "I knew he had to do the city's bidding. We had to move things forward as activists, and we did not do a good job utilizing things on those lines."

The majority of the people who elected me to three terms did so because they saw I was the leader for the entire community.

"Some people wanted to think the mayor could go in and wave a magic wand for the black community and everything would change overnight," said Myrna Durley Crawford. "I really think he did the best he could for African Americans. I know that any time the black community needs him, he's there and will do what he can—within reason."

The one thing overshadowed in the claims that I forgot the black community is that if my administration did things to improve the city as a whole, then all of the residents benefited. When we made sure the trash was picked up on time, when we fixed the potholes in the streets, when we created new summer jobs for youth, Denver became a better place to live for everyone.

When voters approved the $93 million bond issue in 1998, that money was used for new police and fire stations citywide, new recreation centers and recreation renovations citywide, and improvements at parks citywide.

The attention leading up to the May election got diverted by a national tragedy near Denver's city limits. On April 20, 1999, I hosted the National Conference of Black Mayors Convention in Denver. Several mayors were gathered at the Adam's Mark Hotel when my bodyguards said something was going on at Columbine High School located in unincorporated Jefferson County near Littleton.

Our police radios were jammed with requests from other law-enforcement jurisdictions for help, and we sent officers to assist at the high school.

We turned on the television and watched the horror unfold. Colorado now had the distinction of having the most deadly high-school shooting. Two students killed twelve of their classmates and a teacher and injured twenty-four students before killing themselves in the school's library.

The next morning, I marched all of the mayors to Trinity Methodist Church for a prayer session. Inner-city violence among teens had been raging for years, but now that suburban kids were killing each other in Colorado, Tennessee, Arkansas, and Oregon, the nation was finally ready for stricter gun laws.

James Mejia, then serving as my director of human rights and community relations, suggested we hold a healing event.

Denver invited the public to come to the Civic Center, and we asked parents to bring their kids. The media was flying in from all over the nation, and as residents we needed to gather to deal with this tragedy and to mourn the loss of life.

I wasn't sure what I was going to tell the crowd. I wanted to give a message of hope at the first large public gathering after the shooting.

"We have to learn to live together," I said. "Parents, hug your kid or the closest kid next to you because there are lots of parents who wished they had hugged their kids the night before."

The National Rifle Association (NRA) had booked its convention in Denver months before the shooting. I thought it was a mistake for the group to keep its original date, because it landed right after Columbine. I sent NRA president Charlton Heston a letter asking him not to come. It was my thirty seconds of fame in Michael Moore's movie *Bowling for Columbine*: Heston holds up the letter and says, "Well, we're here already."

He still didn't get it. Heston played Moses as an actor, but he sure is no Moses in real life.

People in Colorado were grieving the loss of the twelve students and their teacher. The NRA should have postponed the convention for the healing process to move forward for the traumatized students, teachers, and the community as a whole.

Instead, the NRA convention came to Denver on its original date and members passed out literature of me, Mao Tse-tung, and President William Clinton saying we were un-American because we supported tougher handgun laws. I believe in the right for people to own rifles for hunting, but there was something wrong with kids having easy access to guns to kill each other.

I admired Tom Mauser, whose son, Daniel, was killed at Columbine. He bravely led thousands of people through the streets of Denver and past the NRA convention. The marchers called for tougher handgun laws.

Mauser has continued the fight for tougher handgun laws nationally.

The Colorado legislature responded and supported laws restricting the sale of guns to youths as a direct result of Columbine.

Some people threw the issue back in my face when one of my staff members, Jonnie Bearcub, arranged for me to go buffalo hunting on an Indian reservation. The Indians used a pickup truck to chase down the buffalo, then the hunters killed the buffalo and skinned it the way they did 100 years ago. The meat did not go to waste.

I went to Gart Brothers Sports store to buy a rifle for the trip, and the salesman was stunned to see me. One of our SWAT officers helped me prepare at the firing range, and I enjoyed the new experience.

Something else came up, and I decided to give the trip to my good friend Chuck Williams, who said he had a great time. I guess I'll have to go in the future. One friend joked that if I ever ran for the Senate, I needed to shoot a deer a week to overcome the guaranteed opposition from the NRA.

There were other times I had to forego a personal interest to avoid uncomfortable situations.

Prior to the opening of DIA, Greg Romberg alerted me that *The Denver Post*'s invitation to ride in their corporate jet to a World Series game in Toronto could be dicey. The city was negotiating with the company over newspaper-rack space at the new airport.

"I told him that he should go on the trip because it was a cool trip but not to be surprised if the issue came up," Romberg said. "He canceled the trip. It was hard for him to be a regular person and be mayor. He knew very few people wanted to just be with Wellington and Wilma. It was very lonely. Parties weren't even fun. He was always the mayor."

Five months after the Columbine shooting, another crisis hit the Denver Police Department. SWAT officers executing a no-knock warrant shot and killed an innocent man. Ishmael Mena, forty-five, was sleeping in his second-floor bedroom in northeast Denver when officers acting on a reported $20 sale of crack cocaine mistakenly came to Mena's home. He was in Denver earning wages to send to his wife and nine children in Jalisco, Mexico.

After an investigation, the city admitted the mistake in February 2000. My view was we needed to quickly apologize and give the family a cash settlement.

In a letter sent to Mena's widow, María del Carmen Moreno, I gave her my personal sympathy and the city's sympathy for the loss of her husband. "I am hopeful that the claims on behalf of you and your family can be resolved, and I have directed the city attorney to make this the highest priority."

City attorneys offered the Mena family $150,000, the statutory limit on government liability. The family's attorney requested $5 million. I had to step in when negotiations stalled. The family received $400,000 from the city over twenty years, an amount based on a larger sum than Mena could have earned.

"Webb had been saying for months that the city had an obligation to spare the Mena family a litigation nightmare, if possible, and the mayor made good on that pledge," a *Rocky Mountain News* editorial said.

Frankly, I don't think you can put a price on a human life, but I wanted to make sure that justice was done. I also had to handle this issue carefully because I didn't want to demoralize the police officers who still had to go after the bad guys.

The daily headlines about the tragedy took a toll on many people.

"This was the only time I told the mayor I was taking a week off," recalled my spokesman Andrew Hudson. "Police Chief Tom Sanchez even called me into his office and asked me how I could get the press off his back. I told him that his officers should quit shooting innocent people. He was pissed off at my answer, but it was true."

When former chief Dave Michaud retired in 1998, I was leaning toward promoting Denver officer Gerry Whitman because he was the only candidate dedicated to community policing. Unlike most chiefs who started out in Denver, Whitman began his career as an officer with the nearby Lakewood Police Department. Whitman also was not the choice of Michaud, who often called me "Boss."

I liked Deputy Chief Tommy Sanchez, but I had some misgivings when I named him chief. There were internal problems among his officers, and after the Mena shooting, I knew a change was needed. Sanchez told me he wasn't a good politician, but when you are police chief, you have to know how to not only deal with your officers, but also with the public and politicians.

I named Whitman as the new chief and brought back a longtime officer and former police chief, Ari Zavaras, as manager of safety. I thought the two would complement each other, and I think they made a great team.

I transferred Butch Montoya to oversee the city's Motor Vehicle Department.

Zavaras, who was named police chief by Mayor Federico Peña and worked for Governor Bill Owens as state corrections director, had ambitions to be mayor.

I told him as long as he did his job, I didn't care if he laid the groundwork for the 2003 race. I was term-limited and couldn't run.

As was the case with most mayors in 1999, a lot of my time was focused on getting ready for the turn of the century and the Y2K scare. Communities worldwide spent millions making sure that computer systems were updated properly so that there were no massive blackouts and breakdowns in basic services, including phones, electricity, and water supplies.

I took a lot of heat that year for not having a millennium celebration, but I was more concerned that all of the streetlights would work. I also kept reminding the press that the real millennium year was 2001, but the whining continued about Denver not having a party.

My emergency-operations and mayoral staffs gathered in the basement of city hall on December 31, 1999, to monitor our computer system at 12:01 A.M. Hudson wanted to break the tense mood and switch off the lights. I didn't laugh.

"Everything went fine, but then what were people upset about?" said Deputy Mayor Stephanie Foote. "That we didn't have fireworks that year. No matter what we did, there was never a silver lining."

It was a whole different tune a year later when Denver put on an incredible party. We spent a lot of time in 2000 raising private money to put on two fireworks displays on the Sixteenth Street Mall. We had one early display for families where fireworks were shot from buildings on a ten-block radius at about 9:00 P.M. Another round came at midnight to usher in 2001.

Skeptics and some of the mainstream press said no one would show up because the party was a year late. We had nearly 250,000 packed in downtown. The party was so successful that the business community has sponsored the event every year since. Once again, we showed, as we had during my twelve years, that if you provide a good idea to the public and have tenacity and resilience, the results exceed expectations.

As we welcomed 2001 with style, little did any American know how life would drastically change in nine months.

I was getting ready for work on September 11, 2001, when our oldest son, Keith, called and asked if we knew a plane had hit the World Trade Center in New York City.

I turned on the television and was listening to the broadcaster when I and many other Americans witnessed the second aircraft striking the second tower.

I called my deputy mayor and staff to open the city's emergency-operations room that we used on December 31, 1999, for Y2K. It was clear to me that the nation was under attack and cities would have to focus on security.

Amy Bourgeron, filling in for Aviation Director Bruce Bumgartner, who was out of town, heard shortly after the attacks that the Federal Aviation Administration was closing down airports nationwide.

"He was the first mayor to officially close a major airport," Bourgeron recalled. "Within two hours, we had a lockdown sweep of security, including dogs, in the 6 million square feet of DIA."

Later, I had to make an unpopular decision not to allow the public to park in an underground garage of a new city office building, which later was named for me. The first World Trade Center bombing in 1993 was from a truck filled with explosives in an underground garage. Mayors no longer could afford to take risks that could endanger the public.

9/11 was a pretty frightening time. It was also the only time in my life that I felt that everyone in the country was unified. Color and income status didn't matter, because we all were under attack as Americans.

A few weeks after the attacks, I went to New York City. The mayor's office there arranged for me and some staffers to tour Ground Zero and some nearby buildings that were still standing but damaged.

We looked at the devastation in disbelief. The heavy odor of smoke, destruction, and death hung in the air, and that memory stays with me still.

The United States always responds well to crisis; that's normally when we have our finest hour and pull together as Americans. We tend to slip with the long struggles.

Earlier in 2001, several people approached me about challenging U.S. Senator Wayne Allard, a Colorado Republican and veterinarian, in the 2002 race. At one point in my life, I would have loved running for the Senate. Democrat Tom Strickland, an attorney and my friend, also was thinking of running.

Donna Good wanted me to seek the seat so badly that she had First Lady Hillary Clinton call me. Clinton encouraged me to run, saying I could play a significant role in national politics.

I was torn because I knew how difficult it would be to run a statewide campaign against an incumbent and still serve as an effective mayor. I took a tour with some of my staff around the state to see if I had enough support. We planned to do a major statewide grassroots campaign.

When I ran for mayor, I started in the most-conservative areas of Denver, and I did the same by starting the state tour in the most conservative northeast section of Colorado.

Kevin Flynn of the *Rocky Mountain News* followed us on one of those trips and got nailed with questions about why the *News* was no longer distributed to the rural areas. The newspaper returned to communities statewide later, but I had to chuckle that Flynn got put on the hot seat over this policy.

Ken Salazar didn't agree with some people that I couldn't win a statewide race because I'm black. Other African Americans were elected to statewide positions, including Joe Rogers and George Brown as lieutenant governors; Vicki Buckley as secretary of state; and Rachel Noel as a University of Colorado regent.

I thought being the mayor of the state's largest city was more of an issue than my ethnicity. How could I build coalitions? On one hand, I was excited about the prospect and the competition of running. Then the irritating daily grind of "Will he run? Won't he run?" began.

Wilma wanted me to run for the U.S. Senate. I had also encouraged Wilma to seek Pat Schroeder's congressional seat when she resigned in 1996. The timing, I think, was planned by Schroeder to pave the way for Dianne DeGette. I had just survived a nasty reelection campaign and didn't want to seek her seat, although earlier in my political career, I thought someday I may replace Schroeder.

Frankly, I wish Wilma would have challenged DeGette for the seat. Wilma would have been a dynamic member of Congress. She studies legislation and passionately cares about people. I, in turn, know that sometimes you have to offend people to get things done. I'm more of an executive, which fit me in the role as mayor. Wilma has more patience than me, and that would have served her well in Congress.

Wilma considered running, but in the end, our daughter Stephanie helped her make her decision not to campaign. Stephanie felt she had lost one parent—if not both parents—to politics and didn't want her mother away in Washington, D.C. I always thought Wilma would have been excellent in Congress.

Despite Wilma's encouragement for me to seek the Senate seat, in my heart, I knew my job as mayor wasn't over. As the elected leader of the city, I had to be present to finish what I had started.

You can serve in office and campaign for another position, but one area will suffer. The only way I know how to campaign is by giving 100 percent twenty-four hours a day until the objective is won. You can serve in office and campaign for another position, but you cannot do both well.

I admittedly was obsessed in 1991. I walked 300 miles across the city through snow, rain, and sleet with no money in the bank out of pure desire and determination. I don't know if anyone can reach that level more than once in a lifetime.

I also remembered promising Jennifer Moulton before the 1999 election that I planned to serve the entire four years. She had an opportunity to leave government for a more lucrative private job, but she agreed to remain as my planning director when I told her I would stay until 2003.

"I was disappointed when he didn't run for the U.S. Senate, but I understood his decision," said my friend Ben Jeffers. "He doesn't do anything less than 100 percent, and he couldn't run the city and a grueling statewide race at the same time. I respected his decision, but personally, I really wanted to see him in the U.S. Senate because he would have contributed so much."

I haven't had much regret about not running for the Senate. I am more of an executive-branch person. I can build things. I can put organizations and operations together and make it work. That's what I do, and that's what I do well.

The benefactors of that management style were the Denver Art Museum and the Denver Zoo. Both organizations wanted a bond issue so they could expand. I met with our financial people to get an update on our bonding capacity and then told the boards of the zoo and art museum they could split a $125 million bond but would have to privately raise funds to help pay for other needs outside the bond. I also told them that they would have to increase the diversity on both of their boards. If voters, including those in minority and low-income neighborhoods, were paying $125 million to improve these facilities, then their boards should include people of color.

Once again, voters approved a bond submitted by my administration, in which the city benefited from more parking at the zoo, and an amazing $110 million addition to the Denver Art Museum, of which $62.5 million is from city-bond revenue. Renowned architect Daniel Libeskind was chosen to design and build the Frederic C. Hamilton building, which opened with much fanfare in October 2006.

In addition, my administration provided $26 million for improvements to the city-owned Red Rocks Amphitheatre—the popular mountain concert venue for such performing artists as Bruce Springsteen, U2, and all types of musicians. We also purchased open space near the entrance to Red Rocks, located fourteen miles west of downtown Denver, to assure that no development could obstruct the 300-foot sandstone rock formations and 200-mile panoramic view of Denver and the plains.

Also, under Fabby Hillyard's leadership, a $30 million renovation took place at the Denver Coliseum near downtown.

I thought it was important to address the needs of these historic venues, but that also meant that other groups were upset when their projects didn't get money.

The National Western Stock Show for years wanted the city to present a bond for improvements at their complex. The Botanic Gardens also wanted money for repairs, but there was just so much we could do.

Voters recognized the importance of expanding the Colorado Convention Center and approved a $308 million addition, which opened in December 2004. Voters also endorsed $25 million for the Denver Auditorium Theater, which I later named for former mayor Quigg Newton.

The tricky part came in getting a convention center hotel built. I made sure that the negotiations for the $285 million Hyatt Regency Denver at the Colorado Convention Center were completed on my watch.

The city's agreement with developer Bruce Berger to build a private hotel was going nowhere for several years. Berger's talks with Marriott International, Inc., were stalled, and by 2003 I had to step in.

I knew we had to find another way to finance the hotel because of the high interest rates banks charge private developers.

Another private developer tried to get my support by including minority participation, but I feared he also would face problems with financing. With only six months left in my last term, I couldn't take a chance on the hotel project dying.

Cheryl Cohen-Vader, the city manager of revenue, Liz Orr, special projects manager, and private Denver attorney Dawn Bookhardt advised me that the city could create a hotel authority that could float bonds to build the hotel. Other cities, including Sacramento and Austin, had built hotels this way. Bob Swerling of Piper Jaffray and Mark Tobin of Hospitality Real Estate Counselors explained how the financing would work. The city would own the hotel, but a hotel chain would operate it.

I liked the idea, but first I had to get the prime piece of land for the hotel near the Colorado Convention Center, which was owned by Berger.

I took Berger to the Ship Tavern at the Brown Palace because it had been a lucky spot for me in resolving the Moore lawsuit over condemning downtown property. Berger agreed to sell his land to the city.

I had the land and now I needed a hotel chain, and I wasn't sure if it would be Starwood, Hyatt, or Marriott. I decided to let the companies bid, and Hyatt, a privately owned chain, immediately stepped up to the plate.

Hyatt CEO Nick Pritzker was in Turkey but called me directly to talk about the project. He gave me a dollar amount that the other public companies couldn't match. My only caveat to Pritzker was that Denver people like to promote Denver people. I told him the current Hyatt in Denver had an excellent manager in John Schafer, and if I went with Hyatt, he should get the opportunity to run the new Hyatt. Pritzker agreed.

I had the land and a hotel chain. The last piece was getting city council approval. I met with Councilwoman Cathy Reynolds, who supported the proposal but faced opposition from Councilwoman Susan Barnes-Gelt. I decided to proceed with naming a hotel authority.

Some people criticized the creation of a hotel authority and the city's ownership of the hotel. But I knew we had to have more hotel space in order to compete with other cities for conventions.

Attorney Gail Klapper, who also served with me during Governor Lamm's administration, agreed to be the chair of the hotel authority. Other authority members included Reynolds, Cohen-Vader, developer Odell Barry, business executive and former president of the U.S. Hispanic Chamber of Commerce Ron Montoya, retired investment banker Harry Lewis, and developer Mark Smith.

The Hyatt, with 1,100 rooms, opened in December 2005 and became a landmark in the downtown skyline.

After I left office, I worked on some hotel deals, which included Bookhardt, Swerling, and Tobin.

I worked out another controversial public/private partnership for the Winter Park Ski Resort. Denver's parks department wisely purchased the ski area, sixty-seven miles west of the city's limits, in 1937. When I was auditor, I discovered the private board that ran the facility was paying the city a miserly $7,000 a year and any profits were reportedly going back into the ski area. That payment was beyond ridiculous.

During my second term, I considered selling the ski area and putting the money into an endowment for the city. Two things happened: first, everyone in Denver who hadn't known the city owned the ski area now thought it was a bad idea to sell it. The second was the point that if I wanted to be known as the mayor who created more parks and open space, how could I also sell Winter Park? We put together a task force in my last term to study a public/private partnership for the ski area.

"I never asked Wellington for anything, but one day, he asked Jennifer Moulton what he could do for me, and he put me on the Winter Park board," said Joan Ringel. "It included some white men who needed to be leaned on. They didn't really like Wellington."

After reviewing several large ski-area operators, we chose a partnership with Intrawest Corporation, which runs ski areas in the United States, Canada, and British Columbia. The agreement requires Intrawest to invest $100 million in the ski area through 2013. In addition, the city receives $2 million annually and a percentage of the gross revenue throughout the seventy-five-year life of the lease.

Denver was able to keep its ski area and the city's park department benefits from the yearly payment.

So, I left the city in pretty good shape for the next administration, with the exception of building a new city and county jail complex.

I never really wanted to build a new jail. But I also knew the city jail located downtown and the county jail located ten miles east of downtown were unsafe. Still, it was crystal clear that most of the public didn't want their tax dollars raised to pay for inmates to be comfortable.

Many residents couldn't care less that the county jail was bunking inmates in makeshift plastic cots on the floors because all of the beds were full. The facility built to house 1,350 inmates averaged 1,800 inmates per day.

There was no question that the facility was dilapidated and that the overcrowding was unsafe for the guards. We had to release several nonviolent offenders early.

The city was also facing growing transportation costs for bringing the inmates to the courts downtown.

Denver actually was lucky that no one had filed a federal lawsuit because of the overcrowding. Other cities were forced by judges to build new jails, and the judges chose the sites and sizes of the facilities.

I wanted Denver to make the decision about a new jail. We set up a task force chaired by Ari Zavaras, who by then was clearly running for mayor. We chose a site to relocate the jail in an industrial area near downtown that was strongly opposed by one neighborhood, which we expected, and its council representative.

Then we had to raise money to educate voters on why a jail was needed. That's when the e-mails initiated by the opposition started circulating. They questioned what developers were giving money to the campaign and how the opposition could smear my name. What the opposition didn't know was that members of my staff also were getting the e-mails and we reviewed them daily. We saved the e-mails for posterity.

Historically, it takes communities two or three attempts to get voters to endorse higher taxes to build new jails. That's what happened in Denver. Our proposal in November 2001 failed, with 52 percent of the voters opposed.

The negative e-mails about me from the opposition continued even after the election. But instead of lashing out at them, I looked at alternatives to address the overcrowding problem at the jail.

The first site I chose was a good site, but then a great site became available.

I thought it was a good idea for the city to buy the *Rocky Mountain News* building near the City and County Building. The Denver Newspaper Agency, which jointly operates the *Rocky Mountain News* and *The Denver Post*, sold the site to build another complex to house both operations.

The concept was to move the county jail from east Denver and the downtown city jail to one location, along with some courts, for a centralized justice center.

The new justice center would have everything contained at one site and was strongly supported by sheriff and jail officials, the district attorney, and judges.

Some people still questioned the location after the 2003 election, so Mayor John Hickenlooper hired the Urban Land Institute to review where the justice center should be built. The review cost the city $75,000. They came to the same conclusion as I did, that the *Rocky Mountain News* building is the best location for the justice center.

The proposal was approved by voters in 2005, and I was happy that I had laid the groundwork before leaving office.

The only other bond issue that failed during my tenure was called the Kids Tax. After getting bonds approved for new athletic stadiums, parks, streets, and other physical needs, I wanted to do something for the city's children. We proposed a sales tax that would raise $30 million annually, specifically for children's health needs and before- and after-school programs. Other cities, including Kansas City, had passed similar taxes.

· Donna Good, serving as my human-services director, and Carol

Boigon, my education coordinator, took the lead on the proposal.

The issue was talked to death by Councilwomen Sue Casey and Susan Barnes-Gelt. Instead of embracing the spirit of the program, they started questioning how the money would be spent. Voters in Denver are good about supporting higher taxes for tangible things, such as improved parks and streets.

We didn't make the case that human-services programs are always more difficult to sell to voters. Bricks-and-mortar projects are easier because voters can see the renderings and the designs.

When these two councilwomen put doubts into the minds of the voters, voters answered by defeating the issue, with nearly 59 percent opposed.

Still, Denver was moving in a positive direction, and the 2000 Census showed people were moving back into the city. Mayor Peña had challenged the 1990 Census because it said Denver's population was about 460,000.

By 2000, the city's population had grown to 550,000. State demographer Jim Westkott called the more than 19 percent increase "miraculous" in a *Rocky Mountain News* article. Denver saw its growth at the same time many of America's largest cities lost population to the suburbs.

I felt that this population growth reflected the fact that people felt safer in the city, were drawn to the redevelopment of downtown, Stapleton, and Lowry, had more confidence in Denver Public Schools, and wanted to be closer to the cultural and sports facilities in downtown.

As 2002 wound down, I had the luxury of sitting back and watching the candidates line up for the 2003 mayoral race. For the first time since I ran for the state legislature in 1972, I would not be actively campaigning for myself or anyone else.

The slate of candidates proved to be interesting, and once again Denver voters, always hungry for something unique, showed their independence in choosing my successor.

Chapter Twenty-Five

Wilma's Challenges, Private Businessman, DNC Race

I knew for sure three men would be candidates for mayor in 2003: Ari Zavaras, Auditor Don Mares, and State Senator Penfield Tate.

I also suspected former councilwoman Sue Casey would run, because she had been laying the groundwork, even though she resigned her council seat in 2001. Councilwoman Susan Barnes-Gelt also looked like a possible candidate, but she didn't run.

Ari Zavaras had the backing of Taki Dadiotis, a leader in the Greek community. He and his son, Jimmy, whom I hired as one of my neighborhood liaisons, owned restaurants in Denver. Zavaras's return to city government as the manager of safety helped him build a constituency for his mayoral candidacy.

I had no trouble with Zavaras seeking the job while serving in my cabinet. As a matter of fact, I encouraged three of my staffers—Carol Boigon, Rosemary Rodriguez, and Judy Montero—to seek council seats in 2003. All three women were elected and joined my former staffer Elbra Wedgeworth, who by then was council president.

Zavaras had a lot of money backing his candidacy, and he was the early front-runner.

Mares and I should have been close because we are alike philosophically and believe in the same values and issues. But he made a fatal error in attacking my administration and me personally. As auditor, I had some disagreements with Mayor Federico Peña, which his staff didn't like, but I was not grandstanding, upstaging, or trying to make Mayor Peña or his staff look bad. Mares always acted innocent when reports conveniently got leaked to the press. It was no secret that his staff regularly pitched negative stories to the media and often did the homework for the reporters.

Tate, son of former Boulder mayor Penfield Tate II, was a bright attorney who had worked for Mayor Peña and had a strong voice in the legislature. We met and discussed the mayoral campaign.

I told him that the first thing he should do was to maintain his Senate seat while campaigning. That way, he would have some control over his successor if he won the mayoral race. If he lost, he still had his important Senate seat and more than likely would be chosen as the Senate president.

Not surprisingly, his other advisers told him to resign immediately.

Most minorities have been taught since they were children to never give up one job until they have something else securely in hand. Only people who know that they can easily get another job or another seat in office would give something away so casually. Minorities fight hard to keep what they have because the first opportunity is so difficult to achieve, and a minority may not get another chance.

Tate ignored my advice and resigned his Senate seat.

I also warned Tate that voters likely wouldn't elect another minority.

"I think that after having eight years of Federico Peña and after having twelve years of me, the next mayor of Denver is going to be a white male," I said.

Denver is ready to have a female mayor, but it will take an exceptional candidate. In 2003, former councilwoman Casey and historic preservationist Elizabeth Schlosser did not spark enough interest among voters to get elected.

I also reminded Tate that Denver voters love mavericks.

"You'd better watch out for Hickenlooper," was my last advice offered to Tate.

Businessman John Hickenlooper was a former geologist who opened the Wynkoop Brewing Company in Lower Downtown Denver after the oil and gas bust. He supported me in the 1995 mayoral race and sometimes made the gossip columns for his adventures as a bachelor.

But in 2001, Hickenlooper took up a cause that was near and dear to many people: he fought to keep the Mile High Stadium moniker on the new home of the Denver Broncos.

When I look back, I wish that I would have legally required the Broncos to maintain the stadium's name in order for the team to get out of their lease with the city. But this was the era of naming rights, when big companies paid millions to put brands on football stadiums.

I also wished that I'd kept the mayor's box. Denver's mayor and city council had a private box at Mile High Stadium that wasn't part of the new stadium's plan. Instead, the stadium district provided a box for one game to each of the elected officials in the six-county region that endorsed the sales tax.

I made an error in judgment trying to make a side deal with the Broncos concerning the trademark of Mile High Stadium, owned by the city, in order to get a box for Denver city officials, which we had at the original Mile High Stadium. I quickly dumped the idea and got about six of my friends to raise about $100,000 for the box. Then I found out the box didn't even include food, nor could we bring in our own food.

I initially told the press that the naming-rights issue was the decision of the Metropolitan Football Stadium District, which oversaw construction of the $364.2 million tax-supported facility. But the more I thought about it, the more I didn't like the idea.

Hickenlooper and Lew Cady, a marketer and journalist, were fighting to keep the Mile High Stadium name. They promoted pro–Mile High Stadium bumper stickers and distributed thousands of pro–Mile High Stadium signs at a *Monday Night Football* game.

The stadium district board, including board member Norm Early, had community hearings on the issue. The majority of the residents urged them to keep the Mile High Stadium name.

Hickenlooper had been lobbying me to support the issue, and I was ready to endorse him, when the stadium board gave me a little nudge. I had worked very hard to make sure that the stadium tax passed in 1998 while Governor Bill Owens was neutral on the issue. Yet the first public official who was asked to tour the construction site was Governor Owens.

"That pretty much made up his mind to publicly join John's cause," recalled my spokesman Andrew Hudson.

My press conference endorsing the Mile High Stadium name attracted media attention nationwide. I explained that the Mile High moniker was Denver's identity, not unlike the Big Apple for New York City. The Mile High moniker is invaluable for Denver.

"Everything should not be for sale," I said.

Unfortunately, the stadium district disagreed. They sold the naming rights to a local mutual-fund company, Invesco Global Investment Funds, Ltd. At Early's urging, though, the final name was Invesco Field at Mile High.

The deal for $120 million provides $60 million toward the public's bond debt and $60 million to the Broncos. I thought it was a lousy business deal to sell Denver's identity, which really is worth billions of dollars.

This was Hickenlooper's first time in the spotlight. The group Drive for Mile High Stadium unsuccessfully sued the stadium district. By 2005, Invesco's parent group, AMVESCAP PLC of London, had basically vanquished the Invesco brand, but the name remains on the stadium.

Someday someone may have the courage to get the old Mile High Stadium name back on the facility. To this day, I will only call the facility Mile High Stadium.

In January 2003, Hickenlooper entered the race as a long shot. Then Zavaras shot himself in the foot when he told a reporter that he had graduated from college when, in fact, he had dropped out because of poor grades.

Mares had another problem. He tried to sue the Winter Park board to open their books to the public. One of the board members was Dean Singleton, chairman of the board of the Denver Newspaper Agency, which oversees the joint operations of *The Denver Post* and the *Rocky Mountain News*.

"We may call Don a lot of things, but we will never call him mayor," Singleton told me.

Singleton and I liked each other and had an interesting relationship. He's a conservative Democrat from Texas. I would call him for business advice, and he appreciated it when I appointed him to the Winter Park task force that negotiated the partnership with Intrawest Corporation.

He told me that if I decided to run for the U.S. Senate, I would have the endorsement of both *The Denver Post* and *Rocky Mountain News*. After I left office, I told Singleton my life in politics was over and I wanted to concentrate on being a businessman and making some money.

He told me I could start a business anytime and that I needed to continue in public office. I laughed because only people with money think that way, because they already have money.

Hickenlooper's campaign did some marvelous commercials, with one focusing on his promise to lower Denver parking-meter rates. He looked goofy walking the streets with a coin belt, plugging meters, but it caught the voters' attention.

Hickenlooper and I met privately on the parking-meter issue after the city raised the hourly cost to $1.25. The city was facing a budget crisis, and we needed the revenue from the parking meters to help avoid cutting services or laying off workers.

Hickenlooper hit a nerve with every voter who had to dig for a quarter to avoid a $20 ticket for expired time on a parking meter.

He followed up the commercials with some brilliant budget analysis by Michael Bennet, a bright guy the campaign borrowed from billionaire Phil Anschutz.

It became clear as the May election approached that there would be a runoff with Hickenlooper and either Mares or Tate.

Casey had name recognition from serving on the city council, but she was treading water, and her attacks on Hickenlooper backfired.

Hickenlooper and Mares, whose primary support came from labor, got the highest number of votes in the primary. The runoff wasn't even close, and a bold headline of "Mayor Hick" greeted readers of the *Rocky Mountain News* the day after the election.

Some union people said the election showed Denver's racism. I disagree. Hickenlooper—like Peña and me before him—gave voters something unique. We also showed not only a great interest in the job, but the determination to work hard.

"Denver voters do not want to be told there's an heir apparent to the throne," attorney Steve Farber said. "Likeability also is huge."

The night Hickenlooper won, Wilma and I went to his victory celebration at City Park to keep a tradition alive. Mayor Bill McNichols had congratulated Mayor-Elect Peña, and Peña had done the same for me. Denver is unique in that we have a history of smooth transitions between administrations. We have different styles as leaders, but we often keep on the same course with the same agenda.

Hickenlooper and I were onstage with our wives beside us. And wouldn't you know it, the huge photograph the next day on the front of *The Denver Post* shows me and Hickenlooper and his wife, Helen Thorpe—they had cropped Wilma out.

That photograph symbolized Wilma's twelve years as Denver's first lady. This was no way to treat a public servant who had given so much to Denver, the state, and the country.

"Some people were kind of afraid to attack him, so Wilma became the target," said Fabby Hillyard. "She wanted an office at city hall, something that was never done for a mayor's spouse. He blinked to the opposition. Wilma has been his political partner all along. Wilma is everything that Wellington is not. She will remember everyone's names, their children's names, and the names of their grandmothers. People love her, although she is so misunderstood."

Maria Garcia Berry advised Wilma to keep her seat in the legislature after I got elected. But Wilma and I both worried people would see that as one couple having too much power.

"Wilma was doing a good job in the legislature, and I thought she should have kept that seat," Garcia Berry said. "Federico Peña wasn't married when he was first elected, and Bill McNichols's wife wasn't involved. Many people didn't think we needed an activist first lady."

Wilma did not want to sit by and only show up for ceremonial events. She tackled issues from expanding Denver's art and culture to drug treatment programs and youth and family issues.

"Wellington was the first mayor to promote his wife as the first lady of Denver," said Paul Sandoval. "That didn't happen with McNichols or Hickenlooper. He would introduce her as the first lady, and she made things happen."

Wilma also got unfairly assailed for "politicizing the arts" when she wanted a review of art contracts for Denver International Airport. With about $30 million tax dollars slated for art contracts, most of the artists had been chosen without consideration of a balance of international, national, local, and ethnic talent. Local artists, and specifically black artists, received less than $40,000 of the contracts, or .001 percent of the $30 million budget. Wilma sought to correct this unfair practice.

"We both saw that all of the money was going to mainstream artists," recalled Hillyard. "Wilma said, 'Let's stop and look at this and see if this is happening because of bias or a lack of education. Let's fix it and open it to all artists.' It had nothing to do with getting black artists more money, even though that is how it's perceived. Now this policy is something that has been copied and used around the country."

President William Clinton's administration recognized Wilma's knowledge and talent and appointed her to be the regional director for the U.S. Department of Labor in 1997. She oversaw six states and their share of a $28 billion budget.

Although Wilma didn't get credit for all of her work as first lady, she and other family members share one of my greatest honors. Nine months before the 2003 election, the city named a new $200 million twelve-story public-office complex for me.

The city had outgrown its office space and had leased private buildings throughout downtown Denver. It didn't make sense for residents to have to drive all over downtown to do business with different city departments or to continue paying millions in lease payments. The new building adjacent to the historic City and County Building in Civic Center houses forty governmental agencies and about 1,800 employees.

City Councilwoman Wedgeworth and Jennifer Moulton had discussed naming the building in my honor, but first they had to change a law that wouldn't allow a major city project to bear someone's name until after the person died. (The council viciously approved that law in 1991 as a way to block any attempt to name the new airport after Mayor Peña.)

Sandoval and Elvin Caldwell began circulating petitions in support of naming the building in my honor.

"We were fighting and had to really lobby the council," Sandoval said. "Some people didn't like the idea because they thought Wellington was too powerful. My feeling is that you need to recognize someone while they are alive, not dead."

Wedgeworth successfully garnered enough council votes to change the city's law.

"I told the mayor I thought it was important that children see that an African American mayor was so successful and that he did it on his own," said City Councilwoman Joyce Foster, who was council president at the time. "Many of my friends told me they couldn't believe I was voting for it, but it was the right thing to do."

Planning board chairman Bill Hornby also supported naming the building for me.

"It is a tribute to the black community," Hornby said. "Black children, who may wonder if they can get anywhere in this basically conservative community, can look at that building and know they can."

I felt this was one of the highest honors for me and for my family, who had sacrificed a lot during my thirty-one years in public service.

"After the council voted, we went up to his office and Wilma was crying," Sandoval recalled.

The building was dedicated on September 26, 2002. I felt like every member of my family—living and dead—was either there physically or spiritually that day. My grandmother would have been blown away by the honor.

I imagined her saying, "I knew he was going to be special, but this is beyond anything I could have dreamed of." Then she would have added, "I'm proud of all of my grandchildren," just as my mother would always say, "I am proud of all of my sons."

I still feel pride when I drive by the Wellington E. Webb Municipal Office Building. Most people call it The Webb Building, but I'm pleasantly surprised the newspapers often use the entire name when events or meetings take place there.

My last few months in office were consumed with dealing with the stagnant economy and budget problems. Mayor Hickenlooper had to deal with the budget problems, but overall, I felt that I and the city council left the city in good shape for the new administration.

"It was an era of confidence, and that was because of Wellington," recalled former city councilwoman Foster. "He was always in control, and that was very important to me. I never saw him fall apart, although he could get frustrated, and that was in spite of all the things the city was dealing with, such as the opening of DIA. He was the visionary; he made things happen. He kept building, and we see the results throughout the city."

Once out of office, when I became a private businessman, I finally understood why businesspeople complained about paying taxes.

From the taxes on office furniture to the head tax on employees, it sure adds up, but I was excited to get Webb Group International established shortly after leaving city hall.

As president of Webb Group International, I consult with companies including UnitedHealth Group, the National Education Association, and Forest City Enterprises.

I was busy learning how to be a private businessman when several people urged me to run for the chair of the Democratic National Committee (DNC), where I served as a vice chair.

The election of a DNC chair usually is a vicious internal fight, with the party eventually united behind one candidate.

Following President George W. Bush's reelection in November 2004, the party was at an important crossroads.

We ended up with a slate of seven candidates for the job: Martin Frost, a former Texas congressman; Tim Roemer, a six-term congressman from South Bend, Indiana, who served on the 9/11 Commission; David Leland, an attorney and former chair of the Ohio Democratic Party; Donnie Fowler Jr., Al Gore's 2000 political director; Simon Rosenberg, founder of the New Democratic Network; Howard Dean, former Vermont governor; and me. We were all running in the shadow of Dean, whom I supported when he ran for president before his campaign imploded with "The Scream" in Iowa.

Dean still had his presidential machine in place nationally, unlike the rest of the candidates, who were building constituencies at regional debates.

The DNC chair is elected by 447 national delegates chosen by each state.

I really enjoyed the battle of ideas. Once again, people underestimated me, but I won over many delegates during the debates.

"He did have a lot of people coming up to him and saying, 'If Howard Dean wasn't there, we would have supported you,'" said Tish Maes, my assistant at Webb Group International, who helped with the DNC campaign.

Ben Jeffers also traveled with me to some of the forums.

"Clearly, Wellington became the second choice for many people after they heard him at the forums, but these people had already made up their minds for Dean," Jeffers said. "I watched the audience, and their jaws literally dropped because they were surprised at his answers and that he was so knowledgeable about the issues."

Dean even told me I was taking part of his crowd at one debate.

All of us tried to get support from different constituencies, including the state party chairs, governors, labor, and Congress.

"When none of these groups chose to pick a candidate, they

went in conflicting directions and made it easier for Governor Dean," Martin Frost said. "The key decision was when the governors decided not to be involved. They did not endorse anyone. The governors blinked and chose not to act. That set the tone for everyone else. The governors didn't understand their power or they were paralyzed."

All of us said the Democrats have to return to their roots and basically rebuild the party in all of the states.

"It almost got monotonous because basically we all were saying the same thing," Leland said.

However, Roemer found himself on the defensive because of his antiabortion stance.

"The bloggers and Web sites were ruthless," Roemer said during a March 12, 2005, speech. "My twelve-year-old son, an avid Web-surfer, one night admitted with tears in his eyes, 'Daddy, I knew some Republicans didn't like you, but I didn't ever expect Democrats to hate you.'"

I knew Roemer's beliefs would kill his candidacy, and although I am pro-choice, I don't believe our party should have a litmus test on abortion.

"Mayor Webb personally told me several times that he believed that I showed courage in speaking to the DNC about my beliefs," Roemer said. "He said it took bravery to stand by my values."

Roemer and I agreed that the Democratic Party should be more than anti-Bush and that the party is losing many traditional Democrats, including churchgoing African Americans and Latinos.

"We cannot just give lip service to organizing [Democrats] all over the country; the real grassroots are with state parties," Frost said. "Wellington talked about that. He did very well and had good ideas."

I was able to talk about what I called the "2004 Colorado Miracle." On the national front, Colorado has traditionally been a Republican state, with the Republicans controlling the House and Senate. In 2004, the Democrats regained a U.S. Senate seat when Ken Salazar was elected in Colorado, and another congressional House seat when his brother, John Salazar, also won. The Democrats controlled the state House and Senate for the first time since 1961.

I pointed to the coalitions the Democrats built in Colorado to be successful, and I felt that that could be duplicated as part of the Democratic agenda nationwide.

Although I loved the combat of words, I hated what I have hated in all campaigns: the backstabbing and fund-raising.

As is the case in every election, there are people who you meet who you like and others who you wish you hadn't gotten to know so well. Then there are people who the more you are around them, the more you like them. I found that to be the case with Al Sharpton.

I got to know Sharpton during his campaign for president. I enjoyed his passion, sense of fairness, and sense of humor. Sharpton is a reformer, because he's trying to encourage other African Americans outside of the beltway to get involved.

Also disappointing was discovering through this campaign that there were people I had known for a long time whom I found out I didn't like as much as I thought. It did sting me when people who said they were going to vote for me jumped on the Dean bandwagon, but that is an ugly side of politics.

Maes had worked on my mayoral campaigns and came away a little disillusioned.

"From the beginning, it just seemed that everyone was saying, 'What's in this for me?' Instead of what is good for the party," she said. "And the process of having these 447 people represent the Democrats on a whole doesn't make a lot of sense either. Everyone wanted to be on the winning team because that's how the party has always worked in the past, and they were going to get something out of this deal by supporting the winner."

My concern is that if the Democratic Party does not cater to more of its base outside of the eastern establishment, we will never win back the White House. The road to the White House goes through Colorado, New Mexico, Arizona, Montana, Nevada, and the South.

That's why I thought that the DNC chair should come from the West. The Democratic Party cannot abdicate the West and the South and expect to be a national majority party.

Some people told me they thought Dean was more liberal than me and in some cases, that's true. Being more of a moderate would have attracted back many Democrats and Independents who supported Bush in 2004.

But in the end, I know how to count, and Dean had the numbers. Instead of treading water with the outcome already decided, I endorsed Dean for chair. It was an easy decision because I endorsed his presidency bid before I endorsed John Kerry.

If the Democratic Party gets to the point where African Americans are not being considered for all roles and responsibilities as candidates from all levels—including DNC chair, cabinet members, senators, vice president, and president—then the question comes up as to how much support African Americans should give the party.

The same questions should be asked of the Republican Party.

I have been a Democrat for my entire life. I campaigned for hundreds of Democratic candidates in local, state, and national elections. But the day has passed when anyone can blindly support a party—whether Democratic or Republican—unless the party shows real support for their issues.

African Americans have earned the right to stand tall and dignified and support what's in our best interest.

Conclusion

The Webb Legacy

When the city was debating whether to put my name on the new office building, some people questioned why I was concerned about my legacy.

"He didn't like criticism, and I'd write him notes and tell him to forget it," said longtime friend Ruby Kirk Gray. "Maybe he always feels like he's trying to prove himself. Maybe it's his generation. Or maybe he's still trying to prove himself to his grandmother. I told him his work speaks for itself."

Other supporters understood how history can be rewritten, ignored, or forgotten.

"I have to be candid. I'm nervous about how history will view him," said Charles Rutland, my former aide in the auditor and mayor's offices. "Racists and naysayers may not give him credit because, without a doubt, he was one of the greatest mayors. Pharisees are respected by the number of pyramids they built. Wellington was one of Denver's greatest pyramid builders, but I am concerned that history won't reflect that."

I grew up in a time when there were no history books about African Americans in my school. As a young adult preparing to teach a black-studies class, I found no resources in the public libraries beyond inaccurate statements in history books saying blacks were happy being slaves.

I think some people in Denver misunderstood my administration's mission to include everyone in city government.

"They were misunderstood by the establishment," said former

Being chosen by Denver voters three times to lead this great city, from 1991 to 2003, is one of the highlights of my life. I gave them all I had to give.

director of theatres and arenas Fabby Hillyard. "People were saying, Who is this Wilma Webb, and what does she know about the arts? Who is this Wellington Webb, and why is he demanding 'those people' get a shot at contracts? And why is he appointing 'those people' to boards and commissions? He was doing those things because it was the right thing to do and part of his social agenda."

Although the critical comments about me and Wilma stung, we never let it steer us from our purpose.

I wanted to succeed for every introverted, skinny student in the back of the classroom hoping that the teacher doesn't call on him or her. I'm an example that with work and determination, you can become somebody.

I wanted to succeed to make up for the times that I wasn't there for my family, so that no one could question our achievements over the twelve years.

As mayor, I was building for history. As is the case of all mayors, I was building for the future.

I'm blessed that I can drive around Denver and see the fruits of my twelve years of labor. The Platte Valley was transformed from rail yards into a thriving community with lofts, parks, and numerous businesses.

The Pepsi Center, Six Flags Elitch Gardens, and the new Mile High Stadium bring hundreds of thousands of visitors to the Platte Valley each year.

I know that when I need medical care, I can go to Denver Health Medical Center. But more importantly, the hospital is a safety net for the poor. Denver, unlike other cities, can take pride that its public hospital is financially healthy because we attacked the cancerous tumor of debt before it killed the facility.

Families of all income levels and all ethnic backgrounds will use Denver's parks and open space for decades. My administration made sure that parks and open space grew more than during any other period in Denver's history. We also received strong voter support for bond money to maintain these incredible assets.

My out-of-the-box ideas allowed us to create the public/private partnership to ensure that the Winter Park Ski Resort will continue to prosper and give money back to the city to help the overall park system. The public/private partnership with Hyatt allowed the city to have a new convention center hotel.

Many of my critics scoffed at whether public/private partnerships would work. I believed in both projects, and both have been successful.

I also strongly believed in maintaining and enhancing the basic needs of the city.

All Denver residents and visitors benefit from the additional police, sheriffs, and firefighters we hired to make the city safer.

When people attend a concert, convention, sports event, or art exhibit, they are visiting improved, world-class facilities. Voters embraced increased taxes for the Colorado Convention Center, Denver Art Museum, and Denver Zoo because they agreed with me that these facilities help keep the city viable and stimulating for our children and grandchildren.

I also wasn't afraid to expand the city's economic opportunities beyond the United States when I opened trade offices in London, England, and in Shanghai, China. The trade missions to South Africa may not pay off for a few years; however, business leaders worldwide appreciate the fact that Denver was one of the first cities to extend a friendly hand.

Yet I know there are people who will only remember the times I had to say "no" as mayor.

I was a strong supporter of historic preservation during my entire twelve years, but in 1996, Historic Denver was disappointed when I allowed the Adam's Mark Hotel to demolish architect Ieoh M. Pei's famed hyperbolic paraboloid located on the Sixteenth Street Mall.

"Wellington is a supreme realist," said Bill Hornby, whose wife, Barbara Sudler Hornby, was a preservationist leader. "He doesn't go out and commit suicide on some issues."

Attorney Steve Farber was among a group in 2002 who wanted

the city to bail out Ocean Journey from a $63 million debt. I viewed the large aquarium as the last piece of the Platte Valley restoration and admired founders Bill Fleming and Judy Petersen Fleming for raising $93 million to build the facility. It was the largest aquarium between Chicago and California.

After a grand opening in June 1999, attendance started to fade, partially because of high ticket prices. After my staff ran the numbers every way they could, I saw this as too big of a risk for the city to take on. In March 2003, Ripley Entertainment, Inc.'s Landry's Restaurant, Inc., bought the facility for $13.6 million.

"Wellington felt compelled to listen, and I think he was leaning to get the city involved," Farber said. "But he has an alarm system inside. And when that alarm went off, no matter how much the advocates were on his side, he would not be deterred."

My staff through their recommendations helped me make that tough decision and many others. It was through their loyalty and service, including the police officers on my security detail, that we were able to accomplish so much in twelve years.

"He also told us if we couldn't figure out what we wanted our legacy to be that we should go home," Hillyard said. "He encouraged us to come up with our own ideas [on] how to make Denver a better city."

Although I had high expectations of my staff, the job of mayor has its own expectations that often are hard to meet.

One of the more emotional and difficult duties as mayor is attending funerals for police officers shot in the line of duty or an employee who unexpectedly died. In many cases, I had never met the survivors before but suddenly had to give them comfort in a time of grief.

During my tenure, I attended eleven funerals for city employees, including director of the Department of Public Works William Smith and firefighter Mark Langvardt in 1992; director of Street Maintenance Doug Franssen; Sheriff Deputy Norman Tony Silva III and firefighter Douglas Konecny in 1993; police officer Shawn Leinen in 1995; mayoral aide Deborah Tucker in 1996; police officers

Ronald DeHerrera and Bruce Vanderjagt in 1997; and City Councilmen Hiawatha Davis and Bill Scheitler in 2000.

Two other difficult losses came shortly after I left office in 2003. Jennifer Moulton, my trusted planning director, died from a rare blood disease that July. In September, my longtime political colleague and friend Arie Taylor died.

Although those people can never be replaced, I take pride that since serving in the Colorado legislature, many of my former employees have gone on to make important contributions to city, state, and national policies. Like a proud father, I have watched my staff join me as young adults and grow into respected community and political leaders. They include Denver City Councilwomen Elbra Wedgeworth, Rosemary Rodriguez, Judy Montero, and Carol Boigon. I was proud to see Wayne Cauthen become the city manager of Kansas City and take a handful of Denver employees with him. Adam Brickner, who served as my drug czar, went on to oversee the drug- and alcohol-abuse programs for the city of Baltimore.

Andrew Hudson is the senior director of sales, marketing, and corporate communications for Frontier Airlines.

Mike Musgrave became an executive at MWH, an engineering firm.

James Mejia helped the city finally get the justice center approved and is overseeing the project.

Donna Good went back to Boston as the president and CEO for the nonprofit Center for Women and Enterprise. B. J. Brooks, my former parks director, is the deputy director of parks for the city of Seattle.

Many other staffers have been successful in the private sector.

Some of my staff gathered my quotes over my twelve years, which they refer to as "Webbisms." There were several times I told them, "Stay in your lane" or "Don't outrun your supply wagons."

When we faced obstacles or difficult people, I'd tell my staff, "Ignorance is correctable, stupidity is forever" or "It is what it is."

Several staff members I plain wore out or drove into retirement.

They needed a rest after working for me.

But everyone did not shine, and many people have said that my loyalty to my staff and friends is my biggest strength and my biggest weakness.

"He believes in and took care of people who believed in and took care of him," Paula Herzmark said. "Not all of them deserved him being there for them. At the end of the day, he was used by some people. He's smart and probably knew it, but he chose not to acknowledge it. Loyalty is important and rare in politics, but it became a genuine handicap for him."

"Being around people with power gives others a taste of power," said Charlotte Stephens. "Some people around him abused it more so than others. He has to be blamed for not pulling them back."

Although some of my staff made mistakes, the majority dedicated a large chunk of their lives to the city.

These employees, who sacrificed time away from their families to meet my high expectations, helped me build a modern Denver. We knew these kind of opportunities to shape the future of a city come only once in a lifetime. We went out on the top of our game.

I expect my employees' knowledge will be passed on to other generations of Coloradans who will lead Denver and the state through the end of the century.

I also look for leadership from my grandchildren: my son Allen's children, Allen II, his sister, Jaime, and brothers, Michael and Dialo; my son Anthony's children, Wellington, his sisters, Gabrielle and Shonda, and brothers, Jason and Mack; and my daughter Stephanie's, sons, Patrick and Steven O'Malley.

I have told all of my grandchildren that they have to find their own identity and not tie it to mine. Everyone has to build their own legacy.

As I've gotten older, I also better appreciate the old saying "When your kids are young, they are heavy on the knee. When they are older, they are heavy on the heart."

You can only guide your children and grandchildren in the right direction, and then they have to make their own decisions.

I was blessed through my grandmother's, mother's, father's, brothers', and wife, Wilma's, belief and encouragement to use my intellect and hard work to achieve what God allowed me to do. I also had a little luck along the way, and the faith that people had in me.

I think the only better job than being mayor is being president of the United States.

"Wellington Webb's legacy will include how a black man became nationally and internationally recognized as Denver's mayor," said longtime Denver Planning Board chairman Hornby. "When you look at everything he accomplished in twelve years, he is able to list those accomplishments and tell his story without being arrogant."

One of the most gratifying outcomes of two years spent writing this book is giving my children, grandchildren, and brothers some insight into their roots. My grandmother Helen Brazley Williams Gamble was the trailblazer who had the courage to come West. Without her determination to create a better life for herself and her family, I never would have experienced the joy of growing up in Denver and leading this great city for twelve years.

After every mayoral election, we held up signs on busy downtown streets thanking the voters for electing me. In some ways, this book is my sign thanking my wife, children, family, friends, political supporters, and voters for their love and encouragement.

There's an old rural saying that if you see a frog on a fence post, he likely didn't get there alone.

The same is true for me.

Epilogue

Wellington Webb's Elected-Office History

Colorado State Legislature
House of Representatives, District Eight
1972–1977
(Served as the chairman of the House Democratic Caucus and chairman of the Health, Environment, Welfare and Institutions Committee.)

Community Office: First legislator to establish, at my own expense, a neighborhood office to make it more convenient for constituents to meet with me. The office was later closed due to the lack of operating money.

Antidiscrimination Bills: Successfully sponsored HB-1427, which prohibits the discrimination against any person in the granting of credit due to marital status. Previously, banks would not give loans or credit cards to wives, only to their husbands. I was decades before my time in (unsuccessfully) sponsoring bills that would have protected gays and lesbians against discrimination in the workplace and for housing.

Bills for the Poor: I successfully sponsored several bills that protected the poor. Those included

HB-1340, which established a state program for persons who are needy, blind, elderly, or disabled and do not qualify for the federal Supplemental Security Income act.

HB-1310, which protected people who received more than the correct amount of public assistance from having to repay the money if the additional amount was given by no fault of the receiver.

HB-1405, which provided additional funding to Denver to support its welfare programs. The bill also raised the amount of money provided for funerals and burials for indigent people.

Health Bills: HB-1112 mandates that insurance companies offer group health insurance benefits for the treatment of alcoholism. Other bills that addressed health issues included HB-1437, which required health insurance policies to cover complications of pregnancy or childbirth for all women, regardless of marital status.

Bills Concerning Social Issues: HB-1266 established rules, regulations, and procedures for an interstate compact on the placement of children. I was not successful in trying to help establish a law that would allow adopted adults to contact their birth parents. HB-1078 allowed the legislature to award $15,000 to Kenneth Lee, who had spent nearly three years in prison for a crime the Colorado State Supreme Court said was never committed.

Denver Auditor
1987–1991

Ensuring Prompt Payment: I made sure the city paid its bills promptly or faced penalties. Several business owners had complained to me that the city was always late in paying its bills.

Professionalizing the Auditor's Office: I hired professional CPAs, including Patti Beer, Tom Migaki, Mel Thompson, and Charles Rutland, to make sure that we had sound fiscal rules and to address such issues as contract change orders.

Computerizing the Office: I started the first computerized system in the office, including computerized city-employee paychecks.

Enforcing the Prevailing-Wage Law: My staff made sure that the city's prevailing-wage ordinance was enforced. The law requires that contractors working on city projects pay a wage calculated according to the going rate for federal projects in the same city.

Serving as Liaison to the Mayor's Office: I was the first auditor to have a member of my staff attend the mayor's weekly meetings with city council members and department heads. This allowed me to get up-to-date reports.

Division of Internal Audit: As part of the auditor's role as a "watchdog," I created the Division of Internal Audit, which was the first time an auditor created a way to audit all city agencies with accompanying recommendations for improvements.

Resolving Major Lawsuits: I successfully resolved an outstanding payment from the city for a contract at Stapleton and a general fund payment to Denver General Hospital.

Denver Mayor
1991–2003

Revitalizing Downtown Denver: My goal was to first attract new residents and retail to downtown Denver, which was achieved. In 1991, there were approximately 2,700 downtown residents; that ballooned to more than 8,000 in 2003. The opening of Coors Field for the Colorado Rockies in 1995 spurred restaurant and bar development and later residential growth, with Lower Downtown (LoDo) now a popular destination.

Opening Denver International Airport: After four delayed openings and the replacement of an unworkable automated baggage system, the $4 billion airport opened on February 28, 1995. My policy to open the airport concessions to all businesspeople—as opposed to one main concessionaire, as was done in the past—became controversial but now is a model nationwide.

Redeveloping the Former Stapleton Airport: My administration chose Forest City Development, based in Cleveland, to transform the 4,700-acre former airport into a mixed use of 12,000 homes and 3 million square feet of retail space. I insisted that the redevelopment include 1,100 acres of new parkland. When completed in fifteen to twenty years, the area will be home to nearly 30,000 residents.

Creating the Lowry Authority: The redevelopment of the former Lowry Air Force Base became a poster child for the U.S. Department of Defense. The partnership between myself and longtime Aurora mayor Paul Tauer, along with our city councils, led to the creation of the Lowry Redevelopment Authority. The 1,866 acres will have more than 4,500 houses, condos, and apartments when completed in 2009.

Creating Additional Park Space: In 1993, my administration promised to create the greatest addition to parkland since the "City Beautiful" era of Mayor Robert Speer. I came through with more than 2,350 new acres citywide, including the Stapleton redevelopment and several parks along the South Platte River, including Commons Park.

South Platte River Project: In 1995, my administration began a grand goal of transforming a ten-and-a-half-mile stretch along the South Platte River from an eyesore of abandoned railroad lines and homeless shanties to new park space and recreation areas. I brought together city, state, and federal resources to make the dream become reality.

Denver Health Medical Center: The city's hospital was facing a $39 million deficit when I took office. I supported the creation of the hospital authority, which allowed officials to cut through red tape and run the facility more efficiently. By 2003, the hospital was healthy financially and expanding.

Public Safety: My administration successfully dealt with gang violence in 1993, and by 2003, violent crime had dropped by more than 40 percent since 1991. This helped reflect that Denver was a safer city, and we saw our population grow by 19 percent, to 554,636, while other cities were losing residents to the suburbs.

Neighborhood Issues: I declared 1998 the "Year of the Neighborhood" and then asked neighborhood leaders to decide how to spend a $98 million bond. The projects included improvements to parks citywide and the construction of new recreation centers and police substations citywide. I also leased a vacant city office building adjacent to the Denver City and County Building for $1 a year for thirty years to the Colorado Coalition for the Homeless. The coalition converted the building to provide about 100 apartments for the homeless.

Cultural Facilities Projects: During my tenure, the Denver Central Library addition was completed in 1995 and the $16 million Blair-Caldwell African American Research Library opened in 2003.

My administration supported bond issues for the addition to the Denver Art Museum, addition to the Colorado Convention Center, renovation of the Quigg Newton Auditorium, and improvements to the Denver Zoo. We also allocated money in the general fund for improvements at Red Rocks and the Denver Coliseum. Wilma and I raised $1 million for a new Dr. Martin Luther King Jr. sculpture at City Park.

Hyatt Hotel and Winter Park Ski Area: My administration turned to the private sector for a joint partnership to build the 1,100-bed Hyatt Regency Denver at the Colorado Convention Center and operate the city's ski resort. The creation of the hotel authority moved forward a stalled project to get the city more hotel space. An agreement with Intrawest allows the city to keep ownership of the ski resort, and in turn Intrawest makes annual payments to help maintain our city and mountain parks.

Index